STELLA ADLER

ON IBSEN
STRINDBERG
AND CHEKHOV

STELLA ADLER

ON IBSEN
STRINDBERG
AND CHEKHOV

EDITED AND WITH A PREFACE

BY BARRY PARIS

ALFRED A. KNOPF NEW YORK • 1999

THIS IS A BORZOI BOOK
PUBLISHED BY ALFRED A. KNOPF, INC.

A portion of this work was originally published in
The Yale Review.

Library of Congress Cataloging-in-Publication Data
Adler, Stella.
Stella Adler on Ibsen, Strindberg, and Chekhov /
by Stella Adler : edited by Barry Paris.—1st ed.
p.   cm.
ISBN 0-679-42442-3
1. Drama—Explication.   2. Ibsen, Henrik,
1828–1906—Criticism and interpretation.
3. Strindberg, August, 1849–1912—Criticism and
interpretation.   4. Chekhov, Anton Pavlovich,
1860–1904—Criticism and interpretation.
I. Paris, Barry.   II. Title.
PN1707.A34   1999
809.2'034—dc21   98-38190   CIP

Manufactured in the United States of America

FIRST EDITION

CONTENTS

PREFACE

M Y INTRODUCTION to Stella Adler took place on the perfect California afternoon of October 15, 1992, at her home in Beverly Hills. I was received by the grand lady, grandly reclining on a chaise. She was stunningly beautiful at ninety, with the unlined features of a woman half that age, wearing an elegant pink dressing gown topped by a dramatic pink turban.

Adler means "eagle" in German, and Stella's eyes lived up to the surname. I was there to explore how we might craft a book out of her legendary lectures on theater, and the beguiling smile she bestowed on me did not conceal her real agenda: this was an audition to see if she liked me and thought we could work together. Throughout the initial pleasantries, those eyes bored into and unnerved me. I had never felt so intensely scrutinized and, in self-defense, I got down to business quickly.

Among her voluminous files from a lifetime of teaching were some three thousand pages of transcribed lectures, from the seventies and early eighties, on script analysis as applied to the works of a dozen great modern playwrights. These were the transcripts I was to work with, but there was no way to include them all in one or even two books. The problem would lie in the selection: Ibsen, Strindberg, Shaw, Williams, O'Neill—which ones?

"In your choice lies your talent," Adler often said.

My talents lay in film and Slavic languages and were very modest in the realm of theater. Years earlier, I had translated Chekhov's *Three Sisters* and Griboyedov's *Woe from Wit*. That was about it. For want of a better way to broach the subject, I made a blatant effort to impress her with my Russian. When she responded with enthusiastic fluency, I asked if she agreed that Chekhov should be one of our leading candidates.

"He would be, if you and I thought he was," she replied. "I think Chekhov is most wanted in terms of performance. I analyzed it, pulled it apart, got to the core of what he was. Chekhov. I think it's a good choice, because he's misunderstood. He's the most interesting and most wanting to be understood."

Her democratic, clear-minded approach was striking. She spoke eloquently and at length about Chekhov and of her exposure to the great Russian literature that permeated the work of her parents, Jacob and Sara Adler, in the Yiddish theater. "No curtain in New York goes up without an Adler behind it," people said. In 1939, when Sara celebrated her fiftieth anniversary on stage, there were no fewer than fourteen Adlers active in the theater, including every member of her immediate family. Stella, the youngest daughter, made her debut in 1906, at the age of four, in Jacob's production of *Broken Hearts* at the Grand Street Theater in New York. By the mid-twenties she had performed in more than one hundred plays there and elsewhere.

"I'm so delighted that I come from a family where my parents spoke Yiddish, with all the idioms and aspects of that milieu. My mother played in the theater in Moscow. My father loved the Russian language so much. Russian thinking and feeling was a big thing in my life. The enormous talent. I'm astonished at the output of Russian music, literature—so unbelievably big. I've been reading a great deal of Tolstoy lately.

"The Yiddish theater was not what most people think it was. It was more. The plays were so formidable. I saw them all. Such a pleasure. I'm so familiar with it. Nekhlyudov in Tolstoy's *Resurrection* is *mine!* I know how he dresses, how he walks, how he feels. Damn it all, what a play! My parents brought the greatest literature of the theater to a Yiddish-speaking audience. The names of Jacob and Sara Adler will stay alive forever for their contribution."

After Stella left the Yiddish theater, she found that Broadway and the world of mainstream drama were quite chilly toward Jewish names—okay for character actors, maybe, but not leading ladies. Later, in Hollywood, she would star in a Paramount comedy called *Love on Toast* as Stella *Ardler*, based on the studio brains' notion that the *r* made her surname more Gentile. She switched back to the original immediately afterward, refusing (like her brother Luther) to turn her back on her heritage.

"When they interviewed me on television in London, my opening line was, 'I'm a Jewish broad from Odessa.' I'm deeply understanding of being a Jewish child, a Jewish woman, which has given me my talent and my standards. My parents and grandparents came from Odessa. I am so proud of it!"

She paused to catch her breath. The energy and passion of her testimonial were infectious. I'd been respectfully silent for a long time. Now seemed the time to take advantage of her pause and play the trump card of my credentials. "Guess what?" I said cheerily. "*My grandparents were Jews from Odessa, too.*"

Suddenly, the big eyes that hadn't left mine got bigger and watery. Her benign conversational smile vanished. She held out her hand in the traffic cop's firm palm-up signal of "Halt!" What the hell had I said? I was riveted with alarm to that dramatic hand in the dramatic pause before her dramatic whisper:

"Stop—don't make me cry!"

I replayed it many times on my tape recorder and in my mind, wondering if the tragic tone was real or theatrical, before figuring out it was a precisely equal combination of both. Alone with an audience of one or onstage before hundreds, Stella Adler gave the same performance: Emotion was something felt, not faked. "Real" and "theatrical" must be the same.

This book is the brainchild of Victoria Wilson, my close friend and editor at Knopf. She is the daughter of author Mitchell Wilson. At eighteen she became Stella's stepdaughter when her father married Adler. So there were multiple personal and artistic reasons for the three of us to undertake this massive project—not least that it would be a delightful lot of fun. But to whom, exactly, would the book be aimed? Stella's answer:

"It's for actors. It's for directors. It's for other people. It's for *readers.*

An awful lot of theater people want to know and understand, don't you think?"

We would aim for a general and theatrical audience alike, limiting the student-teacher exchanges in her lecture transcripts to a few of the best and confining most professional "exercises" to the last chapter, tailoring them so that—although primarily for actors and directors—they might interest nontheater people, too. We would do it in two volumes: the first devoted to three great European playwrights, the second to three Americans. For now, we would worry only about volume one and the Europeans. There was no doubt about Chekhov. But which other two?

"Ibsen is the big one," said Stella. "Ibsen wouldn't let us lie. In *A Doll's House,* Nora has the children, she's not allowed to eat macaroons, she's so confined and restricted. But there is a moment where her husband is taking an after-dinner drink, as a banker would, and she watches him through the window. In that moment, she sees he's not a man. I discovered that. It is under the play, not in the words. It is indicated—I found it—that she sees him naked. You watch the way a man takes a drink and you see his conceit. Nora saw it. That observation of the character detail is important in my work as a teacher."

Ibsen was in.

Another Scandinavian came along:

"I translated Strindberg, analyzed him. Such a great, great writer. I'm the only one that undertook him. He's so unknown, so disliked, and I don't blame people. He's a miserable man. He was so against women that he ran through the streets and insulted his wife in public. He screamed so loudly in such a conservative country that they sent him away to France. Strindberg was insane. But he analyzed himself out of insanity. People are weakest in Strindberg. He's not an audience man. People don't read him because he's so insane. His whole life was insanity."

Strindberg was in.

But there would be a fourth person—the one Stella knew personally, who came along for her at a time when her theatrical life was at loose ends and tied those loose ends (and those three playwrights) together not just for Adler but for the whole of twentieth-century theater: Konstantin Stanislavsky.

Stella's road to Stanislavsky and to her own epiphany as a teacher began in the midtwenties at the American Laboratory Theater, an experimental group headed by Richard Boleslavsky and Maria Ouspenskaya, who espoused Stanislavsky's revolutionary acting principles from the Moscow Art Theater. During her two years of intensive work there, she came in contact with the brilliant writer Harold Clurman and director Lee Strasberg.

Stella called Clurman "a savior," the man most responsible for the "opening up of my talent, of my mind." Clurman, in the *Fervent Years,* called her "poetically theatrical—with all the imperious flamboyance of an older European tradition [but] somehow fragile, vulnerable, gay with mother wit and stage fragrance, eager to add knowledge to instinct, spiritually vibrant." The mutual admiration was personal as well as professional. In the future (1942) they would marry.

In the present (1929), Clurman, Strasberg, and Cheryl Crawford cofounded the Group Theater, a permanent ensemble dedicated to producing American plays about American life. The company introduced the works of Clifford Odets, John Howard Lawson, Sidney Kingsley, Irwin Shaw, Dawn Powell, William Saroyan, Maxwell Anderson, and others. Adler joined in its first season and, over the next few years, performed luminously in Maxwell Anderson's *Night Over Taos,* John Howard Lawson's *Success Story* (opposite brother Luther), and most notably Odets's *Awake and Sing* (Clurman's first directing effort) as Bessie Berger, a Jewish mother of complex depth instead of burlesqued stereotype.

The Group's actors were trained by Strasberg according to the Stanislavsky "Method" as he understood it. In *Success Story,* Strasberg's direction and Stella's unique combination of restraint and emotion made her performance so real that such seasoned veterans as John Barrymore repeatedly attended to study her last scene. Noël Coward, for one, came seven times.

However, after the run of John Howard Lawson's *Gentlewoman,* in 1934, in which she hated her own performance and director Strasberg's excessive use of the "affective memory" exercises, Adler left New York for Europe, where she found the founder of "the Method" herself.

"Stanislavsky's attitude toward the theater, the actor, the exchange, has been diminished," she reflected sixty years later. "It was like Roosevelt's attitude—available and enormously intimate:

'What troubles do you have?' I said, 'I couldn't solve *Gentlewoman.*' He said, 'Well, I did *Enemy of the People* and had such trouble I didn't do it again for ten years.' He showed me how he corrected it. It took him ten years to find the key. He was honest, open, intimate—extraordinary qualities for a man of that size and personality.

"It was dangerous to get into an elevator with Stanislavsky because he was so handsome. In his little elevator, you were really on top of him. Once I said, 'It's easy for you to walk in the streets. You're the handsomest man in Russia, you dress like a king.' He said, 'I'll tell you something. When I walk in the streets and there's a crippled man, they look at him not me.' Which is true. The man with the limp gets your attention much faster than the man dressed in tails. Stanislavsky's power of observation was not just to see but to *understand* what he saw.

"It was extraordinary to realize I could talk to him. I came every day for five weeks in Paris and worked with him, until he begged me not to. 'You know, I come here to see my family and you won't let me.' So then I left."

She felt she was leaving not just Paris but "the master teacher of the world, the man whose words were going to flood the world with truth. His sense of how truthful you had to be—this was his heritage, this is what he gave away. I remember thinking, I can't thank you personally, but all my life I will dedicate myself to give other people what you have given me."

In private conversation and in her lectures, Stella often told the end of a story first—the bottom line. If it intrigued you and if you asked and if she felt like it, she would then go back and tell you the beginning.

"How I met Stanislavsky was the greatest thing. Nobody ever had such a meeting. I went with Harold to Mr. Stanislavsky's apartment in Paris. Mme. Chekhova* was there, Stanislavsky's doctor was there, Harold was there, and I was there. Mme. Chekhova suggested we all go to the Champs-Elysées. We all went, Mr. Stanislavsky sat against a tree, and we all sat around him, and there was great laughter and gaiety. . . . I remember him chiding Mme. C. and calling her a ham, and she laughed and he pretended to bully

---

*Olga Knipper, the widow of Anton Chekhov and great actress of the Moscow Art Theater, who originated the role of Masha in *Three Sisters.*

her, and she pretended to be stronger than he was. . . . Stanislavsky spoke and they spoke and then Stanislavsky spoke and then they spoke. I didn't open my mouth. . . .

"Stanislavsky noticed that I did not speak to him. He knew of my family because Jacob Adler had produced Tolstoy's *Living Corpse* and was the first one to play it, even before Stanislavsky! After a while he said, 'Everybody talks to me but you.' I said, 'Well, Mr. Stanislavsky, I loved the theater until you came along, and now I hate it.' He laughed. I didn't like his method because of Strasberg."

The problem wasn't Stanislavsky's method, but how it was being used. Stanislavsky offered to coach her personally. Once he corrected her notion of it, she came home in the midthirties aflame with revelation and a desire to pass it along and correct Strasberg's misinterpretation—a calling to teach that would grow and eventually become even greater than her calling to act.

Stella began to give classes on Stanislavsky in the Group Theater attended by such actors as Robert Lewis, Sanford Meisner, and Elia Kazan. After the Group's demise in 1939, her classes were held at Irwin Piscator's Dramatic Workshop in the New School for Social Research. Those classes would evolve into the Stella Adler Acting Studio (later, Conservatory), her comprehensive two-year program for play analysis and characterization, which opened in New York in 1949.

Another Adler bottom line is typically devoid of self-effacement:

"Thank God Stanislavsky's real method has come over here to a certain degree now. I think maybe he wanted his philosophy to be taken over by an American who understood him. He had done all this work. He didn't want it to be misunderstood. When I first gave him my opinion of his Method, he laughed. He knew something was wrong."

Stella's screen career was limited to three films: the Paramount comedy *Love on Toast* (1937), MGM's *Shadow of the Thin Man* (1941) and United Artists' *My Girl Tisa* (1948). After the second of those, she moved behind the scenes as an assistant to MGM's Arthur Freed on *Du Barry Was a Lady* and *For Me and My Gal* (1942), the latter starring Judy Garland. Adler badgered MGM to cultivate Garland's talent, not squander it on fluff, and to some extent she was heeded.

But Stella at heart was profoundly indifferent to the movies and soon abandoned Hollywood for her true passion. Over the next half-century, she would train thousands of actors in whose subsequent work lies her legacy: many of them remained on stage. Others became directors, playwrights, technicians, and teachers. Some formed their own companies that are part of America's vast regional-theater revival today, while others, among them Marlon Brando, Robert De Niro, and Harvey Keitel, went to Hollywood and became screen actors.

I went home to tackle the two-foot stack of three thousand pages—inspired then as now by Stella's farewell: "Okay, darling. Nothing can break us up because of Odessa."

Our collaboration, projected to take about two years, would in fact consist only of those five hours. Stella died seven weeks later, on December 21, 1992.

My meetings with America's greatest acting teacher were supposed to be business sessions, not "interviews." But I had the tape running, thank God, and they constitute the last recorded conversations with Stella Adler. In a thousand such encounters over thirty years, I never left one flying higher—never left the scene of a literary accident feeling so much a part of the family.

But, then all people who love theater are part of the Adler family.

Barry Paris

HENRIK IBSEN

ONE

IBSEN THE PIONEER

JACOB ADLER said that unless you give the audience something that makes them bigger—better—do not act. Do not go
into theater. Unless you can create something bigger and better,
there is no use climbing around and chattering on a stage. I have a
mission from my parents—right from the old man, who said, "Make
it better for them. Otherwise, why are they here?"

This is not a course in "drama." It is a course in opening up the
vastness in you as a human being, in all your aspects, to understand
your place more than you do—not to be led by the Bible or anything else but the truth of modern life as given to you by certain
genius-authors in the theater who can make you into something
tremendous. That is why you are here. There is no other way to grow
except through an art form today. A few hundred years ago, maybe
religion could do it. But today, only the art form is able to stretch a
human being so he can measure up to his potential to grow and
grow and understand himself and his life until the end. We are here
to get that.

There are two aspects of the theater. One belongs to the author and
the other to the actor. The actor thinks it all belongs to the author.
The aspect that belongs to the actor he knows little or nothing
about. His mistake has grown to such proportions that you cannot
give a play to the actor anymore, because he does not know what his
own contribution is. The curtain goes up and all he knows are the
lines.

It is not enough.

Script interpretation is your profession. What am I? Say, "I am a script interpreter." It is much better to say that than "I am an actor," because unless you can interpret a script you are not an actor. The whole point is interpretation. When the playwright has done his job, then it hangs there, and you come along and say, "Well, he's done it, I'll take it from him and say his words." That is not interpretation.

Interpretation means that I am going to find that playwright in me. I am not going to do Ibsen if it's Chekhov. I am not going to do Strindberg if it's Shaw. I am not going to do Odets if it's Wilder. That makes the interpreter.

Horowitz once said that American pianists don't play the piano, they play their technique. There is a similar problem in theater: instead of employing and imposing my technique on his work, I must find out what the *playwright* wants. How does the playwright affect me as the actor?

In the plays that preceded Ibsen, one always knew who the hero was and could identify with him. It was very difficult to do tragedy without the hero and villain. But Ibsen did something different. Contemporary theater started with Ibsen.

Ibsen changed the whole world of literature. He opened up the drama, which was the most forceful way of making a statement that had to be made. It was time to find a more forceful way, and Ibsen was the one who found it.

You have to understand what he accomplished. There is no important writer after Ibsen who does not utilize his sense of craft and his ability to analyze the human character. The human character is what you find in Ibsen's plays.

We are in danger, all of us, and I will give you an example why—a journalist I knew years ago. He was a good journalist. He went around the world and recorded what he saw and came to various conclusions. He said, Paris is this and London is that—and Greece is worth a couple of days. He felt two days was enough to give him an understanding of Greece.

What that statement reveals is that the basis of our Western culture now, and of professional man, is middle-class. The middle class makes statements and knows nothing. You and I are the middle class and must think of ourselves as middle-class. We are middle-class actors, middle-class journalists, middle-class plumbers and morticians.

The creation of the modern theater took a genius like Ibsen. His formulation goes on and on, stated and restated in creative ways that are profoundly startling. You will be aghast at what is revealed in Ibsen. Every play after him was influenced by him. Miller and Odets and Inge and O'Neill and Williams and Shaw swallowed the whole of him. You cannot escape the influence. Whenever you start a class on a modern playwright, you have to start with Ibsen, because he is the seed. The fertilizer of the egg. Like Mozart in music, and the long line of composers who have taken what Mozart, the seminal genius, did and creatively restated it in a thousand different ways.

Ibsen was a pioneer. "Pioneer," to our ears, sounds like somebody who got in a covered wagon and went West. I think it may be the wrong word, so I will change it: Ibsen was a revolutionary, an anarchist, a nihilist. He broke open everything in order to get to what he wanted to say. What did he want to say? He wanted to say the truth of what he saw. The truth was difficult to find, because until Ibsen came along the forms were romanticized, melodramaticized. Too many things "happened" to the truth along the way.

The Audience and the Middle Class

What did Ibsen want? First and foremost, he wanted the audience. Who was Ibsen's audience?

Ibsen was a pioneer in many ways but primarily because he wrote for a specific class—the middle class—which was created by the institutions of marriage, church, civil life, and law.

Ibsen expressed the middle-class man and his nobility. He thought it important to ennoble the middle class. But he had the problem of creating a great contemporary figure and of redefining tragedy. For Ibsen and his contemporary man, tragedy derives from each man's responsibility for his own fate.

In Ibsen, the hero is in conflict with the social and moral system that he lives under. In the theater of the Greeks and the Elizabethans, man deals with God and society is ordered. If a man broke a law, it was a sin. The aim was always to bring back order. Ibsen felt that contemporary writers must see *through* things and their insights must be seen through the characters in a contemporary human situation.

Ibsen wrote for and about the middle class. He did not speak about the upper class, the aristocracy or royalty. A playwright writes in his own time, and Ibsen's was from 1860 on. Do not always think in terms of you and the late twentieth century. The middle class came along long before you did. You must know whether it is the middle class of 1860 or 1970. There are many changes. It's the largest class in the Western world and the one we are always in connection with.

Ibsen personally had two strong impulses. The first was to get out of his conventional, stuffy, unproductive middle-class surroundings (nevertheless, the environment he wrote about). The second impulse was for freedom—a great desire to exist in his own self-controlled way, not to be controlled from the outside by the government, church, etc. His idea of freedom was not to be imposed on by other people's ideas. To understand him, we must sketch his life and how it lent itself to modern theater.

Ibsen very early in life felt something tremendous: the difference in class. He was from a fairly poor working family. What was rich was usually bureaucratic and business. When he speaks about the middle class, he speaks a great deal about how its bureaucratic institutions rule life. And about money. If you speak a lot about money, you will know it's the middle class.

Most of his plays do not take place in the capital, but in the suburbs. He understood the smallness of suburbs. Norway had not developed industrially, technically, or culturally. It was far behind other European countries in education and literature. Norway was a kind of colony, dependent in every way on Sweden.

Ibsen was up against thinking as small as the towns: less than thirty thousand people in the capital and under ten thousand in any other town. Norway did not gain full status as a country until 1905. Ibsen was a good artist and an art critic. For many years he was manager/director of a small theater, redesigned the costumes—always down to the last button—and began to write plays at a time when only "commercial" plays from Germany and France were done. Norway was horribly claustrophobic, and he would spend no less than twenty-seven years of his life abroad—yet he wrote *only* about middle-class Norway.

The middle class deserved Ibsen but was not ready for him. It was a class that needed but did not want to be analyzed or revealed in all its compromising, destroyed self. Ibsen didn't believe in the structure that created the middle class: love, friendship, etc. He made fun of fidelity in a society that didn't want a problem like that to be opened up. It was the first time that characters talked about themselves from the inside, revealed themselves. He went right to what he thought had to be done because the continuous middle-class lie goes on and on and deserves to go under.

The reaction was violent. The middle-class audience that saw an Ibsen play said, "It's an open drain—a toilet." They called it a public obscenity. When you deal with Ibsen, you deal with what the middle class considered indecent, disgusting, sick, amateurish, poisonous. The criticism of him was furious in the middle-class newspapers.

But there was a percentage of that class who saw the plays and said, "Well, this is it. We are in for it. Some of the truth of our lives is being revealed to us." The public was divided and you will be divided, and that is part of what Ibsen wants. When you get so much excitement about ideas, you are in a new school of playwriting—and you are in for a strong, active, healthy, violent opening up of ideas. Ibsen laughed at what the middle class considered honorable. He attacked the institution of marriage. He was highly skeptical of standard ideals of family and friendship. He said they were all open to discussion.

They said, "Do not open it up." That is a very middle-class thing. "So I don't like my husband. So leave it alone—he's my husband." Ibsen's attacks on values deeply troubled people because his characters and his audiences were the same kind of people. It was not that the audience didn't understand what he was saying, but that they didn't *want* to understand. Ibsen kept saying, "You understand—just stop pretending that you don't."

Ibsen was lost for fifty years, even on the British. The British are experts on words and literary understanding, but they did not dig him at all. They said, "He's a degenerate." It was a devastating putdown, because these were intelligent middle-class critics and literary men. "Leave it alone, we don't want that. We want something comfortable." But Ibsen kept giving them something uncomfortable.

You get much more class behavior in England than in America. Here, we can hardly talk about who we are because we still don't really know. But if you watch any European you know, his behavior will be almost exactly what it was a hundred years ago. He will kiss your hand or behave in a certain way according to whether he is Swiss, Russian, Dutch. He behaves in a traditional way because he has not given it up so easily. We have given it up because we're not sure we ever had it.

If I told you about a family that has an uncle who killed his brother and married the brother's wife, you would be correct to say that it was not a typical middle-class family. It is fine but you don't quite relate to it. You relate to a lawyer or doctor who owns a house. You do not relate to Elsinore and Prince Hamlet. He owns Denmark.

Ibsen wrote about a privileged nineteenth-century class. The audience understood the problems of characters who—for the first time—were people with the same aims and goals, who lived the same life. They were not special people. They resembled the audience and the audience could identify with them. Their problems belonged to the society—and thus to the audience.

The middle class deserves a beating at every stage of its creation. Ibsen tore into it and in each play revealed a different mountain of problems. Ibsen did not "criticize" the middle class—he annihilated it. He said it is simply not to be believed, what it has done to the human race. He is the prophet who made us understand that we were led down every drain in the world, and still are, by the institutionalism of the middle class—its politics, religion, morality, family life, economics. All of us are surrounded by and part of these institutions.

The middle class was very resistant to this analysis. Still is. Some of the truths that will come out will astound you even though you are a hundred years later. It is interesting to see how you came to be. What happened to make you like this? What happened to make you do this?

You must honor your father and mother. You must love your brother. You must love your husband. You must love your wife.

Ibsen said all this was nonsense. You do not have to love your husband or your mother, and your mother does not have to love you. It is not your own idea. It was handed down. He attacks all institutions that are handed down and built up.

In a thousand years, I don't think we will change. I wanted a divorce, but I did not dare divorce until after my mother died. She had divorced but I could not—oh, no. We are not as free as we think we are. Ibsen forces you to rethink every aspect of your life—sex, church, morality, money. He said it was all idealized. A great many people were handed a great many ideals: "My country is the best in the world." "My family is the best family." "I am an honest businessman." It is going to be a long time until you are a person that really thinks for yourself. But at least Ibsen made it possible for people to say, finally, "My God, I have been trapped in conventional thinking and I don't know what to do." You have a big problem. If you give up conventional thinking, where do you go then? That is what Ibsen faces you with—and there are not too many places to go.

A man does one thing at work and another thing at home, and they are not necessarily the things he thinks or *says* that he does. Ibsen makes you see that you are not a function of what you say but of what you do—and of what the society, in many ways, makes you do.

The Discussion

The playwright after Ibsen was not considered serious unless he brought in the discussion. The play which cannot be argued is not a serious play. The argument concerns ideas that cannot be resolved. But they can be discussed. Until Ibsen, the problems were settled by the playwright. Ibsen unsettles you. He challenges the spectator to think and discuss and—from the discussion—to learn who he really is.

The discussion concerns an issue about which the audience has already formulated an opinion, so they go out arguing their opinions with each other and perhaps continue to do so at home. A playwright who knows how to touch that in his audience is a very powerful, successful playwright. He knows that if he can involve you in that way, he has the power to teach you something.

Therefore, the material has to be about moral, social problems that affect the whole of the audience. *An Enemy of the People* and *Ghosts* and *Hedda Gabler* and *A Doll's House* concern problems that existed many years ago. Some have been worked out, although basically I don't think any women's problems have really been "solved"— improved a little, perhaps, not truly resolved. In any case, Ibsen's is a technique of getting at both the social truth and the truth of the individual. For the most part, the problem he poses is not unusual or bizarre. It is a problem or moral question familiar to everybody and in need of illumination.

If a girl wants to leave home and lead her own life, but her father says, "You must stay because it is your duty to care for your mother," who is right? There is serious disagreement about that. Ibsen says it is abhorrent to sacrifice yourself for another person. That person will not thank you.

You may agree or disagree. Either way, when Ibsen deals with family life, the audience is forced to see the problem as its own. For the first time, the audience buys a ticket and in return takes away an idea that stays with them and that they have to deal with. The play's meaning is not available to you unless you follow the argument in the action and involve yourself in the discussion. Ibsen says that unless it is discussed, you cannot find the truth. In an Ibsen play and in every later play, you find the problem discussed in one form or another. Ibsen's is a teaching theater. He pioneered the idea that the audience—and the actors—must see life as more complex than they think.

The villainous character, for example, is just as conscientious as the heroic one, or—if anything—more so. He is just as "true" and as firm in the belief that he is right. Ibsen says, "In the good there is bad, and in the bad there is good." There lies a more profound kind of characterization: how can a character be wrong if there is so much right about him? More important (and more interesting) is *who* the hero and villain are. Ibsen aims to *trap* you. He introduces you to a man who is good and you side with him. But in the second act you recognize that he isn't as good as you thought he was. Ibsen catches you up by making the character both right and wrong. He makes you like or respect something that the discussion may reveal to be hateful and dishonorable. He misleads you so much that in the end, you are uncertain where your opinion lies. Perhaps, then, you go home with some other idea that belongs exclusively to you, to solve it for yourself. Ibsen seldom solves it for you.

The one thing you can hang on to is that an Ibsen play deals with ideas and that they are discussed in front of you. Ibsen changed the theater by including this "discussive element" within the play. Discussion was a new concept in drama—something that makes the play both modern and intellectual. It does not necessarily lead any-where.

There are many truths, and they change: "A wife should obey her husband." "As a man, I am head of the family." "As a priest, I am head of the church." Somebody else comes along and says, "I do not know if you are the head of the family. I don't think you can be the head of anything but yourself. I don't think anybody can own any-body else or ask anybody else to belong to him." If you have the power to arrest somebody, you can do that, but the audience might say, "I do not think you are arresting him because you are right. I think you just have the power."

In the discussion, you have to try to distinguish between truths. You listen to all the truths and then make your own choice. Each person is saying honestly what he believes to be the truth. There is no "solution." You cannot "win." You can only do what you think is right. Truth must be individual for each person—you can only rep-resent yourself. No pastor can represent God. No institution can represent God.

Get the Big Argument in an Ibsen play. The uproar in *Enemy of the People* when the chairman calls on the doctor to withdraw: he says, "Never." Never will the majority in the community prevent him from speaking the truth. The majority never has right on its side. Hovstad: "Stupid people are in the absolute overwhelming majority and govern the few who have absorbed new and vigorous truths for the future."

That illuminates the whole moral-social situation: In the end, none of them will go with the doctor. They can't take the chance. The paper will go under. The town will go under. There's no hope if they reveal this sickness. In the end, Dr. Stockmann becomes the person who does it by himself—without the press, without the majority. He finally understands that he has to do it alone. It is the only way in an Ibsenian situation. You want to be an actor? You go out and look for a job. You are going to be defeated. You are not going to get acclaim. You have to fight your way through to becoming what you want to be—not according to somebody else's standards but to your own. Do you have your own standards? In marriage? In relationship to your profession? Are you willing to fight for them?

Ibsen always has two points of view on the stage in his characters. One says "I believe this" and the other says "I believe that." The audience listens to both sides, but there is usually no way to resolve an Ibsen idea.

If you have two opposite opinions and both contain some truth and the audience listens to both, then the one thing you are not going to get anymore is a hero. That is finished. There will be no "pure" heroes in literature after Ibsen. Before Ibsen, everybody knew who was good and who was bad, who was right and wrong. We didn't have to think about it. From Ibsen on, you have to make up your mind as you leave the theater.

Ibsen never says which character is wrong or right. That is absolutely new. Before, everybody could recognize who the hero was and who the villain was. You always knew, right from the beginning: Iago is the villain. But Ibsen never says anyone is wrong. The characters all have a right to live, a right to their own way. And if nobody is right, you have no hero.

That is a big change. Before Ibsen, there was a hero and a villain. After Ibsen, there isn't. You cannot play Iago or Claudius anymore as pure villains. That is no longer a privilege of the modern actor. You are forced to think about everything in terms of the action and the conflict. Since you cannot play "I am the villain," you are forced to build your character from "I am right." That is terribly challenging for the actor. He has to find the ability to say "Hitler was right" if he is going to play that role. You cannot play Hitler as a villain. First of all, he thought he was right. That leaves you without a certain kind of grandeur—that thing of "I am Lear!" "I am Hamlet!" It leaves you with, "I am Nora," "I am Dr. Stockmann."

The conflict in *Doll's House* is about family life, not personalities. If you are the audience, do not look for a hero or villain. If you are the actor, be on the side of your character.

This is an enormous advance in the theater—not to dictate the solution. After Ibsen, no one wrote a play in which the discussive element was not an important part—understood by playwright, actors, and audience alike. The audience from now on, as Shaw says, is "constantly at a murder trial."*

So the audience has to argue it out, starting in the lobby, and the arguments got pretty violent in the lobby. A playwright who can do that to an audience is revolutionary.

In fashioning and infusing his plays with this argumentative element, Ibsen created not just a whole new form of drama but, arguably, a new way of life. Something more real or at least more realistic.

Realism.

Realism vs. Idealism

If you say "I am unhappy" in a play on a stage, it should not mean that you alone are unhappy, but that millions of people all over the world are unhappy like you. To play it on a purely individual level gives it a pedestrian rather than a poetic quality. If it is *not* pedestrian, then it should be poetic. It should be a search for truth, which is what poetry is. Even when you do it in the simplest terms, do it with that largeness, that dignity, that large searching for the truth that is realism.

Realism is a style that has to have a certain anatomy. Ibsen takes situations of life that are idealized and unrealistic and he works on them. The family, for example: society has to have families to perpetuate civilization. You have to have marriage. You have children; the children have parents. That's the situation—the picture that is presented, but without what is *underneath* the picture.

A man has a yen for a girl, for instance. He says, "I love you." He knows love is not something that can be sustained for twenty-

---

*Curiously, the discussion in Ibsen is almost always at the end of the play; in Shaw, it is almost always in the first act.

four hours, even among the poets. That eventually must be faced. To face it realistically, he should really say, "I want to sleep with you." But society doesn't function that way. It functions by putting a mask on sexual needs. The woman is the outsider. The man can have an affair, but the aim of society is to perpetuate itself, and the only approved way to do that is with the family unit. So he marries her, and she takes her place in a family. She is now a woman because she is a wife and potential mother. The man believes in this form of society.

If you dig into it, says Ibsen, most people are either unaware or actively do not *want* to be aware. They just want to be "happy." They want the illusion. Man dresses it up and says marriage is a romantic thing that lasts forever. He idealizes. *That* man, Ibsen is after. Ibsen says you can go on all your life with that idea, but society does not work that way. The family is a conventional arrangement, legally enforced. The majority says it is good for everybody. Ibsen says there are those for whom marriage is good but a minority, at least, for whom it is not good. The poets and the writers and the society all promote the *illusion* of marriage—not the reality but the idealism of it—when in fact it is not what it is cracked up to be.

Ibsen says that society makes us disguise our primitive instincts in terms of the family. It creates form for us. Suddenly one person says, "Marriage is not for me. I cannot accept it, cannot live with it, do not find a need for it. Let's abolish it." The society replies, "Where would the wives go? Where would the children go? Where would it *all* go?" This person is called an iconoclast and declared mad.

At one time, paying absolute allegiance to the king was unquestioned. He was there by divine right. But time changed that. At one time, you could own as much property as you could grab, without penalty. But eventually one person said no and then another said no, and now all property is taxed. Social progress starts with the criticism of one or two people. Ibsen says it's the only formula for progress—by one person leaving and saying what he thinks, usually at the cost of his or her life. People do not give in easily to change. Social progress is not made by statement, but by sacrifice. During McCarthyism, the American government repressed your political point of view and threw you out of your job.

Idealism emerged with the middle class and the vague concepts of truth, virtue, liberty, responsibility, etc. it inherited but never had in reality. The middle class creates a lot of ideals to hide the drive for material advantage. The idealist puts a mask over the truth, so that he can live with it. He will defend that mask. The idealist prefers that mask to facing the truth, especially when he *knows* the truth. A woman says, "I am happily married." Underneath, she knows something different, but she would rather *believe* that she is happy. She therefore serves the man more than she serves herself.

The realist, on the other hand, says, "I am, by force, made to revolt," either publicly or privately, in the family unit. He sees the evil, denounces it, and wants to tear off the social mask. The society regards a person who stands alone and says "I don't want it and I will fight against it!" as a traitor. In all his plays, some Ibsen character is fighting against the *majority* way of thinking. There are fine examples in history.

Byron, for instance, was a radical realist. He had an affair with his sister, and when a man does a thing like that in the society, he is stoned. Many people want to sleep with or marry their sisters—it's an old urge—but society does not permit it. What happens is that Byron is then ostracized by society.

Ibsen says fiction, poetry, church, marriage, theater—all romanticized institutions and art in middle-class life—need to be examined. If a person announces, "Marriage is a failure and so is the whole ideal family thing"—if he really comes to that conclusion—then he should do what Byron did. The brother-sister yen thing has been around for ages. But still today, even now, nobody will come out and say, "I'm in love with my sister, and we're getting married." Advanced as we are. I remember meeting a man who loved and lived with his sister pretty openly. They were very happy together. Every time I saw them I blushed.

After Ibsen, all plays are based on real social frictions and issues: "You cannot marry your sister." But Byron did. "You cannot open a theater with non-Equity actors." But it's been done. To the extent of becoming actual or potential dramatic material, it all came out of Ibsen.

Ibsen is the Father of Realism, even though the realistic school of thinking actually began with the novelists. Theater always lagged behind the novel. We have to get to know what the hell realism is. It is a form of social criticism—it is the theater of understanding. The realists made fun of the theater formulas. They knew nothing about what to do with a play but they had definite ideas about how to tell a story. An art of playwriting developed that had to do with a certain kind of reality. The basis of realism is the negation of the ideal and everything that flows from it.

Modern theater is a theater of thought. Realism is a thinking theater, a verbal theater. There are not many jokes. Count the jokes in *John Gabriel Borkman* and tell me how many you find. You don't dance much in realism, because if you use your feet you can't also use your mind. You understand better if your feet are quiet and you use your mind instead. Realism needs an intelligent audience to listen to what it has to say.

It is not a good idea to approach the realistic theater as "This will be a barrel of fun—let's see *Ghosts* tonight." But at the end of seeing *Ghosts,* if you understand the play, no one goes out without saying, "My life has to be changed because I have to think differently."

So realism has everything to do with thinking. All serious playwrights now fall into the category of what we call modern realism. Wilder belongs to the class of thinking writers and he is in a line with them. Ibsen, Strindberg, Chekhov, Shaw, O'Neill, Odets, Miller, Williams—these are thinking writers.

It is tough to get away from realism—very tough. Many people have left it and gone back. Realism is a poisonous form for playwrights. It gives up glamour, diction, stardom—those things all had to go, because the middle class does not consist of stars. You cannot have a star in the middle class on the stage. It is oxymoronic. People will say, "She doesn't look like Aunt Harriet at all." She is supposed to look like Aunt Harriet. You are supposed to identify. There have been great attempts to run away from it and get into other styles—symbolism, surrealism and constructivism and poetic this and that—but they go back to realism. So, it is a style which is painful both to the audience, to the actors, and to the playwrights. It is a style that profoundly affected the Russian theater, where it still exists.

It is a style you can kick off from—you can go from realism to poetic realism to surrealism to all the other isms. You can do a lot of shtick with it. It is well over a hundred years old and still going strong. You must understand it and be able to do it once you understand it.

Certainly, you must be able to *speak* it.

Prose vs. Poetry

Most of us lie all the time. We have gotten used to saying things without understanding them. "Oh, what a lovely day." Lovely what? Day? It does not occur to you. You bring this to the theater with you. "Oh, what a lovely day. I didn't notice." Real language has disappeared in us. That is the nature of life. The nature of life is a lie. But the nature of the stage is truth. When you say "Oh, what a lovely day," it must *be* there. You cannot say it unless it is there. You cannot lie on stage. You must begin to realize and admit, "I am a liar in life. But let me get on the stage. Before I die, I will say a couple of truths."

But it is difficult to cast and put an American on stage, because he does not really know what he is saying and does not have the diction. The English don't give a damn about the day, but they can say "Oh, what a lovely day" so nicely and with such conviction that they don't have to worry about sincerity.

In America, we have a greater sense of truth. Maybe that is why we have so little diction. Because our language is so dense, you can say "Won't you have some hot roast beef?" and it does not just mean roast beef. And since it means more than that, you are going to have more fun saying it.

One reason why realism is difficult for you is that you are not used to listening to language. You have been weaned from language. Theater, when it's not singing and dancing, is based on language. Real theater is rarely offered to you. Try to listen in such a way—with your heart, blood, mind—that you get the real meaning of what is being said. What is being said in a play is not "Oh, I'm late for supper." But that is all you will hear until you get used to listening to what is underneath.

Realism does not feature smart language. It uses a common language which has no vulgarity and therefore contains ideas which go in layers and in depth. It is not on top. It is not what you hear. It is what you are going to train yourself to hear as we get to how the language creates characters and ideas.

Because Ibsen is so forceful in modern language without iambic pentameter, the size of his characters is as great as Shakespeare's. You have to understand that in order to act in Ibsen, you will have to build up the size of language to such a degree in yourself that it is on the side of Shakespeare.

Ibsen wrote the two greatest plays in verse after Shakespeare—*Brand* and *Peer Gynt.* Aside from *Faust,* these are the two greatest plays written in verse. He was one of the greatest poets in the world. But he gave up poetry to give you prose in a dining room. I want you to go home, kneel down, and thank God that he gave us a dining room instead of poetry, because it is from that dining room that we will get the truth. I want you to realize that the dining room and the living room are where people live and exchange ideas with each other. It has very little to do with your idea of a living room. You have to say, "What is the center of middle-class family life?" You have got to stop thinking 1981 and who has the ratings.

We are in a field where words are important. In everything that you and I will be dealing with, we will share the importance of text. In music you can just *feel*—it's gay, it's a tango, a waltz, or a fox-trot—you know everything without words.

Imagine that you must know everything through words and that the playwright does what the poet does in a different kind of words. He finds exactly those words which open up the miracle of understanding. You have the habit of using common language to function and not to open up the mind and heart to the deepest understanding of the human race. We are here with this dynamic, important asset man has—the understanding of himself and life through words. Through the text.

Most plays before Ibsen were written in poetic verse. Ibsen was the manager of a theater for many years and put on verse plays. He was a very practical theater man. The problem of the modern playwright was how to give modern man *size* within the confines of a much narrower dramatic form—in the modern dress and modern speech of middle-class man. Theater was now more accessible to general audiences. Industrialism and scientific discoveries made it harder for people to identify with poetic verse plays and the nobility that they portrayed. Society had to change its concept of poetry to conform to Ibsen's concept of poetic prose.

Realism is something arrived at because society has failed to produce another form that serves it as a form for theater or for a novel. It cannot be done—it has to have this essential ability to knock it around until the truth of life exists in this form. It is not a pedestrian form. It should not be done or thought about on that level. It is on a poetic level, in search of the truth. It may take the form of meter and rhyme—doesn't matter. The main thing in poetry is not the meter but the search for the truth. Mr. Ibsen was the poet laureate—there are only two plays equal to Shakespeare, *Peer Gynt* and *Brand.*

When he wrote the realistic plays, which are to find the truth without the rhyme, they said, "But your plays are not poetic, Mr. Ibsen." Ibsen said, "Then you will have to alter your idea of poetry. It is the search for truth—it does not have to have rhyme." If it has this search, then it is poetry.

So Ibsen chose prose over poetry and changed the course of the drama.

The hidden loss of interrelationships with life is an inexhaustible source of material for the theater. Ibsen saw the truths and lies of such loss and then found the dramatic means to project them concretely so the audience could see, too.

A new kind of play consisting of absolute reality would require great conviction to bring off. Saying something truly significant about life required a whole new technique of acting to match the new technique of writing.

Nowadays, authors routinely reproduce what they see and hear around them in an effort to show us contemporary life. This began a century ago—in backwater Norway—and has continued on stage and in film, radio, and television ever since. Such scripts seldom reveal the human situation; in "real" contemporary life, we just chat and trade gossip most of the time—the kind of talk that one would think was of very limited use to a playwright. But Ibsen accepted those limitations and created masterpieces out of them. The old form of theater was gone. In its place, he offered what seemed at first like just a sort of shrunken reality. How could this form be better used? How to enlarge upon it? Ibsen figured it out.

The poets all considered realism to be antipoetic. They said it would lead to a mere dead-end "likeness" of life—no better than those thousands of daily newspaper reports all over the world that are mistaken for reality and that have no poetic qualities at all. They missed the point, of course, which was that the realist form forces a playwright to look for the *truth,* and that the truth has nothing to do with the literary importance or insignificance of poetry.

The new poetry in theater was realistic prose, and its "realization" could only come about through the new actor—a different species of performer with enormous sensibility and the ability to interpret the subtext in performance. Not least among the intimidating components of realism was its total dependence on the art of acting—indispensable in rendering Ibsen and Chekhov and the rest, for one simple but daunting reason: realist plays do not pretend to be art, but life itself.

After Ibsen, all writers are going to deal with the social moment. They are going to investigate the relationship of people to their culture: church, sex, money, war—whatever it is, they are going to talk about it. The modern play is going to talk about what is wrong in the culture. From now on, playwrights are teachers, and from now on you can't act a play without knowing why the playwright wrote it.

Ibsen wrote *A Doll's House,* for example, to show the tragic struggle behind the trivial anxiety of a middle-class housewife: flighty Nora in conflict with the immensely powerful forces of the society. To create the tragedy, Ibsen emphasizes and manipulates certain simple, everyday details. The emphasis on the commonplace leads you to the style of realism.

Ibsen says no institution can tell you anything. Make the rules true for you. Realism is built on self-discovery, self-truth: *find out the truth for yourself.*

No Ibsen play is easily solved. For that matter, few plays from Ibsen on have solved problems. Yet realism is a teaching style, in which the audience learns *something* about themselves and the society they live in. Ibsen's plays are not about a single person with a problem. They are about *all* the people who have that problem and about the idealized social arrangement (often marriage or money) that is the source of the problem. Ibsen neatly divides society into three types of people, based on their *attitude* toward—and response to—the problem:

The Idealist (a vast majority) hides from the truth about life and believes in the illusion—eternal romantic marriage, for example. Most of society wants such idealizations, which is why Ibsen believed there was ultimately no solution; people insist on their illusions.

The Compromiser (a sizable minority) sees the truth but lives and even defends the lie. He creates a family and accepts a good or bad social situation, regardless of whether he believes in it. He knows the truth but settles for something else.

The Realist (a tiny minority) knows the truth but wants and tries to change it. He fights the majority and is thus viewed as a traitor to the society. The man or woman who tears off the mask of conventional life can expect to pay a high price.

Ibsen's men and women usually paid with their lives.

MORALITY, MONEY, AND MARRIAGE

IN THE AMERICAN middle class today, we have a kind of President and a kind of Senate.* They are all middle-class fellows. Their wives are middle-class. They live middle-class lives with problems like yours. The President can go into his own little kitchen, make his own coffee, fry his own egg. He is not the kind of leader Louis XIV was. He has a dining room and a door that opens. Do you see how he is related to you? There are various grades—upper and lower, richer and poorer—but it is all basically the same middle class. If the President needs an operation, he goes to a hospital—you know who the doctor is, or you can find out if you really care. You do not know Louis XIV's doctor and you might be guillotined just for asking. Louis XIV and his doctor have nothing to do with you.

In 1789, during the French Revolution, Napoleon was a common man. A few years later he became the emperor, and then he became a common man again. He did not know where the hell he was going —he went up and down. He is a king one day and they put him on Elba the next. So he was really mixed up. And so is the middle class. Going into the 1800s to 1850, you have the middle class taking over. Very much like our class. It has conservative elements, which is why you must know *An Enemy of the People.* You read the play and see the mayor is a conservative. He is not very different from Alexander Haig. The mayor wears a high hat. Mr. Haig would like to wear one, but he does not dare.

---

*"Today" was 1976, and "a kind of President" was Gerald Ford.

Ibsen introduces you to middle-class society, and you learn that it has many different sides. It has a left wing, a liberal left, a liberal right, a right, a far right. They and we have a very mixed group of people in the middle class. Some are in government, some in professions. It is not just one class, as in *Hamlet*. When you have a middle-class society after 1850 you have a mixed bag. Every character you meet after 1850—ask what he thinks about politics, ethics, religion. You must know how your character thinks. You are not just an actor who has lines. For God's sake, say, "I don't know about politics, and I need to!" What do you think about sex and economics?

STUDENT: Sex is free.
ADLER: Great. I like that.

You are part of the middle class—neurotic, half-baked, half-genius, half-idiot. You can't get out of the middle class, because its situation surrounds you. No one can get out of the middle class, because it's a community setup that does not have Queen Elizabeth. England has Queen Elizabeth. She lives in her small, aristocratic circle, but most of her world is middle-class nevertheless.

So if you transfer a queen from the classical period to today, do not play her as the same queen. Elizabeth II is not Elizabeth I. She is like every other English girl who goes to school. Get this division straight: from 1850 on, you are middle-class. You can have a little of the "upper" or "lower" thing, but not too much. You can be a peasant or a proletarian, but mostly you have the familiar things: we have cars, we belong to trade unions—we're middle-class.

The king can no longer be played the old way. The robes can no longer turn an actor into Henry VIII or Lear. With the downfall of royalty, the robe became just a costume and the sword just a prop. Why? Because something had happened to the *real* king. The king of Norway doesn't wear robes these days. He wears a kind of tuxedo with a diagonal red sash across the front. They let him keep the decoration, but the robes had to come off with the advent of the middle class. The new arrangement was some royalty, some socialists, some Whigs, some Liberal Democrats—some mixed thing. The robes had become a little absurd. Because of that, the costume was taken away, but something else is given to you: the social situation. Each character represents a part of it, and you will in time be able to say, "He's not a conservative, in spite of his tuxedo," or, "The red sash doesn't fool me—he's a scoundrel." He is this or that. You will begin to see his social character.

The success of an actor's work depends a great deal on how deeply he can penetrate into the culture that he is going to act. That is one of the things we are going to work on. Ibsen said very concisely what his aim was: "I will torpedo the arts. I will destroy them." He was a tremendously strong man, and when he said something, he did it.

Ibsen said revolution per se did not interest him. He found that revolutions were not engaging or useful; they were external and political. He stood alone in his political philosophy. The society of the mob was not for him. If the people take over and the crown has to go, then later the crown takes over again and the *people* go, and then the people again and then the crown. It was a tiresome process for thinking people. Groups that advocated such things tired Ibsen's mind and turned him into an independent. "I have no gift for politics," he said. "I don't even have a gift for citizenship."

Ibsen rejected all group thinking. From his individual sense of thinking for himself, he thought political action was no longer terribly useful. No politician or political philosophy could catch him. He would not join any party. He said, "It has become a necessity for me to work entirely on my own."

In every Ibsen play someone says, "I cannot join. I have to stand alone." By standing alone, Ibsen worked out and wants his characters and you and the world to work out a life that belongs completely to oneself and no one else. He is in the artist group. That is his religion. In an Ibsen play, see how people stand—in what groups. You can say, "He is standing with the socialists, she is standing with the conservatives. . . ." Sooner or later, somewhere in the play, someone will emerge with the idea of, What about just standing on your own two feet?

There were no railroads in Norway in Ibsen's day. How did people get around? You cannot go to your own life or your own "instinct" to answer this. You will be forced to do some research, to read and look at pictures. How did people go to work and travel and transport things without a railroad?

The smallness of Norway reflects the smallness of thinking there and in the larger world. The big world was not emancipated. Ibsen was in a historical moment when things were struck down, made small, made provincial by the government, by the thinking of the day. He writes about that—about the smallness of the towns and of people who are surrounded by small, conventional thoughts. He attacks the idealism behind those thoughts. The essence of the entire community is opened up to you by the biographical knowledge of this.

Ibsen's plays deal with the parochial smallness of such European cities. Complaining did no good. Complaining in Ibsen's time brought one catastrophe of revolt and then another catastrophe to overcome that revolt and then a counterrevolt, and then overcoming the counterrevolt. When Ibsen came of age and was writing the plays, he was aware. He read newspapers. When you see pictures or read about him, you see him at a corner table with a newspaper. In those days, a cafe had the newspaper on a stick of wood. It was there for the customers to read.

Ibsen did something that few other people did: he traveled. Extensively. For twenty-seven years. I don't know if he went to Greece, but if he did, you can bet he spent more than two days. In all that traveling, he observed the similarities and differences between his own community and the communities of the world. It proved very useful to him. He discovered that European middle-class morality in his day was on a very low level. To be honest, good, faithful—the moral values of the society were on a very low level. The cultural level was not very progressive, either.

In 1891, when *Ghosts* was performed in London (ten years after he wrote it), the scandal was enormous. By 1891, the Industrial Revolution had long since happened. There was already Marx and Darwin, and Freud was in the wings—there were large thinking patterns in the world. But in 1891 England, the play was scourged. They called it syphilitic and vile, unfit for human beings. The public insults were uncontrolled. The critics published them in all the major literary magazines so that the whole world could have a chance to hate Ibsen.

Before 1900, if a woman left her husband it was considered dirty. You have to find out and understand the difference between then and now. If you look at any social period more than ten years later, you will be hopelessly out of date and out of touch with it. If you have a play written in the thirties and you are doing it in the forties, you have to go back to the thirties or your efforts will be absurd. The play comes out of a unique time and place, which the actor has to know.

You *must* know the social situation.

Society, through industrialization, has become competitive. Certain economic benefits have resulted. But the drive to compete grinds down the spirit into something smaller and less than its capacity and grinds out the capacity to love.

After the Age of Reason and Darwin, man's spirit was divided. Thenceforth, he translated the love of God to the love of his neighbor, at least in theory. But he lived in a highly competitive society and could *not* love his neighbor, because he was also trying to beat him out at the same time.

It is not easy to love, says Ibsen, and the middle-class husband is not at peace with himself. He says he loves his neighbor and his family, but he is under a strain. Love and life are not easy for him. His domestic and religious ideals are constantly being undermined. Society is now being held up by man rather than by God. Worship of God is replaced by conformity to society. To be a success, to have power, your good name must not be spoiled. Society has a powerful hold on you. Society has largely displaced God as the moral and spiritual authority figure and High Power to whom man owes obeisance and allegiance. Society supposedly has a reciprocal duty to serve the whole community in certain ways, but it can usually be counted on to serve only the elite and the monied interests in the community and—insult to injury—often in corrupt ways. Man seems to have much more duty to society than society has to man.

Among the duties society and its institutions require is conformity. Conformity results in immaturity and childishness. Ibsen says there is no maturity unless the first duty is to oneself. He says a mature man will allow nothing to happen to him until he first faces what his duty is to himself. *First,* duty to oneself, and *then* to society. Duty to society first is what he is fighting.

If at the end of a play the husband says, "Don't you know that your first duty is as a wife and mother?" The girl answers, "No, I think my first duty is to myself, then to my husband and baby." That is a tremendous change in thinking.

We still have not progressed so very far from a thousand years ago—the automatic notion of duty to father, mother, and children first. I still believe it is. I don't care what Ibsen says. My middle-class thinking is too ingrained to fight it.

Ibsen is strong enough to fight it.

Things have changed. The middle class used to have much more support. One hundred years ago there was no revolution against the establishment. People lived with a structure—security, home, respectability. There was an external form to middle-class life. The porter touched his hat. People knew how to act toward one another. Servants knew how to behave toward the master and vice versa. Children had nurses, the mother had leisure.

When Nora was a little girl, she spent a lot of time in the servants' quarters. They're very different downstairs. Children learned the truth from servants. Nora learned about her father. She had a good knowledge of the servant class, which knew and could tear off the mask of the middle class if it wanted to.

The revolution happened fast in France. But in England? Absolute politeness. In England, you have a king and queen and people live up to the image. Without it, we live down. There is snobbism in servant life when there is a king—the upstairs maid won't talk to the downstairs maid. The maid doesn't feel that the porter is as important as she is.

Nora shops. She has small activities, like little streams flowing. To go from home is a little dangerous—there is a certain sense that the outside is precarious. The wind is blowing. Her jolliness is brought in from the outside. The outside has in it the great magic of buying. She brings the outside into her provincial life. People know her name—like a little girl. She has the ability to fraternize with the other class. Men don't have that so much. She brings this inside.

The middle class must spend money—acquire things. Money

and Nora go together. She is the buyer in the family. What she buys has nothing to do with stability—she doesn't buy stocks or land. She is relegated to buying toys, clothes—everything is part of her doll's house. Whatever she buys turns into a toy. She is not allowed to know about the other world. What she buys, she must give up at the end of the play. She shops for chocolate and macaroons and baby clothes. The more she does this, the happier she is. The love supplied by her husband comes in the form of money. Her allegiance is to the source of pleasure—the father who gives me a pony ride, the mother who gives me extra candy. The husband is the source—of the money.

But on the other hand, in this moneyed class there is also a great emphasis on *not* spending money. That is the social moment you have to understand and contrast to your own. It is the opposite of what the aristocratic class wants; they don't want a bargain, they want the best. The middle class wants to *save.*

She says, "This is the first Christmas where we don't need to economize. I can buy all the fruit in the world. We can buy more clothes for the children, more hand-embroidered linen." Write out ten things which she won't economize on. *Then* you can say the line. Know what she doesn't have to economize on.

Torvald says, "Tell me, Nora, you extravagant little person, what would you like for yourself?" He is always at her about money. Extravagance in the middle class is equal to flagrancy, to showing off. The middle class is not for show. It is conservative: "It's a sweet little spendthrift, but she uses up a deal of money. One would hardly believe how expensive such little persons are." The language here is clear. He is buying a marriage. Wives are expensive, children are expensive. What kind of attitude is that? It is a middle-class attitude.

Everything has its price. Money puts a value on everything in the middle class. There is not one character in Shakespeare who talks about money except Shylock. They do not deal in money. If you deal in a moneyed class, part of it rubs off. If you play a middle-class man, from Ibsen on, you must know that the middle class thinks differently. You must think the way every middle-class man thinks. The Pope thinks differently from the way a rich man who supports the Pope thinks. Know the difference between the character and you. Understand yourself in relation to the play, your class and the class you are playing.

Ibsen attacked middle-class rules because they were "given." If Nora walks out, it causes chaos. There was no revolutionary group in Norway one hundred years ago, no jobs for women except servant or perhaps schoolteacher or nurse. The difference between a man and his wife: the husband must not be disturbed. The wife can be disturbed. He is strong, she is weak. Nora is ignorant of money and how it functions. Nora is not in a position to understand how middle-class life works. Man's attitude is one of dominance: he treats her like a child. Nora is a child-wife.

When Ibsen decided to deal with the middle class, he knew about the influence of money on men as well as women. He had a sense of the man being exploited, too. "I'm stuck with it and I know I'm stuck with it." She says, "I wish I had inherited more of Papa's qualities." She sasses him. Whenever she is serious, he laughs: "I wouldn't want you any different because you are my own little lark. You're my puppy and you must not wet anymore." He wants her this way. "Are you sure you didn't get anything in town today?" Nora thinks, "You don't know what I am and you never will. I love you because you're innocent compared to me, and I'll say it the way you want me to."

The scrutinies of Darwin, Marx, and Freud broke new ground and pretty much covered the scientific and social territory. By the 1880s, everything was being openly questioned—except morality. Social life was ahead of personal life. Man in the private sphere was not secure, and neither were his morals. Religion was in retreat. Many still believed, but more and more didn't. The "honor century" would soon be over.

The new man in history would have to be his own moralist. Social structures were collapsing all around. There weren't too many lies left. But "love" was one of them.

For the gentleman of culture who read Voltaire in the eighteenth century, gallantry ruled the game of love. Passion was kept at a distance. Molière came out of the wars and the need to replace that precious quality with something more serious based not on chivalry but on the real conflicting motives and deceptions of passion, the stern dialectic of moral ideas.

The concentrated romantic novel of modern times revolves around the fate of a principal character who absorbs the reader's interest. This was the new style of the nineteenth century—the age of psychology—exposing the spiritual attitudes and motives of its characters, who lost their stereotypical quality and became more complicated, more contradictory, more self-unraveling. The dramatists of the classical period were moralists who represented external happenings, split up their characters, and took out a few abstract principles but not the total context of their life.

The rococo is the final phase of the culture of taste, where beauty and art are synonymous, as with Mozart. With Beethoven, art becomes combative, striving for expression, and violates style. No more canon of universal form. Each artist has a personal struggle for his means of expression. Individualism and its passion for originality put an end to the idea of style as something held in common by the cultural community.

The nineteenth century gives us a new character, the progress of psychological naturalism, the pathological features of love, the fight of badly mated people. Now the social castes are mixed; the bourgeoisie has to defend itself. Now the incalculable love passion threatens the social order.

The "realistic" understanding of love is that a human being can't be truly dedicated to work and at the same time be fully identified with another person. You cannot realize love if you primarily realize your ambition. That main drive doesn't permit you to love. The big mixup in middle-class man's life is that only a small part of it is dedicated to love. His "I love you" is weakened by his drive for power and self-achievement. Ibsen's banker very much wants to love, but if you reach out only for personal achievement, you lose understanding of your wife.

What happened in the man who created such a strong system of government, hospitals, waterways, and things—the way middle-class men live with family and money—is that his spiritual side was diminished. It was first threatened with Galileo and then with Darwin, who said, "You are really not so grand—you are actually a monkey." If Darwin says you are a monkey and the church says, "No, when you die you'll be in heaven," it mixes people up. Then Marx came along and said, "Forget it—let's have a society of workers." Then Freud came along and said, "It doesn't matter what you think—it's all in your head."

Middle-class man in the late 1800s and early 1900s had to find a way to hold himself up more securely. He couldn't depend on God alone, but he could understand government and he could depend on the rules: You must go to school. You must be a lawyer or a doctor. God forbid you should be an actor. It's not good to be an actor in the rules of middle-class society. It is still not good. Art is frowned upon by the middle class.

Man has to mask against the realities he is faced with like death, failure. "I have to get along in this world." The way he establishes himself most strongly is the family—a strong aspect of middle-class life. Family life is a strong institution, and Ibsen deals very much with it. Your generation has opened up the idealized institution of marriage more than it has ever been opened up before, but you have to treat it in its time. Ibsen says the sexual instinct in middle-class society reveals itself as too difficult to deal with; in its nakedness it is too brutal.

Ibsen says love exists only in spurts. Dante loved Beatrice, but he was not faithful to her. He married another woman, and he was not faithful to her, either. But he was able to say "I love her" and to put it over on everybody. We still say "Beatrice and Dante," but they and their love are a myth created by the novelists and the church. The honeymoon. The romance. There's a great deal of idealizing about it in order to make it function. Marriage and family life have a special way of dealing with sex. Otherwise, it is too hard on society. It says that in marriage you love the family better than other people. The woman you desire is better than anybody.

But the love buds do not flourish from nine to five in business. You don't fight all day to get the best of your competitor and then come home and say, "I love my little boy and I adore my wife and, by the way, where is my sister?" Middle-class man seeks and expects love. His wife wants love. But the husband is incapable of giving it. The only person who can do it is Jimmy Carter. That man works eighteen hours a day there and knows politics and then appears with this angel and goes to church. He wants Ted Kennedy to die—he must. Yet he is so sweet with Rosalynn—he really is. But aside from Jimmy, Ibsen says men are wounded by their success. You cannot fight and still be a lover.

People whose marriages fail don't say the institution of marriage failed but "I" failed—they blame themselves. Ibsen says the whole love deal is a mistake which must be reshuffled and started all over again. Nobody knows how to do it. They asked him what would have been the best thing. He said the best thing would have been if Noah's ark had sunk.

Society says a woman is only at her best if she fulfills the ideal of wife and serves her husband and the marriage, not herself. But then, of course, she has lost her right to live, says Ibsen. If society does not threaten her with unemployment and if she is not socially ostracized, she may rebel, which has happened often in the last thirty years. The revolt of women for independence is natural—the desire to achieve something other than domesticity.

But Ibsen doesn't just want to free women, there is something deeper. Something concerned with temperament.

If you are by nature affectionate, faithful, and passive, you are perhaps the domestic type—happy with home and children. On the other hand, if you are by temperament nervous and restless and energetic, this is not a good sign for domesticity. Every businessman woos in terms of the romantic illusion "You will be my wife and we will have a family together and I love you and you are beautiful and I have chosen you above all other women and our marriage will carry out this romantic ideal." Immediately after the marriage, the wife is neglected for the business, and nine-tenths of the man's life lies away from the home.

Ibsen depicted a man and a woman of opposite temperaments, who therefore have a different reality. Nora is scatterbrained, bright, impulsive, romantic. Torvald is stuffy and compulsive. It is improbable that two such people could ever understand each other. Because of their differences, they lose touch with one another. There are two kinds of conscience—one in man and another, altogether different, in woman. They can never really be reconciled. Ibsen says they are doomed with this difference. After living with him for nine years, she has found out a lot of these differences. One of these differences is that she will never stop responding and he will never respond. He will bring everything down to where he needs it to be reasonable.

Ibsen is not talking of an aristocratic society, but a middle-class one, where men do not stay home. The wife has nothing to do until the children come. She then becomes very powerful. The man knows that the moment the children come, the woman will settle down, because she is needed by them, the grocer, the butcher, the doctor. She says either "Now I get down to business" or "What happened to me? Who am I?" If she has the temperament for it, she stays. If she wants self-fulfillment, she will be a failure. Society tells her she is supposed to be a good wife and good mother—an illusion. She lives with this convention imposed upon her until she discovers something else.

Ibsen says, "Find out what you are."

Men and women don't understand one another.

Women are judged as if they were men, Ibsen says. But they have different patterns, psyches. It is unjust to judge women by male standards and men's laws. Women don't have a society—the society is for men. Ibsen sways you toward her. He says women are kinder. They are not out hardening themselves. A man says, "I mustn't cry"—part of the outside ethic—"I have to be strong." Ibsen says that strength is overestimated. A woman can love more, care more. A man squeezes that out of himself. He is out in the world, needing to be hard, and doesn't know the price he pays for that. He can't share in the love of the children like she does. When the courts give the children to the mother, they know what they are doing. The man doesn't have the time.

Ibsen says it is impossible for man to face reality. Modern man has created a social structure to defend himself against reality and intervene for him. He hates or refuses to say, "I am going to die." He has created a whole way of escaping from facing death—masks the truth through religion and God and concept of family to perpetuate himself. Having a family is the best thing in the middle class. If you don't have a family, you're not so good, so complete, so socially acceptable. He creates the mask of love—idealized marriage. Sexual instinct is disguised, masked. Ibsen is after the man that sustains this illusion of marriage and family life.

Ibsen smashes the mask. When you smash the mask of the illusion, you arrive at a form of reality: love must be faced realistically. Marriage is a convention, a social institution, legally arranged and enforced. Society presents it as a natural and "holy" institution, but the business of marriage has a great deal to do with money. Matrimony is holy only if somebody says it is. A woman in the 1870s doesn't know "holy." She knows the idea of children and the need to be happy and show her happiness. Inside, she has problems understanding the "big things."

In the marriage ceremony, husband says to wife, "I'll love, honor, and obey." Ibsen questions that. The same man who says he loves his neighbor and spends eight hours a day fighting to make his way in a cutthroat world is in competition with himself.

Each man has the potential for living a full life. He hopes to win by achieving success only to find that the specialization required for this success adds up to failure. In Ibsen, the character of the man turns to his profession—his public life. Ibsen says it is the misfortune of the modern man that he is fated to become an exaggerated, one-sided being no matter what he chooses to do. He develops his professional power at the expense of the home. As a result, the whole man ceases to exist.

Society promises fulfillment in both areas of life, but it doesn't deliver. Man's hopes are unattainable. His dedication to his profession brings the neglect of his obligations at home, which reflects the social trap in which he must brutally cut off sides of himself to realize his outside ambitions. This ruins the man and forces him to ruin the woman.

In the eighteenth century, marriage promised to be a stabilizing force. By the late nineteenth, in Ibsen, one partner's interest is in conflict with the other's, and marriage is a disaster. The men in Ibsen's world use the same techniques at home as they do in their social and business life: Torvald's struggle to succeed makes him treat all other things in the same acquisitive manner, including his wife. The character of the woman goes to pieces because of the complete isolation into which she is driven by the man's professionalism. The whole thing is nothing. The only thing that remains is loneliness without hope.

*   *   *

Duty to society is the focus of *A Doll's House, Ghosts,* and *An Enemy of the People.* It culminates in the woman sacrificing herself for her duty—the false middle-class values of truth, responsibility, virtue, etc. The man lives by the principle of ambition and personal profit. Nora tries to save herself—she does not *want* to kill herself. But Ibsen's people frequently sacrifice themselves to what they see as their duty.

A "natural woman" is thought to have a heart of love and a soul that finds total satisfaction in self-sacrifice, serving the family. But Ibsen says that is a mask. The woman who is self-sacrificing is taken advantage of and is disliked for her pain, because if she sacrifices herself, she denies the man a certain positive attribute that he needs and must act upon. Everybody feels self-sacrifice is a drag and a reproach to the other person. You must have some willfulness to be yourself. You must be unscrupulous, true to what you feel, to be yourself and you must be conscientious about what you want to be.

Ibsen in his plays says love loses its charm when it is not free. If you are tied compulsorily or legally to someone, that person becomes abhorrent: "You cannot love me and possess me and take away my freedom, because you make me dislike you," says the Ibsen character. It is not "natural" to use a person that way. It is only natural for a person to have his own life. Marriage demands such unnatural conditions, says Ibsen, and mandates possessiveness. In fact, it is just a way to make the society go on, but in its idealized form it makes a man think, "I *have* to possess you and you *have* to belong to me because I love you." But love doesn't function that way, says Ibsen. Love is not manifested in continuity. It exists in brief glimpses. It is not in the nature of love to last forever.

Nora, the ideal wife, is expected to pose for Torvald. She sacrifices herself for him. Will he sacrifice himself for her? Live up to her nobility? The man Nora loves is a creature of fantasy with ideal qualities. When this proves false, she is left with a stranger in which she has no interest. She realizes she has been masquerading as a child and he as a father. Nora was taken in by his and her own pose.

Nora's sacrifice is futile. Ibsen says the sacrifice of a human being—self-destruction—is absurd unless it is for a cause that is bigger than yourself.

*   *   *

In realism, make sure to find that part of the plot that paves the way for the reversal of the situation.

Torvald is a caricature of the archetype of father; Nora, of the rebellious daughter. Characters conceived this way have symbolic significance: Nora the impulsive, Torvald the compulsive, human nature. The essence of what Ibsen gives you is opposites: light and dark, day and night, man and woman, kind and cruel—the antithetical forces of the universal character. Those cosmic opposites exist in the outside society and are thus brought into the situation of marriage. The failure of society manifests itself most in marriage. Ibsen puts marriage in a complex way but in simple language. He says marriage is where conflict occurs most. The home becomes a battleground.

Your instinct is to make the play about a "fight." But the problem in *Doll's House* transcends the normal opposition of husband and wife. What Ibsen perceives in this difficult marriage is something bigger—the irreconcilable difference between man and woman, the clash of cosmic forces. Nora's revolt takes on a certain universality, which gives tragic size to what might otherwise be only a simple story of incompatibility. It is a kind of metaphor for the vast irreconcilable viewpoints that resolve into a separation of the union.

Man is mind, woman is spirit. They are opposite right from Adam and Eve. Nora and Torvald are archetypes, not stereotypes. The size must come through. Understand that the man represents the inflated ego, the dominant character on earth. This is not only in Ibsen. Yeats reveals the pompous, self-centered side of man, built up through the ages.

Torvald doesn't want Nora to eat sweets. He wants to control her childish ways. He has an enormous need for her to "mind" him. But he is ambivalent, lets her get away with some things and not others. Now is not too different from one hundred years ago: the man needs to dominate. The "boss" encourages a certain sneakiness—in marriage and in work—in order to keep control. But Nora goes against the rules. She lies about everything. It is the only way for her to survive.

"Happiness" was another lie, as we shall see—the great middle-class illusion and the most haunting motif in realist theater ever after.

Reality is working against Torvald and Nora.

Truth and Lies

IBSEN SAYS no truth lasts longer than seventeen or eighteen years. After that, another truth comes along. He has no illusions about the permanence of truth. No matter how persuasive, all intellectual postulates are invariably reduced to lifeless conventions in time. The ultimate truth lies only in the perpetual conflict of truth.

Great writers rarely answer the great questions they ask, except to preach resignation. Ibsen, on the other hand, clearly stated not just what he believed the problem to be—willingness to let oneself be dominated by one's past—but the answer that we can become ourselves by throwing off the past. It's a theme he was to develop through his final twelve plays.

The word "liberty," for example, meant something special for him, not just "We want freedom." Ibsen made an important point about the Jewish nation that you will have to think about. He calls it the most noble of the human race. ("Thank God," the Jews say, "he's on our side.") It preserved itself in its isolation. It did not belong to any state. In spite of the barbarity toward them, the Jews have nobility because they had no state to turn to. They were not constructing a state and so they did not get corrupted by governments and senates. They maintained themselves. Ibsen calls Jews an aristocracy of the human race because they had no state to burden them—they had a spiritual aristocracy, not one by birth. Ibsen says the state must be abolished or we will be caught in its trap forever. You may or may not agree with it. It is Mr. Ibsen, not Miss Adler, talking.

The aristocrat of birth has certain privileges. If he does not want to say good morning, he does not have to. Only the middle class has to. Another privilege of the aristocrat is that it does not matter if he has no money. He is accepted because he is in a line that will accept him with or without money. We in the middle class do not have that. Fine if we have some money, but God help us if we don't. Just try going to your rich aunt or to a Madison Avenue party and saying, "I'm an actor, I don't have any clothes," and see how much help you get.

Ibsen speaks a great deal about the aristocracy of the spirit—the self, the will. Being an aristocrat of soul is the only weapon against all lies. Ibsen said, "Appear indifferent—never answer newspapers. Act as if you had no idea anyone was opposed to you." I used to read the attacks and say, "I'm finished —I will never be able to hold up my head." But no one remembers what they wrote, and neither do I. Don't cheapen yourself in mud slinging. Start a new series of work. Be contemptuous of everything that is crumbling around you.

Ibsen means he is able to think for himself, which is aristocratic. He is under no obligation to think the way anybody else thinks. You ask, how should I think? About the country, the President, the oil business? If you are middle class, you will think what *The New York Times* or certainly *Time* magazine tells you to think. The middle class does not think for itself, it is too busy. Mr. Ibsen is after this class, Mr. Ibsen and me. His constant clamor, constant aim was the freedom to be himself. That is what he put into his plays. You have to be true and faithful to your own self and your own thinking, not to mass thinking. Mr. Ibsen says you have to do that.

His entire career gave him the possibility of not joining up. Because Ibsen did not join up, the extreme right and extreme left wanted him in some way and could not get him.

Good for Mr. Ibsen.

Ibsen knew if he had an unpopular opinion and stood by it, around the corner he would be bashed in the head, ostracized. Being alone and standing alone meant giving up something. If you could make a great sacrifice, Ibsen felt you were a sincere person. Otherwise, it was probably just an intellectual idea. People are very facile about what they say. "I would die for my country." "I'd rather die than do that." But if you really mean it, Ibsen said, you will die for what you want. You will not succeed without this sacrifice.

In social criticism, the majority is always right. The majority elects a President and says, "If we elected him, he's right." Institutions like the church always have a majority opinion. Every mother knows what is right. I never heard a mother say, "You know, I'm all wrong." Every teacher says, "I know." There is a lack of self-criticism in the majority. The institutions of church, government, learning, etc. all tell us to think the way they think. An individual can't live outside the community. He somehow or other has to be part of the community whether he wants to or not.

But there is something about the majority that really aggravates a thinker. A minority evolves: *the will to individualism.* Man is responsible for his own fate. But most of us have not got control of our own fate. There is no way you can exist within an institution without conforming to the institutional thinking. This is middle-class life.

At one time everybody had absolute allegiance to the king. And then somebody said, "I repudiate that. I do not, myself, want to have allegiance to this king." That created a lot of trouble, a lot of heads rolled, but in time you were no longer required to have absolute allegiance to a king. It took a long time. Time alters the rules in society. It happened with Martin Luther. "I take away the vow of chastity." He created a lot of trouble, but now in Christianity you do not have to take the vow of chastity. Those are historical examples of how society changes from majority-rule conformity— how it has to alter. A man says, "I personally take it upon myself to defy the idea of allegiance to the king." Probably he had to die or be killed for it. But the desire to change the society makes us think that we will win: "How nice it will be if we change and it gets to be *our* way."

Ibsen points out that anybody who takes a minority position in his play loses. It is only many, many years later, after other people take up the thread, that a woman has the right to leave her home. When Nora leaves, there is nobody there for her. Nora leaves and is destitute. The person who takes it upon himself to refute the conformity is the victim of society, not the hero. That takes out a little of the romantic notion. These are Ibsen's truths that emerge in the plays.

In *Enemy of the People*, a man who does not conform says, "I don't want to make money out of the baths. They are contaminated. I want to close them." He sees the truth and fights about it. Once the truth is revealed, there are a lot of objections to it. Ibsen says the middle class lives by lies. He says it is important to reveal the truth. The man who has the courage to do that is the realist.

Galileo—a very good example—says, "The world is not flat." That is very disappointing. Even to me. I prefer it to be flat so you fall off. But instead of that, it was round. That was a very tough business for Christianity to admit. You have to be against Christianity to admit a scientific fact like that. Science comes a great deal into the mixup.

The fight is painful. Ibsen is after the man with inherited ideas who idealizes problems. If a man says, "I'm going to live and work and then I'm going to die—there is nothing I can hope for," that is pretty grim. Ibsen knew that man had to protect himself against the grimness of fate. He understands the man who builds up illusions, but he also understands that illusions create lies in middle-class life. Certain lies have to be supplanted so maybe certain other ideas can take their place.

Ibsen believes the exceptional man has to abandon duty to institutions—to think through for himself how he wants to relate to the church, his landlord, his marriage, his children. He cannot take the rules that are given to him. Ibsen says each man must have his own reality. He cannot have the reality of the group. When you read an Ibsen play, see how the reality of the group takes over. Everybody is with the peer group of either the mother, the head of the family, the businessman, the uncle. Everybody is part of some institution that comes in to make him accept the rules of the institution above his own thinking.

We do not know if Nora is right when she walks out. Some say she is right. The men say she is wrong. A lot of people say, "Where the hell is she going?" But there is no doubt that when she opened the door and said "Here are the keys, and here is the ring," the world changed after that play. The Western world understood something about marriage that will never, never come back: "I am leaving." When Ibsen says something, it rings through the whole world. That is why it is very good for you to get it, because you will also get it in

Miller, Odets, in the modern plays, certainly O'Neill, Tennessee Williams. It is big.

Ibsen says man is on the wrong track. Ibsen thinks man is consistently trapped. The inner self is the only master that a man should put into action. He must work from his own center. If you find your own reality, you are a realist—one who tries to push through to his own truth.

Ibsen says there is hope for mankind only when every individual becomes an authentic person. All his acts must stem from his deeper self. The individual is forced to subordinate himself to the society as a whole, or more precisely, to those authorities responsible for the well-being of that society. In *Enemy of the People,* Dr. Stockmann discovers that the resources are polluted—the social institutions, the whole community is built on a cesspool of lies. The filth of modern life. Both the conservative view and the liberal press are corrupt. The play is full of the tension of community life. Not to affirm it, but to purify it. The rights of the individual versus the claims of the community. What is promised versus what is practiced. The play is about the tyranny of the institutions that control people. Ibsen's attacks in *Enemy of the People* are aimed at the lies that form the basis of modern institutions.

He says, don't conform to them.

The middle class says, "Thou shalt not lie." But it is easy to tell a lie and we think nothing of it. We lie every minute of the day. Nora's lying is second nature for her. Ibsen gives you a person who is forced to recognize that lying makes her have no self. She *wants* to tell the truth: "I didn't love you—I was merry, not happy. I haven't got the temperament to be a mother. I don't know what to teach my children. I am a mess."

In this play, he says that it is bad to lie. In another play, it is wrong to tell the truth—you are a fanatic, people need illusions. Ibsen is not laying down moral laws. He is saying, in this instance she lost herself. In *The Wild Duck,* the girl needs illusions, the grandfather needs dreams. Ibsen does not proselytize in each play the same way. Find out what each play says that is truthful for the situation.

In *Doll's House,* Nora starts to see some of the big lies in some of the big "truths." Nora lies as a way of life, but she tells the truth in the end.

The truth is, men's conduct is undermined by always competing for their own success. They preach the ideals of humanity but rarely live up to what they preach. They never admit to the principle by which they live—the materialism of personal profit. In Ibsen, the women develop a nobility of character superior to their material needs. Women, due to their greater distance from the public life, are capable of expressing human traits of rising above the limitations of society. Their removal from business life protects them from complete surrender to social and economic pressures. The unique quality of women is their superior ability to cling to the truth.

The women in Ibsen love to the point of self-sacrifice. The men never do. The conflict in Ibsen is between the ambitious man and the humanity of the woman. Both men and women talk about values, but there is no truth in men's talk about ideals. There is truth in women's talk.

Somewhere a realistic, independent individual has always been there inside Nora. Her childlike pose was a pretense by which she herself was taken in. Once she understands this, a reevaluation of her position is inescapable. The difference between her way of thought and the masculine society Torvald represents is fundamental: "The laws are different than what I thought. They can't be right." Nora is other than she seems. So is Torvald. He is no longer the man she thought he was or the man he thought himself to be. Torvald is the declination of the patriarchal idea. He was at one time right. But he is fated, as a husband, to go down with that point of view, which he unworthily represents. Nora says, "Stay the way you are if you want, but let me out." She can't accept the size of the male ego once she sees he is a coward, dependent on what others say. When Torvald sees he is not the image he believes himself to be, it is a terrible blow for him, too. What is he going to do? Ibsen gives you the man who is lost—who has been destroyed.

The home is the one great "reality" as well as the symbol. If you leave that, there is nothing else. The idea of the play is that Nora must leave something that will cost her her life in order to break from it. You must pay the price. It's like going to jail, being beheaded. That is the price for change. The home is what generations have built up. The chair means something. It must have a quality that is worth saving and passing on to your children. The home guarantees and is the symbol of continuity. Break it, and you break the continuity of home life forever. The home no longer is taken with the same seriousness after Nora leaves. She has cracked open forever the religiosity of home life. Torvald says, "You cannot leave your home and children," but Nora does. Once Nora is no longer taken in by the "integrity" of the husband, neither law nor custom nor religion will suffice to keep her in line.

You can't say Ibsen looked to the advancement of women's rights; he says it's the nature of the woman to get her freedom but not desert her base, the home. But what is new in the play is that the whole notion of male authority is called into question. Torvald and Nora are equally matched, equally doomed, equal objects of sympathy. The moment she starts to doubt the validity of what she did for Torvald, she no longer accepts the authority of a father or priest or husband. She has to think for herself. Nora throws off her servitude, becomes emancipated and strengthened. She became herself—a feminist.*

You have to understand how you got to modern plays. All modern plays have Ibsenian needs. The actor learns from Ibsen what is modern in the modern theater. There are no villains, no heroes. He understands, more than anything, there is more than one truth.

What is modern are the problems. In Odets's *Golden Boy,* a man wants to beat the system, but he also wants to be true to himself. That's a modern problem: I want to go to Hollywood and make a lot of money, but I also want to play Ibsen. Miller's play *The Price* is Ibsenian: one brother says you shouldn't have cared for Father, you should have been a doctor. The other says, I have the responsibility

*So did Ibsen. The thrust of Stella Adler's analysis is that Ibsen was the most profoundly feminist male writer up to his time—without benefit of psychology, just sociology and cultural-political history, intuiting the psychological essence through his own prescient, firsthand observations. Henrik Ibsen (1828–1906) and his greatest plays—*A Doll's House* (1879), *Ghosts* (1881), *An Enemy of the People* (1882), *The Wild Duck* (1884), and *Hedda Gabler* (1890)— predated Sigmund Freud (1856–1939) and the first major publication of Freud's psychoanalytical theories in 1892–95.

to care for Father. There is a fight on stage—who is right? This is Ibsen's contribution to theater. No modern problems are really solvable. Ibsen makes you understand that the overall thinking in a modern play is muddled. There are really no ground rules.

Torvald doesn't really respect Nora or her life. He thinks of her as a "little person." A *real* person to him is the manager of the bank, men who run the utilities. Theirs is a marriage without understanding—no perception or investigation of the relationship. There are two points of view, two truths. His truth is that if she saved enough, he could take the money and invest it for her. Nora's is that she does what she can, given her nature—she does what is important. She is on another level of money. Both points of view are valid.

When Torvald says "Is that my little lark twittering out there?" it is important to see that, to a certain degree, the woman is less strong and capable than the man. The man has a sense of power and the woman is more decorative in the society. Ibsen says it's the woman's job to fix that.

Women in Nora's time, by virtue of being in the home, twitter and chirp. Nora has accepted the role the man wants her to play and has given the man the powerful, traditional role of historical father, as in the Bible. Nobody threatened that role. Nora allows him to say, "Quiet, please—Father is working, the leader is working." She gives him this power and believes he has the power. She suppresses the sense of what she knows. She lets him play it and he believes it. In doing so, she stays childish and feminine to please. This still goes on.

In act two, Nora's aim is to save her "doll's house." In act three, she enters in a costume—the disguise of a black cloak, the symbol of death. Ibsen chooses the tarantella spider dance—the dance of disease and death. Nora's dancing excites Torvald. He is involved with sex. She is involved with her death.

Dr. Rank reveals that he, like Nora, has an awful secret: the syphilitic spinal disease he inherited from his father. Ibsen parallels his physical illness with Nora's moral illness, which Torvald says she "inherited" from her father. Nora and Dr. Rank are both carrying a poison that is killing them.

Nora feels morally ill. Lost in her unworldliness, she did something wrong "for love"—in a desperate attempt to protect her "doll's house" reality. It is "inexcusable" to borrow money in those days. Today it's not. Everything is on credit. She is guilty of a crime—forging—then borrows and makes everything worse by concealing it, lying. She knows she lies, worries that she's going to pass on her "disease" to her children. Nora feels like a leper, morally unsuitable, after she learns the consequences of the forgery. It poisons her home. Nora is hysterical with fear to know that she is carrying a spiritual disease inside her. She is slowly dying from her disease. She believes she is deeply injurious to her family.

But she must have money and raises it secretly so that her husband can get back his health. She lies because his life is at stake and gets the money from a moneylender, signs her father's name and does not think this is out of order. She pays back the debt by copying at night and deprives herself, steals from the housekeeping money and children's clothes budget. When the moneylender wants a job with her husband, Nora is faced with the truth. She realizes she has done something dishonest out of her own ignorance of the world. She begins to doubt her way of life. She, her children, her husband will go down to the worst disgrace because of her deceitfulness.

Nora's disease, like Dr. Rank's, is something that cannot be remedied. Her last chance to save herself and her husband is to get money from Dr. Rank, who has one more investigation to make about his own disease—to know the time of his death. Both of them are now victims of time. Side by side, they are both waiting as their diseases creep on to a fatal ending. She is coquettish with him. When he gets excited and says he'd do anything for her, she refuses the money because of her innermost decency. One side flirts, wants the money. The other side slaps her own vulgarity and recognizes her way with men. Nora has the makings of a real woman, a realist. She begins to edit herself. She wants to stand on her own two feet. There are now two Noras on stage: the spoiled woman who flirts and the heroic woman underneath, who stops this vulgarity when it begins to offend her sense of what is right, a woman of fundamental sound principles. The meeting with Rank is her last chance of salvation. It is an important scene because we see her in an act of heroism.

Nora is finished but realizes she is not right to kill herself, that Torvald and her father are responsible. She was sheltered from the world. The men who run the society made her a moral cripple. The real crime is not a forgery but a way of life that debases the female.

This attitude must not be transmitted. She must go into the hostile world and educate herself.

Torvald romantically promises to shoulder his wife's burdens. A romantic gesture. Her dollhouse values were all romantic. The husband does not perform this romantic miracle. After this, if anyone else said he would sacrifice himself for her, Nora would know not to believe it. Nora and Torvald both start out as idealists in the beginning. She becomes a realist, learns she has been living an illusion. You do not die for illusions if you recognize them as illusions. Nora realizes her life is an elaborate make-believe. As she discards her fancy dress, she discards her illusions. She appears in everyday dress—a symbol of her going into the world of reality.

She decides to leave the house, Torvald, and the children. Once out in the world she will become like Mrs. Linde: a worn-out woman who has to pay the price to find the truth in herself. Mrs. Linde had nothing to live for. She earned her own living, mixed with the world, found life aimless without the anchor of husband and children. This scene makes us realize what a void Nora faces at the end.

Nearer and nearer the scene goes toward doom. Like the victim of the tarantula, she can only dance a mad dance to vomit out the poison. She can no longer avoid the inevitable, only postpone the moment—wonderful, terrible—when she kills herself to prevent Torvald taking on the burden of her sin. Nora leaves the play as Mrs. Linde entered it, lonely, unhappy, with no one to live for and much, much older. We get a real sense of her going into an alien world—beyond the doll's house. Her life with the outer world will be a life in death.

Nora's exit denies the marriage, motherhood, responsibility. She must find it all out for herself, follow her own judgment and go against the standards of the society. Ibsen does not decide what is the right thing for Nora to do—you must decide that for yourself. You achieve your own truth not by thinking about it, but by doing it.

Ibsen says it is dangerous to deal with a man who represents some abstract thinking—the husband, priest or doctor when they represent their *institutions.* The basic principles that infuse Ibsen's plays are that institutions bring about conformity, that no man can speak for another man, and that you are responsible for yourself. Then you are a realist.

But today's realist is tomorrow's conservative. To Ibsen, progress is made by one man leaving the social situation and getting a few others together to change it. But once it changes, he believes fiercely in that change and refuses to recognize the next man who comes along and opposes it.

It became clear to Ibsen that the pursuit of happiness in middle-class life had to be questioned like the social situation that produced it. Ibsen says that as a society we idealize. If you don't have a family, you're not so good, and having a family is the best thing in the middle class. Torvald must present the "perfect" home to the world. He hides things from himself, keeps Nora a child, doesn't allow her to grow up. Nora has to lie—to buy an expensive present for old Anne-Marie, the servant, and then lie about its being cheap because of Torvald. To Nora it is perfectly normal to lie. Society forces her to do so. Nora doesn't even realize that she is lying.

Ibsen says every ideal situation is a lie and that "happiness" is the last great shared lie growing out of middle-class moral values. Happiness is the most tenacious of them. It has survived all the Marxian-Darwinian upheavals and intellectual ferment. The society gives the individual the aim of happiness. It is not questioned, just mindlessly handed down from one generation to the next. Overspecialization has brought about the failure of marriage—the center of private life. Ibsen's men are all in one form or another specialists, which affects their private lives. Because of it, nothing is really built. The love bugs are not at their most sensuous if you spend most of your life away on business. The love bugs die out. You don't come home with the most fervent material to be a husband.

But the worst failures of society cannot dissuade people from their quest for happiness—marital happiness, most of all. Home and family life are the testing ground for the search.

Man fails the test.

The middle class pays a high price for its favorite myth. Happiness is the great goal—but not the reality. Ibsen reveals the defeat of each individual in his search for happiness. His characters fail in everyday life, in profession and marriage alike. The most specific thing they fail to get is the thing they most want: happiness.

The bedrock of nineteenth-century middle-class life is the quest of happiness. But everyone fails in the attempt to achieve it. Ibsen reveals the contradictions that prevent the individual from achieving happiness. Self-interest makes it impossible to extend oneself in love: Torvald cannot establish a relationship or identify with anyone. At the end he is willing to sacrifice Nora for his reputation. Ibsen says a man's private and public interest cannot be reconciled in modern society. Middle-class idealism promises happiness in both areas but can't deliver.

The whole man ceases to exist in the idealized home situation because he obsesses on his profession at the expense of his family life. The more you become a success, the more you fail. The main social aim of family is to be a stabilizing force to keep away the brutality of outside life. Ibsen was first to discover that this stabilizing force doesn't work.

Ibsen attacks middle-class institutions with a great deal of anger and animosity. From the attack comes a gradual change in the institution. History doesn't leap forward. It grows inch by inch. Progress is difficult. Ibsen doesn't want you to have the melodramatic belief "Oh, the problem is solved! They will be happy ever after." He will give you an extra act to show you why happiness—the aim of the middle class—is not achieved.

The "happiness" Nora is able to create for Torvald and for herself is happiness without reality. She plays with her husband and dances and acts out sketches for him. She behaves like an animal. There is a sense of "I will not take on the real role of wife and mother." The play is not much interested in sex. The sexual instinct contains a brutality. Her playing is a postponement of what is grown-up. What is basic and historical for the woman is that her temperament in marriage is totally different from his. He is playful only when it delights him in an off-moment. Otherwise, he feels it is just wasting time.

Torvald in *Doll's House* is an idealist—irreproachable from the standpoint of society's morality. He is of the highest order in his business and family life—a model father, husband, and citizen. He has a fine wife and three fine children. The wife is loving and affectionate. She believes in this reality and in herself as a wife and mother. There is a sweet house, a motherly woman, a womanly wife and a happy family. Nora believes she has achieved happiness and believes her life is true.

Ibsen tears off the idealism. For the first time, Ibsen shows that a woman can be married and know she is unhappy. If she knows she is unhappy, maybe she can do something about it. The illusion is a way to hide from reality. The reality is, Torvald has no idea that Nora is anything but something to play with. She is what he wants to see. Ibsen created a school of theater where you must understand you are not as great as you think you are. He is not good to Nora; he calls his best friend a bore. Ibsen says he shouldn't have really married. He can't share a life with another person. He has the *illusion* that they are married. He says, "You needn't ruin your dear eyes and your pretty little hands." She is dear to him. Nora says, "It's wonderfully lovely to hear you say so!" Both of them are in the illusion of happiness.

At the end of *Doll's House,* Nora feels in the depths of her soul that she is too corrupt. She must leave.

On the other hand—by futile contrast—Ibsen in *Ghosts* shows us a woman who *stayed* in the home and still didn't find herself. But *Ghosts* is not about defeat. It is about what Mrs. Alving feels mankind needs: the spiritual quest outside the materialistic middle class. Can there be a decent home life without marriage? Why can't children be in a situation where their parents aren't married? Mrs. Alving is in search of the truth. She makes the great attempt to break through the institutions to which she has been subjected and surrounded by her "ghosts"—inherited opinions from parents, dead doctrines like patriotism, belief in God, respect for authority—ideas that aren't alive in us but hang on just the same.

Mrs. Alving, a simple middle-class woman, has a profound awareness of the trap she is in. There is no way for her to escape. She is every woman after Nora who stays in the marriage twenty years later. Society is so strong, an individual can't break from its pattern. The consolation prize is not "happiness" but self-awareness. Either way, Nora's or Mrs. Alving's—willingly or unwittingly, both of them have managed to break the illusion of happiness. Ibsen says man has a chance if he can break through all the ghosts and start again in the wilderness.

*   *   *

In the end, a good case can be made that happiness isn't really a "value" at all, just something related to the pleasure principle. At the very least, it does not come from man, money, or marriage. All those things have been idealized. Where men dominate the economic and social life, women get the short end. In Ibsen, it is women who have the nobility of character to create a way of life superior to the existing one. He says the reshaping of social conditions will be done largely by women.

Ibsen takes it upon himself to question whether the idealized home can ever exist. The threat to the idealized family comes when the individual begins to examine things. To Ibsen, the greatest happening—if not "happiness"—comes when a person begins to look for the truth. What is love? What is happiness? Do you understand what marriage is? Do you know enough about yourself to know what marriage does?

Ibsen's plays open up the whole bag of these realistic social and moral problems. They deal with, how I am going to resolve this problem realistically and not according to the law or the government or my grandmother or the church? "I will deal with this from my own point of view." The problem in a realistic play is to resolve the problem for yourself in relation to your own life. Convention has to go, idealism has to go—things that have blinded us and still blind us to how we live. These problems have not yet basically been solved.

Mr. Ibsen is after you—he will not let you go. You do not want to be caught up by him. But he will catch you. He uses his own techniques to get at the truth. In *A Doll's House*, Nora has to resolve whether she is going to be a mother or her own person. In *An Enemy of the People*, is Dr. Stockmann going to be defeated by the political groups? In *Ghosts*, the minister who is always able to settle matters—is he right or wrong? You have to judge. The wife who stayed in a marriage beyond her need to stay in it: should she have left or shouldn't she?

What Ibsen says about Nora or Dr. Stockmann does not pertain to an individual. He is not anxious to solve a play about a man and a woman. He is out to resolve the problem of Man and Woman, the problem of Man and Society. It is big time. That sense of epic size is something that has waned in the realistic theater, and so have actors who play it. When they do *Death of a Salesman*, they search—where is the man who can play Willy Loman? There are very few. It's because actors today think that being true is being nice, or being some other "set" thing.

That is not the truth. That is your miserable habit of boring everybody to death. It has nothing to do with truth. It has to do with the limitations of the modern actor who does not know how to express a big idea in language that is not iambic pentameter. I am in search of the *big* actor.

If you say in an Ibsen play "I am unhappy," it is not that *you* are unhappy but that millions of people like you in the world have the same problem and are unhappy. To play it without lifting up the cosmic problem is wrong. You have it in you but you must know that within as you work on it. Knowing that it has this size will make you not play it as if it were personal.

Ibsen's search for truth, even in its simplest terms, has largeness, has dignity. A large searching is the basis of life. It is the most important way you can solve yourself as an actor in a size that is modern, because you cannot go back to costume and wearing a crown. Having to do it in this way is the only way you can achieve the modern epic.

The play and its characters are a skeleton. The author takes the chance with this skeletal form that his play will come through with the histrionic art of the actor. The skeletal makes no sense unless the actor puts in the layers of understanding. So now we have the play— its history, ideology, circumstances. The brain is certainly there.

But we need the external flesh and blood.

FOUR

THE NEW CHARACTER IN REALISM

A PLAYWRIGHT IS like God. He makes a world, needs man and woman to live in it, and creates them in his own image. Ibsen, unlike God, looked at the world he created and said, "It's not so good—no Garden of Eden." His Adam and Eve started out without innocence. His human inventions were the opposite of God's: they started out mortal, not immortal—real, not ideal human beings. Ibsen populated his earth with people so "ordinary" they were extraordinary. He created them out of himself and his own society, experience, and observation.

"Before I write one word," he said, "I must know the character through and through. I must penetrate into the last wrinkle of his soul. I always proceed from the individual. As soon as I am certain of every aspect of his humanity, I have to also have his exterior in mind down to the last button. How he stands and walks, how he bears himself, what his voice sounds like. I do not let him go until his fate is fulfilled."

Ibsen described his work process this way:

"Stage I: I approach my characters from a railway journey. Preliminary acquaintances chatted about this and that. Stage II: I see everything much more clearly—I know the people as if I had spent a month with them at the sea shore. I have discovered the fundamentals of their character and little peculiarities. Stage III: I have reached the limit of knowledge—I know my characters from close and long acquaintances. They are my intimate friends who will no longer disappoint me. As I see them now, I shall always see them."

Ibsen not only noticed people's appearance and peculiar characteristics but picked up bits of their private conversation. He was interested in people's ways of speech. Women, he observed, answered a question with a word of two or three syllables—men answered with a single syllable.

"In looking inward—which I did—one sees the sediment of one's personality," Ibsen said. "No man can write anything [for] which he does not to some degree find the model in himself. . . . Where is the man among us who has not sensed in himself the contradiction in himself between word and deed, between will and duty, between life and doctrine?"

There is not a single person that Ibsen writes about that is not in him. He writes about some bastards and some great men.

However idiosyncratic and individual his characters, the problem in an Ibsen play is everybody's problem. It is not about a single character. Nora is every woman. Dr. Stockmann is every man. They are archetypes. They have a universality.

I have an example of an Ibsen social problem:

A boy and girl get married because the father wanted her to marry a rich boy. The boy finds out she married him because he was rich and says, "I am going to divorce you." This is not a play that involves the audience. It is a story about some particular boy and girl. It's a different story if she says, "I married a man because my parents wanted me to marry him and I always did what they wanted me to do—did everything 'right.'" He finds out that she married him for money and says, "Leave my house—you betrayed me. You didn't love me." The girl says, "But you should have understood that I was not in love with you. You should have known that." He says, "Why did you behave as if you were in love?" She says, "Because I couldn't get married unless I behaved that way." He says, "But you are supposed to love your husband when you get married." She says, "But you are also not supposed to be an old maid in the society."

That is a social problem. That affects many people in the relationship of love and marriage and the relationship of father and mother and what marriage really is. Marriage never was built on love. It was built on something else. But in the middle class, it has turned into love. "I'm under the jurisdiction of my father. I'm not free enough to fight my father." Then the husband is trapped with a universal moral situation.

The conflict in modern theater must be clear. The modern playwright is a dreamer. He sees a conflict between the dream and reality. In one phase of life or work, the hero criticizes and rebels against reality. The hero does not win. The characters are pulled backward or forward into the world they hate and they try to escape back into their dreams. The author looks for the link between the active and the imaginative world.

The aim of Ibsen and his characters is not to deal with random personal problems. The object is to portray a human being's moods and destinies, conditioned by relevant social conditions. Conditions close him in. The hero is caught in the same jam as everybody else. He has the same ambitions and desires. He has average size. Chekhov's gentle people are paralyzed by apathy. Ibsen says the human possibility is dwindling—the people are dwindling. Survival becomes their way.

Ibsen's modern man comes in a variety of attitudes and dramatic archetypes:

- *Plays of simple realism,* in which he is set in a world of probable reality that one can believe. The middle-class speech is unlovely. The language is flat. The character cannot heighten it. He is imprisoned by the reality. He struggles with the tedious. He fights, he complains, he makes painful demands.
- *Social-realistic plays,* in which he rebels against his entire situation—and tries to replace God.
- *Prophetic plays,* with epic structure and short scenes, set in an unlocalized, dreamlike place. The hero is superior to the environment; his qualities raise him from the commonplace. The epic aspect of Ibsen involves an aristocracy of character, will, and mind, and lofty language—heightened prose or verse.
- *Plays of social revolt (epic and realistic),* such as those of Synge, Dürrenmatt, Odets, Miller, Osborne. Man is in conflict with the government, family, and society. Such social plays are written in a realistic or naturalistic style. The action permits the ideas to take place.

There are no greater examples of the new characters in realism than the major figures in *A Doll's House* and *Enemy of the People*. Let us examine them in detail for the archetypes they are, for their temperaments and traits, for the subtleties of how Ibsen constructed them, for what the actor must learn from them—and what questions he must ask—in order to render and make them come alive on the stage.

A Doll's House: Behind the Marital Masks

[Synopsis of *A Doll's House:* Nora and Torvald are the happily married occupants of *A Doll's House,* or so it seems in the opening festive Christmas scenes. Nora is childishly adorable, the "perfect wife" and mother. Torvald is an upstanding citizen and "model husband." But beneath the domestic bliss are dark secrets that belie their illusions of one other. Nora got some money by forgery and now needs more to pay it back lest a scandal ruin Torvald's bank career. She tries but fails to borrow it from the seedy Dr. Rank. The strain is terrific. An epic confrontation with her husband is in the works. To further unsettle things, her widow friend Kristine shows up just ahead of Kristine's rejected lover, Krogstad. They choose this moment and this crumbling doll house for an epic confrontation of their own.

—B.P.]

What is the character of a middle-class banker? You can dress Torvald, the husband, in absolutely conventional clothes. He is from a middle class that had schools and a sense of handed-down achievement. His father paid for it. If he studied, he became honorable. But he liked a certain girl whose father was not so honorable by middle-class standards.

Build the character of a husband who is not subjected to very difficult rules. The church is easy. Work is hard, but he knows he can make it. His attitude to money, morality, sex, love—all are attitudes of middle-class society that he must answer to. What is his attitude to tipping? To saving money? Does he spend money on clothes? Think through every single moment. Does he go to church? Where was he married?

What kind of mother did he have, what kind of upbringing? Did he marry a woman like his mother? What is the joy he wants out of life? Work is not joy. It gives a sense of power, not joy. Joy is with another person. He is married, with the possibility of sharing his life. A man requires the house to be gay and charming. A woman's job is to bring that to him.

Nora, his wife, is a woman who knows how to get around a man. By instinct, she supplies what he doesn't bring in from outside. Historically, she is the element of playfulness in life. She has been betrayed for hundreds of years—held down, not allowed to surface. Ibsen says middle-class life is built on the premise that woman is by nature kinder, more sensitive, loving and feeling than man.

"You are an odd little soul," Torvald says—he always uses the word "little" for her—"very like your father. It is in the blood; for, indeed, it is true that you can inherit these things." What is he talking about? What did the father do? He speculated with money. He died leaving debts.

Society has to operate without chaos. In 1933, after the banks closed, Roosevelt did things so that kind of financial disaster wouldn't happen again. Torvald is the kind of man who worries about this. He sees that Nora's father speculated, was careless with money, spoiled her. Nora's father is a symbol to Torvald of instability in the society. Yet knowing this, he married her. He saw she was spoiled but thought that by marrying her, he would make things different. Torvald with his Lutheran stability would change her—a teaching process. But her temperament doesn't want to be that way.

"Hasn't Miss Sweet Tooth been breaking rules?" he chides and patronizes her. "No, what makes you think that? Torvald, I assure you, really. . . . I should not think of going against your wishes." She won't ever challenge him. But everything he tells her to do, she does the opposite.

She lies. She tiptoes—a symptom of somebody "bigger" being

around. If a person tiptoes in her walk, she also tiptoes in her mind. If she is on tiptoe level with the man, her thinking is not robust, full. Build the character from how she tiptoes—how she smiles, how she keeps her closets, plays with the children. Her character has the playfulness of Christmas, her swirling movement. She is like snow falling—tripping across the stage. He gives you darkness; she gives you the swirling. The lines alone are dead. Act the warmth in the house. That is what he wants: the melody on a charmed level—that lovely melody of home. That melody sounds good in the home when it is without reality, with the illusion of happiness.

So she tiptoes across the room. That's physical. It comes from the past. She needs it, because some people have a semi-bully quality about them. My secretary comes over to me half-apologetically and says, "I'm sorry to disturb you"—I'm an authority figure. I have a desk that makes her do it; if I'm on the street, it's different. You adjust to people who have a desk, and the way you adjust is, you talk halfway. Get Nora from this constant adjustment: "I won't disturb him." Develop her walk. Don't use *your* walk—use the gaiety of someone always on her toes. In giving you that she tiptoes, Ibsen gives you her whole character. She tiptoes in her mind, her opinions, in her pleasures with candy. She is Miss Tiptoe. The tiptoeing must affect everything she does—the way she opens a door, the way she doesn't intrude herself onto other people. Work on the walk so when she comes on stage you don't have to worry about it. I would use a sort of lightness. I would use it for a lot of parts in Shakespeare and Shaw. A very delicate quality.

She manipulates him. That trait has to be translated into action. If you can't do it, don't take the part. When you manipulate, you aren't direct. Men and women do it differently. Learn how to manipulate. When you have an action you are not familiar with, go away from the play—get it in ten different situations and then go back to the play. Nora says, "You might give me money, Torvald." Manipulate the line. Pass it through your imagination—add something. You must contribute to the line. Experience it, don't just say it.

There is joy in manipulating. It amuses people. He enjoys her. "But if you spend on unnecessary things, I have to pay again. It's a sweet little spendthrift, but she uses up a deal of money!" If something isn't necessary, it is not respected. It is not in the nature of a man of the outside to evaluate the inside. Her "little" world gives him and his world the sense of being "big." He doesn't bother with the inside. Ibsen touched on something that is still going on between men and women.

As long as Nora does her tricks, she is fine. "Let us do as I suggest, Torvald, and then I shall have time to think what I am most in want of. That is a very sensible plan, isn't it?" If he has a pair of eyeglasses, she might put them on. He loves her playing. *Do,* instead of *say.* How do people learn to manipulate? As children. When Nora was little, she cried and her father gave her candy and let her stay up all night. She got around people with tricks—she would cry and then laugh. With the nurse, she would play sick. She saw the weakness in everybody. Find out how she manipulates the other characters—Dr. Rank, Mrs. Linde, Krogstad. She inherited her feminine wiles.

She needs them in order to deal with his masculine power drive—something Ibsen touches on in every play. In *Doll's House,* how far does the problem go? Torvald's drive for power exceeds every other drive, and when he is in trouble, Nora goes down with the ship. She needs all the feminine wiles she can muster to compensate for her ignorance.

According to Ibsen, you can have either love or power, but not both. The power drive in middle-class life is stronger and is destroying love, the center. In Ibsen, man is in turmoil. He is dissatisfied with himself. He wants to exercise the cosmic mysterious drive of wife, father, and child. It's a joke. In the end, man has to propagate. It is all a trick.

Nora is the best kind of wife, doing what a wife should do, saving money to please him. Her own temperament is to waste it, give it away. Her temperament led her to go into the world and get a big loan. But she is different from what she seems. Nora is not truthfully that kind of woman. Nora would like to do things that are not conservative. But when she wants to get out of her middle-class role later on, there is no place to go.

In the last act, she says, "I don't know who I am." Which self am I—the little bird that wants to please you or the extravagant self I have to hide? In order to achieve a self, you cannot take the rules that are handed down. You accept them because you believe in the social order, you vote because you believe the people are good. You won't vote if you don't believe in the politics. Ibsen examined it. He says you can choose what you are going to do with your vote, with your marriage.

Torvald says, "What are little people called that are always wasting money?" She says, "I know—spendthrifts." Inside, she says, "Stop with that game—we need the dough, we need to pay a debt." It is not in the line. Very little is in the lines. The line is, "Let us do as I suggest. . . ." It means, I will be reasonable if you give me the money. She is manipulative. Her situation is that of a wife that cannot tell the truth. You play games, you go around it. Judge all wives and all situations in realistic plays differently. Ibsen gives you different wives in different situations.

Ibsen says that what you marry is the illusion, the ideal—"He's a fine man." We need these illusions. We cannot face the reality. He is a lawyer who courts her and speaks to her father and is the image of a fine, upright husband. "You must not waste money. You must not borrow money. Don't eat sweet things." All these things he believes. But when she comes to him in the end, the man of everybody's dreams doesn't feel anything like that.

Torvald is a symbol of the wise, monumental male. Nora, conditioned by her upbringing, accepts his pose. When she finds herself in an emergency, she turns to this "ideal" Torvald. She sacrificed herself when he needed her and believes he will do the same. But Torvald is a humbug; he thinks only of himself. The man Nora loves is a creature of her fantasy. When her ideal notion of him evaporates, she is left with a stranger in whom she has no interest. Nora finds herself bankrupt.

She realizes then that she has been masquerading as a child because Torvald has been posing as a father. The moment she becomes aware that she is more masculine than her husband, their relationship becomes impossible. She no longer can endure the passive role her position entails, mentally or physically. She declares the marriage at an end.

When she gets to the last scene, Nora says, "My father didn't let me grow up—you didn't either. You have done me a great injustice." It has been hundreds of years that women have been arrested in their development.

From Ibsen on, it is very important to get the point of view in each character. The author does not make the points of view. *You* make the point of view. Think about it in a personal way. Get impressions from Mrs. Linde, for example.

Kristine Linde arrives wearing traveling clothes—comes into their Christmas. There is nothing holiday about her. She comes from the north; we know the climate. She has made an awful trip—a trip to change your life. We don't really want her here. She is sober, heavy. We instinctively feel against her. We prefer the illusion of Christmas that Nora creates—family, tricks, presents. But now Ibsen introduces a character we have a resistance to. There is an aloneness about her. She hasn't seen Nora in ten years. She is Nora's age, but you wouldn't think so to look at her.

The ten years Nora has added are the years of a schoolgirl. The ten years added to Mrs. Linde are grown-up. Nora remained a child. She says, "You look the same as ever." Nora lies—tries to soften reality. Kristine repeats "older"—she's not afraid of the word. She has no fear of the truth. Nora is speaking to someone who is not afraid of truth. Nora says, "You're a widow now." To say that to a widow has a brutality. It's because she doesn't understand. There is no sense of sadness in Nora. She says "You're a widow" without knowing what that is. We push widows away. Nobody needs an extra woman. You don't go alone to a party. A woman alone has no place in the society. A widow is not wanted. Those ten years have done something to Kristine. She arrives at an important "family time" in traditional Christian life. She is not afraid of intruding. She is strong. Why?

We have to find out.

Nora had put off writing to her. Kristine says, "That's all right, I understand." How much she understands about the other side. Nora is part of the society, marriage; she looks younger; everything is warm and sunny in her life. No wonder she didn't write. Kristine understands this happy world. Ten years—the last three without a husband—have given her maturity.

Nora asks, "Did he leave you anything to live on?" No. No

money, no children—"not even grief, not even a lingering regret." This is such a strong statement that you say, "I don't want to hear it." Where did Kristine get the strength? She had a mother and two brothers to think of. She turned down Krogstad because his prospects were shaky. Kristine's journey has to do with leaving tradition—a whole history—behind. Sometimes a complete change happens in people. A tremendous thing happened to give her this power. In contrast to Nora, she is a complete person who faces the truth in spite of the middle class.

When a man offers to marry you, it is a realistic social situation. Ibsen presents this problem for the first time: did Kristine have the right to marry without love? Now it becomes the audience's problem, too. You have a mother and two young brothers, but if someone offers to marry you, you shouldn't *have* to say yes. What's the alternative? You scrubbed floors. Nora was helpless—she forged. Was it right? Her husband was dying and she forged a check. You know the moral code: society would break down if forging were legal.

Ibsen says you have to make a decision.

Think about the economics of love: The marriage offer includes money. Marriage to a poor man couldn't work. A marriage offer is not a romantic gesture. It has conditions. Even today, finances and class are important issues—you don't marry too far out of your class. Ibsen says it's a serious social issue: what is the marriage offer really about? Nora thinks she has everything; thinks her life isn't precarious. But in another ten minutes, she has no home. Her whole marriage collapses; everything changes.

Kristine lived in a community where it was possible to work in a shop, lower-middle-class. A shop or school were her only exits. She is the opposite of Nora. Nora is a toy, not really needed. Ibsen presents you with two kinds of woman—one is needed and does difficult things, the other does it without being needed. He brings up a big problem in modern society: the woman tries to find a self, the family is not enough, on a big level of what a woman is. With Kristine the challenge is to penetrate her depth, size, experience, thinking. Ibsen says something in Kristine is deeply womanly. She isn't married but she is needed. She wants a job, she has to do something. She doesn't want to be the head of the office—just to be needed, not to take over the man's job. Nora and Kristine live in different worlds. Nora has no sense of Kristine at all.

The situation is that Kristine now has Krogstad's position in the bank. His prospects were shaky when she turned down his proposal. She not only said "I'm going to marry somebody else"—the cosmic rejection of the male: who dares to say no?—but now she has supplanted and taken his place in the outside world. How does he feel toward the world? Antagonistic, doesn't trust it. He is a man of passion, in belief and disbelief alike. He is not a romantic. This driven man comes in and has to face a woman in the home of his competitor. Kristine is prematurely older, no mask of a woman but a woman who is secure. He sees not the old glowing, romantic, beautiful girl he used to know but somebody who is almost unrecognizable. When Kristine first sees Krogstad, she turns away, shaken—couldn't be more shocked if he'd come back from the war without an arm or leg.

If I were acting the part of Krogstad, I would come in—start to leave—wait—think, should I go?—hesitate—go back? He is not quite ready to sit down and talk. Start to go out, turn around in the corridor. There is something about a man in a doorway—to go or stay?—something threatening. Man has size. Kristine looks at this giant standing there. She is smaller—that sense of his power comes over her. In terms of the cosmic force between man and woman, don't try to equal him. Krogstad comes in and tears the place apart, takes over—big—right in her face. It is not a little scene.

The unpredictability of the modern character rarely speaks in such a big way. Krogstad has saved himself from the middle class by temperament. He has risked it all. He is a very big middle-class man. He speaks from the heart and understands his truth. He begins to see it isn't true that she didn't love him—that the whole disaster wasn't due to that. Kristine for the first time has the key to his rejection: she has injured this man much more than she realized.

Ibsen says dissect the human situation and apply it so you can survive middle-class life. The actor's great crime in realism is to bring it down. You must experience the moment—the moment you realized she didn't love you destroyed your life. Sink down on "Why did you do that to me?" Completely break. In realism, *experience* what is said, don't *say* it. It could not be done with the old technique. That is what Stanislavsky helped to develop, and that is what you are responsible for.

She needed money. She sold herself to save her mother. Kristine gives him the reality of the situation. Krogstad was dismissed from his job, took a radical position helping peasants and the jobless. He risked something in life for his passion about things. Did Kristine have the right to put herself against the tradition of male dominance in society? Krogstad says, "When you did that I lost you—when you put something in front of my power, I lost my mate." The mate gives the man his size. When the man loses grip on the woman, he will flounder. Without love, a big man loses the ground that holds him up.

Krogstad allowed himself the passionate nature—a different temperament from Torvald's cool. In this case, the temperament of the man made him flounder. The temperament of Kristine kept her up. Krogstad's "shipwrecked man" had nothing to hold on to, paid the price for loving. He crumbled after losing the woman he loved, lost his integrity, lost his trust. Maybe he will be able to pick himself up . . . maybe not.

Ibsen is saying the ultimate thing for a real man is to know the power of love in his life—the force it gives him. Torvald's conflict is with himself. Out of his ambition to succeed, pursuit of self-interest, comes ruin, not fulfillment. Torvald tried to get it from the bank. Krogstad at no point in his life thought there'd be a substitute for it. Will Torvald continue in the bank? Will he understand he is shipwrecked?

In realism, the discussion remains in the audience.

An Enemy of the People: A Tale of Two Brothers

[Synopsis of *An Enemy of the People:* Dr. Stockmann is a big-hearted dynamo of a man, a socialist who has worked tirelessly for public health. His outspoken passion delights the town's liberal newspaper but enrages its conservative Mayor—who happens to be his brother. The Doctor's good, loving wife tries to keep everyone happy and cannot understand their daughter Petra, a proto-feminist schoolteacher who shares her father's radical views. The current big project in this community is the baths, on which the Doctor is an expert. When he learns that its water is polluted, the money-minded Mayor insists he suppress the information. Their escalating war forces everyone to take sides.

—B.P.]

The play deals with social conformity. When Dr. Stockmann discovers that it isn't really honest—in reality the baths are dangerous—the people in charge don't want to know. They have a commitment to money. Money alters their personality and makes them unable to see the truth. Vested interests are very strong.

Dr. Stockmann represents the power of progress. The Mayor represents the power of money—the name of the game in bourgeois society. Hovstad represents a power, too—the paper. Mrs. Stockmann represents family life.

Ibsen sets it up brilliantly in the action of the very first scene:

Mrs. Stockmann takes care of her house well. She has the temperament for being a wife. She is giving, serves the best roast beef, relates to other people—attentive. "If you come an hour late, Mr. Billing, you have to put up with cold meat." We see she is connected with womanly serving. She makes the home run. By the second or third line you know that Mrs. Stockmann is aware of every need in the house. It's not just that she gives him the meat, but that it should be hot. She is aware of what he needs. Ibsen builds her from her talents. He says not everybody is talented for the same thing. Mrs. Stockmann has a talent to be a mother, a wife, a housekeeper. He'll show you women who don't have that talent, like Hedda Gabler. Realism opens up what your real line of behavior is. Nothing in realism is accidental.

Mrs. Stockmann says, "I expect Mr. Hovstad is coming too." She is aware of everything. She knows what should be fixed, who's coming. She's alive in a sense of doing. She doesn't just give someone more meat, she pushes over the gravy. She sees that there isn't enough wine. She is aware of what to do.

Billing is immediately introduced to you as a man with a napkin. He is a man who's eating good meat and he's appreciating it: "It's uncommonly good, remarkably good." He is interested in food and not much in anything else. What does he do at the table as a realist? If he just eats, it's not your school. Select! If he picks up his fork and just says "It's good," flatly—that remarkably good meat?—that's a bad actor. It needs a bit more salt? The gravy? Hmmmm, marvelous. What about the bread and the butter? . . . Play him as a man who eats.

Mrs. Stockmann says, "My husband makes a point of having his meals punctually." From that you get several character colors: Billing comes in when he likes to eat. He's not aware of these things. His hostess is saying, "We do eat on time but I'm polite and I'll feed you." He's a newspaper man, he'll eat late, maybe go to a coffee house at night. He says, "I think I almost enjoy a meal better when I can sit down and eat by myself, undisturbed." You know a man like that isn't married or connected with children. He's not going to say "What can I do for you?"; you're going to say "What can I do for *him?*" All through the play you have to watch, in realism, the development of his character's leanings. If he got into a streetcar, what would he do? Would he get up and give you his seat or look for a comfortable corner in the back, read his newspaper, be by himself with his interests?

Next, the Mayor enters—Peter Stockmann, her brother-in-law—wearing an overcoat, an official hat, carrying a stick. That is realism. Clothes in that period are worn carefully. A man who wears a high hat has respect; his cane and handkerchief are in the right place. Go look for pictures of an official in 1870. He's an Ibsenian man—a man of the institution. The man of the institution has a uniform. It's the outside of what he is inside. "How good of you to come and see us," she says. He is a man who needs praise. "How well you're looking." There are some people to whom you just say "Come in." And others to whom you say "What a lovely dress you have on." You cater to them.

He says, "I happened to be passing and—you have company, eh?" Even though you don't know the action, you sense it's a false line. In three more lines, you see that it's false.

"You have company, I see." He sees fast. Mrs. Stockmann is embarrassed. She didn't expect him. She tries to adjust. Oh, please stay to dinner. He is formal, uncomfortable. He makes her uncomfortable, too. She must do things—make room for his hat on a table, move a chair—to counteract her embarrassment. We see he's not an easy person for her to deal with. He presents a social problem for her. Ibsen makes him chronically nervous. He's on the outside very correct, but on the inside everything is a potential source of upset. "Good gracious, a hot meal at night? Not with my digestion. No, my dear lady, I stick to tea and bread and butter. It's much more wholesome and economical." It is not middle-class form to eat late at night. This middle-class home has an extraordinary freedom in it. Does this interest you? How carefully good realistic plays are put down, how uncareless they are? How every line creates a build of character, of situation, of clarity?

Now she says, "You must not think that Thomas and I are spendthrifts." He says, "No, not you, my dear." Who does he think it of? The doctor. Now you have the attitude. Find out what money is in middle-class European society at that time. Your *own* point of view on money won't do you any good. This middle class is conservative. They don't eat later than six and people do not drop in. It has to be arranged. Dr. Stockmann's household is breaking the form, the convention.

Then Hovstad comes in and says, "Good evening, Mr. Mayor." Peter says, "You've come on business, no doubt?" He is stilted. He bows "a little distantly." He doesn't say, "I'm glad to see you. Let's have a drink." He immediately goes to "You've come on business?"—goes right to what he needs to know.

Hovstad: "It's about an article in the paper." This is a snooping journalist. What is the action here? It's political maneuvering. Both men are doing it. They don't shake hands. They are suspicious of each other. One is conservative; the other is a liberal. What's he printing? The Mayor is an important man. He's got a cane and a cap. He's not relaxed with this fellow. We get they have two different points of view.

The hostess cannot bring these two together. There is friction on the stage. She's caught between trying to make these disparate elements come together. Actions of embarrassment. It's hard for her. Build that. It's your business as an actor. Would she move chairs? Fix a pillow? In the choice is the talent. In Ibsen you choose things to reveal the character and not just something that comes into your head. This is what you get in the realism school of acting. You don't simply embroider. You sit or spit because it has something to do with your character. You don't just do graceful things. That is not Ibsenian. You pick what to do from the character.

Peter is not only coming in and being unfriendly, he is also a man who comments on people's behavior. "I know what and when and how to eat, how to live an economical life—and you don't." That is why she is embarrassed—the attitude you have toward someone who is always going to criticize you. So when he comes in, she is thrown. It is like a priest who comes in and sees you drinking. He embarrasses you.

Through the Mayor, his brother the Doctor is created: extravagant, eats late, takes walks. The Mayor thinks it's not good to take a late-night walk—the Doctor should be home studying a journal. The Doctor is not practical. He comes in with a stranger, warm-hearted and giving. The Doctor lets you be an individual, doesn't understand the officialdom of the Mayor's life. He's a man at home, busy with family, recognizes the playfulness of life—a very full, rounded figure of a man.

The Doctor has lived with the people, believes they must be educated. He is a socialist in the best sense of the word, full of optimism: it's wonderful to live in a world of new science. He went where there was the greatest need for a doctor, like Schweitzer, met with poverty and resistance to learning. The masses are always ignorant. Flaubert said stupidity creates evil. Ibsen said no, evil creates stupidity. The masses tend to go toward religion and superstition.

Nevertheless, the Doctor is in love with progress. He is between his brother and the people. He worked on his research—therapy of the water, chemicals—under the worst conditions, with very little staff. His work became renowned. He knows how to build the baths. He is naive: he advocates that scientists get the same wages as a chief justice. He writes for the leftist paper. He's frightfully busy getting into trouble. Peter says of his brother, "You have a restless, rebellious disposition." Other characters always give you the key to your character. The Doctor is active, uncontrolled. He might bang the door, not intentionally but just because there is too much world around him not to bump into someone. He's always helping somebody. Have another drink! Where are the boys? Dining? He butters a piece of bread for them. He's doing, whereas his brother isn't.

You have two highly contrasting brothers, so well drawn by

Ibsen. One feels he has the right to comment on the other's way of life, on how he lives, what food he serves, when he serves it. The official takes upon himself the right to tell you how to live in your own house—the "mask" of what is right. Why a mask? Because if he says "It's right for me," he would be speaking as an individual. But the moment someone says "I say you're wrong, in the name of the Church," the moment he talks in the name of an organization, the state, that person is without an experience of his own. Thus he is wrong to say what is wise for other people.

Ibsen builds this very carefully. You do not. You right away see the Mayor as a villain. He is not the villain. Be very careful of that. He is simply *practical.* Ibsen gives you an absolutely valid argument of an official man who represents an official idea that is excellent. Has the doctor been writing an article? He has to know what people are doing. That's the job of political people. No individual is bigger than the thing he represents. When the press says "We owe the baths to the Doctor," that is a threat. Society is not built that way. The Church and the government are bigger than anything you say about them.

How you act in your professional life reflects on how you act privately. Ibsen's thinking is represented by what the Doctor says to the journalist: "Without you, the public would not be informed, without your integrity they'd be misled. I believe you will resist the temptation to sensationalize or twist truth to serve partisanship." The Doctor believes the paper will tell the truth—money should not be in control. The Mayor speaks of the baths in terms of real estate and profit. He does not care whether people get sick, so long as they come to the baths.

The Mayor thinks the Doctor is dangerous because he is individualistic. He is a doctor, valid in his profession. He comes in with laughing and commotion—that's a clue. Nothing in Ibsen is an accident. The Doctor is a symbol of middle-class achievement: children, friends, happiness, exuberance. He greets his daughter, Petra, with "Get a drink"—he taught her how to drink. He gives the kids a little wine. His son steals a cigar, but he doesn't do anything about it. He has a tolerant attitude toward his children.

The Doctor has it all—wife, family, the support of the newspaper. He is a doctor who heals. He represents the middle-class ideal of home and happiness. He has spontaneity. Ibsen likes that as a character trait. He made him a whole person. Most men in Ibsen are overprofessionalized. Competition and their need for success leave them nothing for the family. Ibsen lets the Doctor off the hook—he works all day but is with his sons at night, aware of them and his wife. It is the last happy family in a realistic play. He is the portrait of an ideal man. Dr. Stockmann is probably Ibsen's first and maybe only positive hero. He is completely unaware that he is so threatening to the world of his brother, which is broken into pieces by the end of the play.

The Mayor's attitude is, "Shut your mouth! I represent what is right. Don't bring revolution." Darwin predicts change, Freud wants the investigation of the mind, Marx wants to take society away from the wealthy. The Mayor feels his brother is the enemy, even though both came out of the same mother and family. This makes it bigger than just different opinions.

Petra, the Doctor's daughter, is a teacher. Teachers are paid nothing (people revolt with too much education). She has an active mind, sees a new world ahead, joins the freedom fight. Her ecstasy comes from involvement in the movement. She can't even sit down to dinner, she is so busy with her work and alive with new ideas. Ibsen made the Doctor a healer and his daughter a teacher—they lead morality and culture in Western society. She is not like today's teachers; she has a position where she can help change society. Her teaching is not "instructing"—she is of the Aristotle, Socrates, Moses line of teachers. Think epic. She is a doctor's daughter; her mind has been exposed to ideas. She gets her independence in 1882 from doing that work.

Her relationship with her father is tremendously close. She is very sympathetic toward him. Against her mother's wishes, he sent her abroad to broaden her vision—to London, where she became part of the Norwegian exile freedom movement. She knows how to drink and think. Build a girl who can start a revolution with her father. She's not virginal. If a girl knows how to pour her own drink, she knows other things, too.

Her mother is very sheltered. They are not the same species. She thinks Petra should get married, be quiet, not speak of dangerous political matters in the house. Petra tells her the country will send the boys to war. They have to know what is going on, be able to protest. If she had the means, she would open her own school. Open your own school? Might as well try to open your own government! The idea is very radical, and so is Petra. She is a part of the women's liberation movement.

She is the only one who tells her father "Do it." But she differs from him in one key respect: she is a realist. She knows there is a chance of failure. He does not. He is an idealist almost until the end. That is the Ibsenian formula: the idealist does not see what is going on. Not until the last act does the Doctor face it realistically.

There is always a figure in Ibsen that cannot be spelled out. In *An Enemy of the People,* it is Captain Horster. Do not ground him! Being a creature of the open seas, he has a universality. Something about him is bigger—an Ibsen figure who rises above himself and nature. Enigmatic. If his ship is taken away, he will find another—he will never land. He is not bound to a place. He is in charge. He doesn't vote in the town elections. He doesn't accept such institutions as politics and voting. He is a stranger who comes in and is not part of the society.

The Doctor, too, is rebellious against conventions. That is why Ibsen brings in the captain. My God, that Ibsen is brilliant! He's got the most rebellious nature in the world in the captain. He doesn't even want to be a citizen. He wants to float in mid-ocean. He doesn't want any of this crap. He is the Doctor's best friend. His spirit is special. The discussion is taking place. The argument in Ibsen is never about an individual. It is always for or against a way of life. This gives every realistic play a bigger-than-life proportion. It's what we call epic realism—that large thing. A brave little middle-class human being striving for an idea. That is why I keep saying, don't be pedestrian on the stage.

The tradition of father, leadership—gone by this time. The middle class does not produce such figures—except for the Doctor. There is no other symbol in any of the plays that can lead the young people. Moses, the biblical father image, has been destroyed. The father who gave us the rules—his house is now empty. Captain Horster wants to fill the father's empty house with new ideas. Look for the epic things. The size of what Ibsen says is as big as Shakespeare.

Ibsen says that if a man cannot deal honestly with the way he makes his money, then in order to fight society he must leave it. Dr. Stockmann becomes the "enemy" of the people, a traitor. No one in any of the political factions backs him up. The Doctor doesn't care if the world caves in, he'll sacrifice his family and himself for principles. By the end, his children are fighting in school, stones are thrown at the house, but he refuses to give in, says the masses won't prevent him from speaking the truth. Ibsen: majority is never right. Individual must recognize the wrongness of the situation. He becomes a symbol that people will join twenty years later. The victor is also the victim if he succeeds. Sacrifice is made for the truth.

In Ibsen, those who revolt against the society create suffering for their family. Mrs. Stockmann says it is not his place to change the world—"You should not have had children, you should have been a monk." What is to become of the family? Does Dr. Stockmann have a responsibility only to himself? Isn't it willful or plain stupid for a man to take it all upon himself alone? Even the truth is ineffective. In modern tragedy, society is going to condemn you. You are not going to win. A man sacrifices his family, and nine times out of ten the point still won't be won.

Ibsen says you have to be able to do that. A man cannot be part of the society and also challenge it. Ibsen says he must get out of it. If you are to build a new society, you must live as a realist and free man even if it means sacrificing your family. One person is sacrificed, then two other people, then twenty, until you get a minority, and then they become the majority, and then somebody else breaks away. The man who most rebels must be careful not to institutionalize his revolt.

And if a man *fails* to meet the challenge? Ibsen says, recognize that you don't have the moral courage to go through with it. In a realistic play, when a man gives his life, he is the "hero," but he is as guilty as the people who took his life. He's wishy-washy in *Enemy*. He says, I'll take the banquet, I'll take the majority. All this he has to lose before he becomes a true hero. One thing after another must be taken away. He must pay with his life for his action and in the end say, I need nobody. He doesn't always carry this out. Nora carries it out in *A Doll's House.* Hedda loses one thing after another, everything goes, but in the end has nothing and kills herself. There is no such thing in a realistic play as the hero or the villain, because they are all socially provoked.

In *Enemy of the People,* the journalists Billing and Hovstad represent the liberals against the aristocracy of money. The system is bad, they want to pull it down. Are they good people? Are you on their side—the side of the people—at first? Yes. Then Ibsen makes a fool of you. It is a typical Ibsen trick to show you the people are not what they say they are.

Are you for the rich owners or the people? At the end of the second act, the Mayor offers his brother money to shut up. The Doctor says, I will not shut up. No element of the society is willing to sacrifice money except Stockmann. He is not for the owner class or liberal class, he is for the class that fights and sacrifices. There is no solution for the individual except to be alone and prove by sacrifice what he believes. Ibsen says the only thing a man owes himself is his own conviction that he is right. He doesn't say the man who strikes out is right; he may well be wrong. He just says the truth needs sacrifice and that one should live in such a way so as to be socially useful. This is Mr. Roosevelt. It is Mrs. Roosevelt, too, by the way. She says be careful if you're not part of your community. You can't be head of your house unless you are part of the community, taking part in something bigger than your own personal issue, achieving your full mature expression.

Is the fickle journalist going to win? I don't think so. If you think so, then go ahead and play him that way. It doesn't matter. I just think he's an Ibsen character. He goes out alone and gets stoned, but at least he's telling his own truth.

Ibsen presents both sides. You can never say who is right or wrong, who is true. After Ibsen, to be truthful, you have to have freedom. He makes it clear that to be an honest man is not easy. It is not about "honesty"—it is about his own truth.

Ibsen's genius is that in one sentence he can establish a character. Nothing is wasted. I tried to cut some of Ibsen once, and it was terrible. I asked that the lines be put back again. Someone in the first act is marvelous, but by the third act, he is not that man at all. Ibsen has the reversal always. You think one thing and then he leads you slowly to think the opposite thing. You are always on the character's side, but the situation doesn't always permit you to be right. In each act the character will do something different, until at the end he will be complete. His behavior is not to be anticipated the way it is in melodramas or comedies.

We think Hovstad is right in act two: The little people have to be raised up. The rich elite should be overthrown. He is right. Then he does a complete about-face. In act four he says, "A man must be a public enemy to wish to ruin a whole community—the people cannot think for themselves." He is also right. You cannot build Hovstad as a character you're with in the first act and against in the second, then with in the third act but against in the fourth. Ibsen does not build him straight the way through. He reverses. If you build Stockmann as the hero, you are not going to get an Ibsen character. There is always a flaw. You must always, in realism, look for the opposite side of the character—his weaknesses—in order to play a real man.

Torvald says Nora is odd, "but your faults are something I have to put up with." A man says that in the marriage ceremony. But in the last act, Torvald doesn't put up with anything. If an Ibsen character says he'll put up with a woman just as she is, it means that he won't. Look for the reversal. If he says, "I will take care of you," something will happen to change that.

What does Torvald do? He makes money. To Nora when you make money, you make magic. The intrigue here is terrible. She builds up the money until he says, "I'll give it to you." Her tricks to get money are fantastic. She counts it and says thank you, that will hold off the outside misery for a while. He thinks he is being the most generous man in the world. She says, "I will be reasonable if you give me the money." She is manipulative. Very little is in the lines. She is a wife that cannot tell the truth. So you play games, go around it. Judge all wives and all situations differently in all realistic plays.

She feels, "If I didn't borrow, you'd be ten feet under—I'm not the little squirrel you think I am, and I did it all to save you." She couldn't possibly tell him—he's too big to be saved. It would ruin the game. "All right Torvald, you live your dream, but it is I who'll stay up at night to get us out of debt." Nora is exhausted from being unable to talk to him, let alone tell him the truth. One of them lives in the idealistic world, the other in the realistic. They are living in two different planes.

Nora's attitude is "I don't care if we owe money or not." She found it very easy to borrow—it saved a life. She didn't know or care if she did right or wrong. Torvald says, "That is like a woman!" He puts her down, saying she has no capacity to understand. He says, "There can be no freedom or beauty about a home that depends on borrowing and debt." Her borrowing saved his life. But she is afraid to tell him the truth, that she forged. He won't love her unless she is the ideal "little woman." Their realistic life depended on borrowed money. His prestige is built on a lie. The whole life is built on a lie.

A rock falls on his head when she says, "I don't respect you, I don't think you are a man." The slate is not that she leaves him but that she forces him to realize he is not the man he thought he was. "I would have killed myself for you and you said you would kill yourself for me—but you only think about yourself, pretending." He brought to the marriage a sense of himself that he was not. When he finds out he is not that kind of man, his idealistic mask is torn off. Torvald said, "I will take care of you as long as you are my tootsie." The minute she is not, he is not so full of love. It is important for the middle class to understand the lie that goes on in family, marriage, government.

You have a different kind of reversal for Krogstad. In the first act, he is bitter, hurtful. In the second act, he looks for the strength to be a whole man. The idealist became a cynic. Kristine was crushed too, but becomes a realist.

What is the future of Torvald? "He will do nicely." For Nora? Today, we are still very attracted to the helplessness of women.

Ibsen has a reversal from first to last act. The character is always able to change. He becomes unsettled by what modern man is. The complete opposite can happen.

Ibsen says: Play the character. Play the truth.

These new characters are the product of a mindless, soulless reality. The society now has lost its faith. They become what the external conditions make them due to the power of money. They are controlled. A man's social standing is more relevant than his personal habits. Whether he is a judge or a merchant by profession is more important than the sum total of his individual qualities. Only his profession gives him qualities.

The play became more and more intimate and intellectualized. The characters lost their formal sharpness and definition. They became richer but less clear, more true to life but harder for the audience to understand. It is precisely this element of difficulty that is the main attraction of the modern theater. The conflicts are more obscure. The ethics are ambiguous, and there is no uniform standard of moral values as there used to be. The author has two points of view, two ideologies, and leaves the problem unsolved. Sometimes the audience can solve it. But most of the time, the "discussion" weakens the element of inevitability in the conflict and there is no clear-cut solution.

Now, no character is accountable for his actions except to himself.

We need a new kind of performer for a new kind of character.

FIVE

THE NEW PERFORMER IN REALISM

It is essential to see, not to mirror—the latter is an indulgence.
— IBSEN

THE REALISTIC STYLE has certain problems that do not have an easy solution. It is dead on the page. The actor has to create it. The text has to be filled. The emptiness of the text is nobody's fault. It is not within the means of the author or the style to fill in and give you everything you want in a modern text outright. Family life on stage before was unrealistic, because it was always idealized. Ibsen's plays take away this idealization and work it down to the people, for them to face the truth which comes only from realistic analysis. The situation today is that actors—especially American actors—are extremely unclear about how to solve realism.

Know the difference between the literary and the histrionic side. I said at the outset that there are two aspects of the theater: the first belongs to the author and the second to the actor. You must understand the acting side of this profession, and you don't. You run from class to class all over the world and still go back to the lines. You think it is in the lines, and it is not. The lines belong to the literary side. Many great things come out of that side, but it belongs to the author, and if he is dead, that's great, because he cannot bother you. The best author is a dead author, because he's out of your way and you own the play. Take what he has given you and use it for what you need.

The characters of realism are new and powerful. Ibsen risks having you play them from what is on top. The *real* play is in the actor and behind the words. The words are just a diagram of where the actor has to go interiorly and exteriorly. Plays need actors to put in layers of understanding, to fill an ordinary script with such vitality and life that the audience thinks it's a good play.

The playwright gives you the circumstances. The actor has to fulfill and make the circumstances important, no matter how strange. Make them concrete, live in them. Nora lives in a community that celebrates Christmas. What happened at Christmas in 1885 Norway? What kind of music did they play? How did they dance? Understand the way of life and the words will disappear.

The novelist can give you all aspects of the period. But a play only really exists in the author's mind and the actor's being. Facts stimulate thought. The imagination is closer to the actor than real life—more agreeable, more comfortable. The actor can draw on the life of other people. He must be expansive and observant. What he knows is minimal compared to his imagination, which contains his experience. The art of theater depends on the imagination, which contains the experience.

The audience identifies, in Ibsen, with the undramatic. He takes drama out of the sphere of the aristocratic class and puts it into the class of the people. The main human element in Ibsen and realism is the provincial family—people who do what the average middle-class family does in a well-developed family culture. These new characters had to be as real as the audience. For that reason, you had to have a new school of actors.

It was an important decision on Ibsen's part to get the semblance of life—true life—on stage. How does realism affect the actor? What does he need to act in this style?

Ibsen says the actor has to have eyes to see the world. He must take in, suck in life. He must not walk around and say "I'm bored." Find this ability to take in colors, dirt on the street, cigarettes, traffic, buses, advertisements—such is the way life comes in, fragile and otherwise. This is important for you because you have to use yourself in a play—a lot of what you know and a lot of what you do not know.

Ideas are expressed through actions. These ideas must be clear, not blurred. You are imprisoned in an average situation where there are large social conflicts. The rebellion is against what people call reality. It is hard to live in this reality. People in this society think the same. This creates problems.

Where the action is truly full of suspense or emotion, the acting must shock and leap over the footlights—but not by means of acting "tricks." The most important thing for the new actor is that his vanity has to go. Like Ibsen, he must think. He must ask questions.

A play consisting of absolute reality requires great conviction to bring off. Poetic realism requires seeing a thing and taking it in— understanding and experiencing the problem. Saying something significant about life required a new technique. No actor before Ibsen had to truly *experience* his part.

In realism, the past must be built. The past will give you the character. Build the biography of each character. Think like the character. Unless you know the difference between the way your character thinks and the way you think, you are not an actor, you are a *pischer*—go home and ask somebody to translate it for you.* Know the difference between how you and the character think. The character will take over if your mind says, "I can play this character because I know how he thinks, but I can also think the way the *other* character thinks." You can play it if you are flexible enough to use the difference between yourself and the character.

I want to work with you to build a craft and an approach to a play and a part which will give you greater security, because there is no security at all in the written page. It doesn't say anything about making you happy or good. It is a big secret. That big secret has to be solved by the actor.

It is important for you to know about the author. If you know something about the author's life, you will also know something about what made him write. The author writes out of his time. Every author is surrounded by his time. For an actor to say "I'm going to work on an Ibsen play" without thinking about the author and his time leaves you unaware that the time made him say something that may help you.

---

*To save you the trouble: *pischer* is the derogatory Yiddish word for "bed wetter," literally; a loser or dullard, figuratively.

Always know the author intimately through some biographical material—understand his moment in history. You know, I had a department at Yale University. They finally realized an actor had something to say to other actors that the academic could not say. I don't want you to be driven to read one hundred books, but I want you to choose carefully and not leave it all to the director.

Don't go to you instead of going to the playwright. He expresses the ideas of the play through his characters. When you read the play, see where his ideas are. They must appeal to your mind. The actor must be full of the playwright's thoughts. Go to the author. See where he is going. Don't go to yourself. Don't be bigger than the author. Don't impose on the author. Don't stray away from the author.

What would you do in *Enemy of the People?* Are you with Dr. Stockmann—that he has to destroy the town? His opponents have a persuasive argument, too. Are you only interested in the plot or are you interested in the moral issue of whether a man should or should not do this? In the school of realism, you and the audience must think about the moral situation and take part in the discussion. If you act in the school of realism, it is not because you have a good technique. It is because you understand the issue. If you are going to be able to act the issue, you must first understand it.

Know how to study a scene: in a quiet room alone, concentrated. Your first help is your mind. Thought provokes understanding. The author can only appeal to the actor's thoughts. The thoughts lead to the actor's experiencing the emotions inside. To know the thoughts is to feel and experience the idea of the play.

When you read the text, I want you to be alone, quietly, and read it and reread it. The most important thing is to be quiet and concentrated and not to come to it with opinions. "I heard the play was terrible." Do not ever take anybody's opinion about a play. Do not live by what other people say. People do not know what the hell they are saying most of the time, including the critics.

Understand as an actor, you have one thing and that is your mind. If you cannot think, do not act. You cannot be an idiot and act. There is no such thing as a stupid actor. Actors used to be very intelligent. If they are not so intelligent anymore, it is because they want to go to the words. They like a lot of words. Go to a conservatory if you want to act; do not go to a college. In college they will teach you a lot that you won't be able to apply to acting. In a conservatory of music, they will teach you history as it affects Mozart. In a conservatory of acting they will teach you the nineteenth century as it affects Ibsen. God bless you, but you will never act unless you put your mind together and say, "I must understand when and where this is happening."

In 1890, if a student came into a classroom and sat with her legs crossed and wore her hair down, she would have been thrown out of school, because only crazy people walked around with their hair down. It was a convention that no woman wore her hair down outside unless she was crazy. All through opera, you see a woman walking that way, you say she went crazy.

Today, you have a right to wear your hair down and to sit the way you sit and to say, "I don't have to behave the way everybody else behaves." Years ago, you did not. Nobody thirty, forty years ago talked about abortion—wouldn't dream of it. You had to travel two thousand miles to find some crazy man who knew how to give you an abortion with a hairpin. You only live in your own period with the morality and stuff around you of your own time. I must understand the sociological life of the period I am acting in. We are robots living by what society tells us to do.

Think about your social institutions. That is your first job as an actor. Don't be dumb and go to the lines. You do not know how Mrs. Stockmann thinks, and until you do, you won't be able to act her. The actor has to use and make up his mind how he thinks about his social situation, what he is surrounded with. If you are a builder, you only think about building. A surgeon only thinks about bones. "Yes, you have to fix his bones, but he's Franklin D. Roosevelt!" "Oh, I didn't know that." The surgeon doesn't associate a bone with FDR—to him, a bone is a bone. An actor can't be that way. Always draw a difference between yourself and the character you are dealing with.

The social situation is so strong, it gets you. It pushes you and your character psychologically into understanding your world—its morality, love, sex. Every character has to deal with these situations in order to know who he is in great depth. From this depth, you can then get to your talent. It isn't too far under the surface if you understand how your character is conditioned and how *you* are conditioned in life. You want to play good theater, you want to understand the playwrights, but mostly you are given movies, and the movies are not giving you any way in which your soul is helped.

Every person here—his soul—has been injured because the theater is shifting over into movies. Everybody here is injured by this social fact. What are you going to do? Are you going to be actors or not? Are you going to have to be trained in the movies or television or the funnies? The social impact of the movies is going to affect your life whether you are an actor, a director, or a scholar.

When I go to California, I am a great celebrity—big star. Why? Because Stella is the only one who talks about Chekhov. The others talk about movies. They talk about *Star Wars* and I talk about Ibsen. Everybody sits down and talks about the last movie, how many millions it will make. But they say, "Stella, tell us about Strindberg." I get to be a star in a different way.

Try to answer questions yourself, without the prejudices of other people's opinions and emotions. Then later put questions to others. Begin with yourself. Find the truth for yourself.

How does your character *think?* There is a necessity of knowing a character fully. If Ibsen has to know, so do you. You must know what you do and how you think about many things. How do you and the character think about every aspect of community life? Contrast those two ways of thinking. If you know how the character thinks, you will know how to act him—how to think as you play him. Learn how to choose things that reveal character.

What is Hovstad's action in *Enemy of the People,* for example? Give me the scoop. He's a journalist. Cynical. He's looking for something. We have to get to the thing he does. We'll talk about him more later.

Ibsen finds the thing in everybody that is interesting—especially to an actor. Do that, too. Find the thing that interests you about the character. Then personalize it. Realize that you have to be smart in order to be able to act in realism. You must act smart. You can't act stupid. It won't come over. The play is a bore and you're a lousy actor unless you know the issues. You have to know the issue to make war on. Hovstad is talking about pestilence. Exactly what kind of journalist is he? Take it further. This is the most interesting aspect of acting.

But first, you must fully master the background—from the physics to the metaphysics. Your clues are in the text.

Words help. They don't do everything, but they help. Begin with the external words and draw from them for stimulation: the words and circumstances given by the playwright lead to the feelings and the character development. Work backwards from the words to the acts to the thoughts.

When and where does the action take place?

What season?

Day or night?

Are you inland? In a sea town? In the country?

The facts push you to a deeper level of thinking. They show you the way of a human life. Know the kind of life they led versus your own. Use that knowledge to find the same kind of material—the most helpful material—within yourself. An actor's feelings are analogous to a character's feelings. The side benefit is that as you inspect your own life through the character's, you begin to know yourself better, too.

Go to the details. Underline every fact in minute detail, using present tense—always, the past of your role comes from the present tense. No play is written in the past tense. It is written about yesterday but it takes place today. It is always *now.* So you have a real problem, because the play is in the present but it deals one million percent with the past, which is not in the play. The past is the actor's job. His talent is to create a past that helps him create a character in the present.

Your past is in your play.

The facts of the play give you the external level, which you must know—the land, the social and political situation, the historical setting, the religion and moral system. All these things will lead you later to the psychological levels and inner actions of the characterization, to what is beneath the words and the facts—everything the author doesn't spell out.

The social situation has to take you to the deeper level. If the playwright is Ibsen—just the *word* "Ibsen" is very serious. I know immediately the difference between Simon and Ibsen. I know immediately I am in a provincial town in Norway in 1870. I am responsive to that. Norway takes me away from New York.

We know the larger circumstances. *A Doll's House* takes place in provincial Norway, a home. Keep it always in the present tense. People are in a room, the bell rings, the door is opened, there are servants. . . .

The circumstances lead you to making sense of the words. Actors often react too quickly to the play. That is dangerous, because you will push the lines. Don't force yourself on the lines. Never read the part out with feeling unless it comes to you and you can do it with what you feel is inside. Until then, do not fake it or force it. Do not do all that shtick. Leave it quietly in you for a while. Get a sense of where the play is going. Go from one thing to another carefully. Get a sense of building the play and each scene. Go from your impressions to the circumstances.

I want you to know the political situation beneath *A Doll's House.* There is no vote for women. Know the religion. If you don't know their religion, you do not know anything. Each character has his point of view on religion. Reflect on "What are the spiritual materials in my part?" But don't stray too far from the playwright's basic theme, as expressed through the character's thoughts.

What are the industries? Forestry and agriculture. Later on, they developed shipping. You will see different business problems; it is the beginning of industry here. The rich people live off shipping. You will see political and money differences.

Scandinavia has kings and queens. There is a royal house you have to deal with. Before the twentieth century, when you have royalty you have poverty. It takes a lot of money to support the royalty. Ninety percent of the land is owned by ten percent of the people. Poverty means hunger, sleeping in the streets. It means the poorhouse, where men labored for twenty-five cents a day. There were no hospitals, no money for medicine. Norway was in great conflict. Political exiles like Hovstad and Billing in *Enemy of the People* were sent away. Norway was in a war with Denmark and Sweden—cut off from them. By the end of the nineteenth century there was enough disturbance to give people more of a voice, but people like the Mayor still have the strongest voice. The workers are not revolutionary. The class that needs money must always compromise.

Wars are going on in this country. You will find that there is conscription here because the king has to protect the country. Men of a certain age act a certain way. In *Enemy of the People,* when the mother talks about the children, you must see they are children who are about to be conscripted. That is a layer of thinking there. None of this is in the text but in the situation. All of this must be in the actor. This is what we call the histrionic side of the play. If you know this, you will act good. If you do not know this, you will act lousy.

What is the land like? The topography is mountainous, craggy, lots of water. I get this because I looked it up. It's a landscape that is dark. The writing that comes out of Norway, in general, is dark. The writers are serious. There is no musical-comedy spirit about it. I don't see folk dancing in the street. It is not congenial to outdoor life. This leads me to the first social situation:

The play takes place indoors, the living room of a middle-class family. The family in the middle class is made up of husband and wife, children and servants. What is middle-class social morality? What is their relationship to the Lutheran Church? The church says duty comes first. Christian morality has been around for a long time: family life is moral, marriage is moral. Even in a primitive society, in order not to have extinction, you have to have rules that make the community work. What are the rules in this society? If I live in a house, I can't do anything I want. I can't have dancing all night. . . .

In the 1870s, in middle-class marriage, someone has to pay the rent. Money in my own life—as an artist—is something different. I can't do this play from my life. I have to go to their life in the 1870s. It is not the morality of the 1400s. I have to study a little to understand the play. The primitive moral system after a time broke down. People started to question God. The church took over and said, "We'll tell you what's right." The government said, "We'll tell you." The government doesn't go too far away from the church.

Torvald is a banker. Find out what makes a banker in 1870s society. The bank says, "Keep money—invest." It gives you an economic sense you are in control. This large thing going around you—this aspect of money—is important. Nobody in the bank is an artist. No artist is responsible for knowing what money is. The man in the bank is responsible, and so is his wife.

We are dealing with the middle-class male and female. The

female is responsible for the indoors—housekeeping, raising a family. She could be a teacher or an old maid, but otherwise she has no other way except marriage. The wife is in the home. The husband is outside of the home. Most of the rules were the same for the middle class as for the aristocracy: the woman has the responsibility to the home and children. In the world of the 1870s, like the 1770s, the woman is inside.

The reason why actors nowadays are perplexed about how to solve realism is that they are middle-class or have come up from the working class, which today has money. If you were a student in 1880, your school would contain no one from the working class. You only understand how to dress, what school is available to you, etc., from your own class. You know your own class and who you are in it. You do not understand another class or your own class in another period because your own class is too mixed up to deal with. Democracy isolates everybody from everybody else because we are all alike. Nobody knows who anybody is—either by the way they speak or by what they wear or by what they do.

You cannot play without knowing the class. Reread *A Doll's House* to find the differences among the classes then. The peasant class has no education. They come from the north. The servants have no education. That is why the servants are cared for in many ways by middle-class families. That is the way it used to be. The way it will be now with the Polish people and the Russians coming over to America. They will be servants in the middle class.

In Ibsen, the servant class is divided into two types, represented by the nurse and the housemaid. Do not lump them together or generalize. Find out the difference between the nurse and the maid. Otherwise, you will play them the same way, as they do on Broadway. There is a doctor and a banker. In the bank he is a lawyer. There is a woman who has worked and a woman who has never worked. Those are very important things for you to recognize right away. How do they think differently about life?

Their middle class is not *your* middle class. Ibsen's plays were written from 1860. He analyzed that society. Do not always think it is you. It is very good for you, as actors, to penetrate another society and another way of life because, God knows, you are not actors in order to be *you.* You are actors to be many different kinds of complex people, and you will have to understand each one of them.

I want you to be able to tell me how many archetypes there are in *Enemy of the People.* There is the Mayor, who represents the government. The Doctor, who heals people. See what the different people do. You know the wife is not in business because she is serving people at the table, taking care of the house. There is a newspaper person. On your own, investigate. What do you mean by "newspaper person"? You do not know. Go to *The New York Times* or *New York Post* and watch them work. You cannot just say, "I'm going to play a newspaper person." Do that immediately. Reading *The New York Times* on Sunday is not as important as seeing it. Go to the cafes and see where the newspaper people hang out. Find out how they live with each other. Do some research. Get enough out of it to understand these newspaper people better. Do some work.

The teacher teaches in underprivileged schools. It would be good for you to go to Harlem and see children being taught. Stop being without the profession. Bring in the profession. Do as much as you can do and a thousand times more. That is what acting means. That is what being in the theater means. We have very little time and a lot of work to cover. It is all up to you. Every character must be traced as best you can trace them. Go to the public library and look up the press in a small town in Norway or Sweden. Look at pictures of how they worked.

You can not work with yesterday or today only. You have to combine them.

Are you getting a sense of the truth in realism? Are you getting a sense of its size?

To execute Ibsen's brand of realism in family life and society, the actor must incorporate the *size* of the conflict into his understanding of the situation. He must find the answers to the following questions about his scene, either in the scene itself or elsewhere in the play, and then illustrate those answers in his scenes:

In every scene, what is the conflict about? Is it large or small? Does the revolt reach an extremity in your scene? Where does the scene lead to more conflict and debate?

Where does your character seem alienated or suffer from spiritual loss? Where do you find in the character a hatred of reality? Where is he trapped by the reality? In which scenes or situation do you find the degeneration of the hero?

You have to learn the size of Ibsen. The size of the conflict. The size of the land and how it stuck out into the sea. The size of the darkness. The snowfalls and the sparkling glaciers. The mountains. Surrounded by water, oceans, the largest ice floes in the world. The sea is so deep you could take the tallest building and sink it without leaving a ripple on the surface. The rocks, the sea, the crags, the waterfalls. Do not play it small. You play too local, too little. Stretch it, because that is what is in the mind of the playwright.

Ibsen plays have a strongly symbolic framework. His prose is heavily charged with ambiguity, with dragging oneself up through the terror of competition. Strindberg writes of educated modern man crawling between heaven and earth—trying to find values in a forsaken universe of delusion and nightmare. They are both auto-biographical writers. Both have powerful spiritual conflicts. Things must be blasted, demolished. It is a revolt against modern life. Their works have a psychological complexity of circumstances. Seek a solution to them—an opening of perspective.

The significance and perspective stem from the actor's thought. The richer the thoughts the actor gives to the circumstances, the more eloquent and better the play. The actor has to think. The richer his thoughts and how he directs them, the grander his acting. The closer to filling the depth of the play's content to the fullest. Content of play equals content of actor. Actors must be filled them-selves—and thus fill their characters, as living persons—with the given circumstances.

The actor must absorb this idea.

You will recall that Ibsen never says which character is wrong and he never says which character is right. You do all the time. You say, "Yes, this one is right. . . . No, that one is wrong. . . . Now he's right again. . . . Here he is wrong again." Ibsen gives you for the first time a character whose center is not set like Iago. He gives you a character who is in flux between good and bad—never good or bad. That is something new. You think, "Oh, I know him," but you don't. Find that good and bad part in him; otherwise you will be playing the cliche of the character, not the character. If you think you have solved right away that he is wrong, you will be playing every scene with that in mind and we will get an imitation of the truth but not the truth.

It is your job from now on to see that the character has both sides in him. This gives you profound characters who are made up of psychological truth. You are not interested in hero and villain. We want not to dwell on that anymore. That gives us banal acting—acting that is too fast understandable. I do not care what you know about Stella. You do not know me. You only know one side of me. You do not know the side my daughters know when they say, "Oh, don't be so stupid." You don't know how stupid I can be.

How do you get the truth in realism?

Find the intolerable aspect of the situation and then find the truthfulness in your acting. In realism, the actor—like the character—is a man who thinks. Only then can the audience understand the problem. This kind of understanding is the actor's goal in the action. Out of his understandable action and reaction comes the right attitude toward his partner and the ability to live in the circumstances truthfully.

Do not go to the words. They will spill out naturally as part of the whole action. Do not do the part, do not open your mouth and say the words, until you feel that you have *got* to say them. Do not say it out until you feel that it is really in you.

We have talked a lot about place and atmosphere already, but they are so essential that we must do so again before moving on to specific matters of *craft*.

The sense of place—nature, the scenery—had to be truthful in realism. Where you were had to be as truthful as the new dialogue. Ibsen desired to replace stilted language by the unbeautiful, unemotional language of every day. To tone down the loudness of tragic, classical acting. To tone down the stage effects with the bourgeois fondness for the intimate and homey. This is the end of the reign of complete illusion in the theater. From now on, the effort is to conceal the fictitious nature of how a play is acted and presented. Classical acting portrayed a man with contact to the exterior world but never influenced by it. The bourgeois drama portrays him as a part and function of his environment and shows him not to be controlling reality, as in classical plays, but being controlled and absorbed by it. From now on, the place where the action happens isn't just background. It takes an active part in shaping him on the stage. There is no more break between the inner and outer world; now all action and feeling contain powerful elements of the external world.

In most of Norway, there are only two real months of daylight. People live without the sun—seventeen hours of night. This affects their temperaments, how their houses are lit. How do you light your house when it's dark outside all day? That is up to you to find out. Ibsen says the lines should sound different depending on whether they are said in the morning or evening. You must know whether your scene is taking place in day or night. Otherwise you will just walk in, out of—and into—nowhere.

An actor who gets up to act without knowing when and where he is is insane. Everybody is somewhere. Except an actor, often. He's the only one who can be somewhere and not know where.

Navigation in Norway is very dangerous. It is continuously stormy. The nervousness of the weather affects the personality of the people, dating back to the Vikings. They are dominated by darkness and blackness. The plays are influenced by that. There are very few musical comedies that come out of Norway.

What does "twenty miles south of Oslo" mean? I could say, get fifteen books on Oslo, on the Vikings, on the history of the royalty there. I'll give you this free of charge. But for Christ's sake, learn where you are going to do your acting. Be interested in the fact that Norway has the largest ice fields in the world and that it's very difficult to travel except by sleigh. I like that. I like knowing that Nora comes home by sleigh. People pass each other on the narrow road. I know that a sleigh has bells and that sleigh bells have a kind of gaiety in them. If it is dark eight months of the year, they must give themselves something to make them happy. They recognize each other's sleigh bells. Twilight is at noon. That affects you, if night lasts seventeen hours. If you know this, it will affect your acting. It will make you understand certain things you need to understand.

They have hailstones of a size we can't imagine. These hailstones will be used in the last act of *Enemy of the People.* People throw them at Dr. Stockmann's house. You have to know such things. You must not be so much with *you.* Whatever is left of my *me,* you can have. I do not give a goddamn about my *me,* only what I can give you. That is what is important. That is why my life has been important. I am interested in acting, not "being a professional."

When you look out your stage window, you must see water—fjords and water running along the streets. It's 1880, but it's not an 1880 street. It's a 1780 street with planks. The water runs along these planked streets. You can only cross them a certain way. It is not easy going. You can go by horse or maybe by stagecoach. You come home late because you had to catch the coach. If you're late just because the words say so, you are in trouble. But not if you know that it's because there was too much baggage to put on the coach. Don't act from the words. Act from knowing whether you arrive by coach or whether you have money enough to hire a sleigh.

The fjords are very threatening. They are black and contain bodies that have been disintegrating very slowly for years because the water is so cold. It is a country with a great many psychological problems. Everybody is in trouble. The churches date from the twelfth century. The twelfth century in this crazy Scandinavia produced a very special kind of architecture. It's a big thing about the churches there. Look them up. They have great gargoyles. Do not think of your own pretty little church in East Hampton. You have to see that church people go to with the gargoyles and the frightening things inside it.

Their unique landscape is unduplicated anywhere on earth. What made Ibsen so great is that he used this unusual place to give him such great truths. So when you think of this space, think of it not as your space. Think of the mountains, the water. It must inspire awe in you, so when you get to a difficult scene you will have the help of the landscape. So that if you get to a scene where someone has to flee, you will see the waterfalls, the difficulties.

All of a sudden, now, I want to cry. . . . Why should I tell you everything? When you are a teacher, you have to give everything away. When you are not a teacher, keep it all secret. Give nothing away. Keep it for yourself. It is not your job to share it; it is to keep it. I have a right to tell you because I am a teacher. You have a right to tell nobody because you are not a teacher: *The landscape has to inspire you with awe!*

The fingers of water reach seventy miles into the land from the sea. That makes quite an obstacle if you are thinking of leaving Norway. To cross the sea from the north and come south means that you have risked death to get there, and when you arrive you must arrive with death in you. In Mrs. Linde's entrance, when she says, "I have just arrived from the North," and somebody says, "How did you do it?"—it does not mean by what conveyance. It means, "How did you *survive?*"

If the country has no railroads, what do you think a doctor has? He does not have anesthetics, he does not have machines and technology. Always try to see the difference between you and him—between then and now. Try, all through the play, to see how this can open things up to you. You cannot do without it. If you do not know these things, you cannot act. You must know. What does it mean to live in a small town in Norway 110 years ago? What is it like in summer and winter there? What does "Norway" mean? Norway is three quarters water, surrounded by dark sea. It is different from any concept you have. Look up pictures of its water and mountains. Get an idea for yourself where these people live. Understand that the landscape is always used by the author. Before Ibsen, actors had never been told that—never knew it, never thought about it, never learned how to use it.

Chekhov and O'Neill always use the landscape. You cannot move without it. You must know how to behave inland—know what O'Neill means by inland when his captain in *Anna Christie* keeps saying, "I want to get to the sea!" You will have to understand Mr. O'Neill's sense of inland like you have to understand Ibsen's sense of rain and water. From now on, the landscape always plays an important part. Your responsibility is to find out how it is different from your own.

I will give an illustration or two.

The title *Enemy of the People* is big. In Dr. Stockmann, the people have produced a god. This is large. There is nothing pedestrian in it. You will say "'Enemy of the People'—what does that mean?" At least you have a question. When you read the play, you will see how it develops. The answers will come.

You immediately know the time and class. It is 1880. Don't read it as if it were 1980. You immediately know you are in a middle-class living room. You think, because of your own experience in the theater, "Plays always open in a living room." They *never* opened in a living room. They were phony. In France, they opened in a garden—anywhere at all. The living room is the express room Ibsen uses for a reason. All of his ideas are going to come out of the living room. The family is of the living room, and from the family all the problems of politics and morality will open up. The living room is the opening up for you, like the Bible. It will give you the key to the middle-class way of life. It is where Ibsen expresses all his ideas. Therefore, be careful how you read about the living room.

If it says the living room is attractively furnished, let us have a table with a lot of books on it—a large round table. I want you to furnish a middle-class room. I do not want you to hurry it. In the back there is a dining room with the doors rolled open. That is where people dine. The dining room in a play says a lot about the middle class. It is not a studio apartment. A middle-class house has a kitchen and a dining room. It has a place to feed the family.

So in the front you have a living room with a sofa and a mirror. In the back you have a dining room and table. The table is set for dinner. Do not pass over that. Dinner is the meeting place—the one moment in which the entire family comes together. Do not put it down as just a dining room. Lift it to its larger level; then you can bring it down later. The dining room gives you a ritual that has been there for thousands of years—the table, the Last Supper. It is better for you to think that way than the way you think. You think everything is nothing—unimportant. When I say "you," I mean "us." We do not think of the table as representing a ritual. Unless we do, it is not going to serve its purpose. The living room is where people live and exchange ideas with each other. It has very little to do with *your* idea of a living room.

You have to think, "I am now entering the beginning of modern life to do Ibsen with a house where people live, and he will reveal a truth that will go on for more than 125 years." What he gives you will not be just a table or a stove or a lamp, and from it you will be able to get a great deal more than from the line. See the circumstances of the dining room, the living room. Do not skip them. Do not say, "It has a lamp, it has a mirror, it has a tablecloth." *See* them. Know that the peasant ate from the ground; the workingman ate from a table of wood, without a tablecloth. It is the middle class that started to decorate the table. The tablecloth is what makes it the middle class.

Become a member of the place and its physicalized objects. What does the lamp do? It gives the ritual of light, gives happiness to the end of the day. It gives it a glow. It is not just a lamp. It becomes more valuable if you know what it does. It is not just *there,* it *does*—it *behaves.* It creates a glow at the end of the day when the family comes together. That glow comes from the lamp.

Don't think, when you read the description of the Stockmanns' dining room, "Yes, it's a dining room, a table with chairs around it—just a room where people eat, a door leads to the kitchen. . . ." You accept this. The more you accept it, the more you do not know what you are doing.

It is a good idea to have in your mind what this place really is— and to have it immediately. If you are a middle-class human being today, you do not need words. You need a kitchen, a dining room, and a door that slides open. You do not need this in Shakespeare, because you have other things. There, you are in Elsinore and you have a castle and the queen comes in. You need not bother about where she comes from—whether she comes from the bathroom— because it is not necessary for her to have a bathroom. She exists in a different kind of place. She is a queen in the Renaissance. She knows about morality and ethics and when ethics are broken. She lives on a plane that does not need the bathroom.

You, on the other hand, live on a plane where you need a dining room and a kitchen. In your plane, you do not know a goddamn thing about ethics or history. You just *live.* Your approach to the theater is mindless, without thought. Modern theater is modern in that it introduces things that are identifiable with the audience, such as a kitchen. Nobody who watches *Macbeth* knows about the three witches. The audience says, "Lady Macbeth knows about them. I don't." That is the classical Elizabethan theater, and it is on a plane of large philosophical ideas. It does not deal with what we call "petty reality."

You say, "Well, I have a dining room, and Stella said everybody has a dining room after Louis XIV. So I'm like them." What you do not understand is that this dining room has nothing to do with yours or you. *When* is this dining room? Do not be dumb! Get away from *you.* Your greatest problem is you. Your biggest asset is that you can get away from you and say, "In 1750, they built different dining rooms." You know a dining room has four walls, but how it is made—what kind of wood, what kind of workmen did it—you do not know anything about.

All this comes before the words. If you find yourself on stage in Dr. Stockmann's dining room, you better say, "When is it?" I myself say, "I'm afraid of Ibsen. I better learn something—how to spell his name, why he is important, why some people talk about him, why most people do not. I have to understand more, educate myself. I cannot be an idiot if I am an actor."

Enemy of the People is about a community with liberal journalists, a traditional housewife, a doctor who does not belong to anything. I do not know them. I have to find out about them. When? 1880. Where? The south of Norway. You do not know anything about the south of Norway. You think, "I bet the south of Norway is like Tennessee."

Begin to find out about Norway twenty miles south of Oslo. Is this inland or outland? Do I live near the sea or the mountains? I have to know where I live, so nobody can fool me. I am not playing me. I cannot use where *I* live. You would like to do that. You like to go to Mr. Strasberg, who says, "Take everything you know about yourself and use it to make Oslo." But you do not *know* Oslo, let alone how to use Oslo. Unless you look up Oslo and find out, you will live in some dream world that you cannot use. If you play a Russian during the Napoleonic revolution it is a good thing to read Tolstoy. It cannot hurt you. Your whole thing is *words,* and I say leave them alone—for Christ's sake, leave them alone! Find something out about Oslo!

It is very far north, surrounded by three oceans—the Atlantic, the North Sea, and the Arctic Ocean—full of rapid rivers and ocean storms and hurricanes coming in. It has nothing at all to do with your life or your weather. They have the highest mountains in the world. Sixteen thousand feet is baby stuff to them. I cannot travel inland because there are no roads. How can I travel inland if the mountains are sixteen thousand feet with endless seas of frozen snow on them? Inquire about those mountains. Aren't you interested in anything?

{During her dramatic pause at this point, an offended actor made the mistake of not just interrupting but challenging Adler's passionate rhetoric. Their exchange:}

STUDENT: We are here as professionals and sometimes you address us as rank students. I am sorry I have to say this. . . .

ADLER: Listen, I'll tell you what we do. You don't say anything rotten about me and I won't say anything rotten about you. I am talking to you as a professional even though I don't think there is a professional in America. How do you like that?

STUDENT: I classify somebody who owes his livelihood—

ADLER: We are in Ibsenian dialectics—you have your truth and I have mine. I am treating you like students because I feel that you need this work. I do not want to treat professionals like students, and I do not want to treat students like professionals. I am going to treat you like I *feel* like treating you, and one of the things I want to say is that I have very little respect for your ability to call yourselves professional. "Professional" means to me something else than it means to you. "Professional" does not mean belonging to Equity. "Professional" also does not mean having jobs. When I am acting and involved with the snow, I don't give a good goddamn about it.

I am involved with acting, with the play, with the different snows. If you want to be professional, get involved with the snow. I'd like to treat you with greater politeness, but that is not how I was treated. Different people treat you differently. There are very polite people from England. I will introduce you to them, and they will be extremely elegant with you. But I am a pretty important teacher. There is nobody giving this class better that I know in America. You are stuck with me. So you better take what is good about me and shut up about the rest.

I am giving you everything, and I do not want to apologize to you because you are professional. I want you to know that there *is* no "professional." You always start from nothing and always finish up with "I didn't get it." Very few big actors say "I got it—I really did Richard." I saw Gielgud do *King Lear* for the third time up in Stratford. I went backstage and he said, "I didn't get it. I still didn't get it." *That* is professional. *That* is working on the play and the part.

Ibsen or Williams. Oslo or New Orleans. A specific author in a specific moment in history has a specific style that he needs, a specific time and place and class and set of circumstances he is talking about. Once you understand him in his time, it is your profession to interpret. You have to ask yourself, very quietly, inside, "Do I have the craft to do this?"

Among the English actors, you would say Olivier has got a lot of craft. Outside of being able to act, he knows how to handle the part. Richardson, you would say, knows how to handle the part—you don't have to worry about them. You know already, when you speak about certain people, that there is a layer that they have. We say, "He knows how to handle it. Let him have a chance at Lear, he'll get around."

We trust him—not because he has talent. We trust his craft. Maybe he'll be a great Lear, maybe not, but he is able to keep the curtain up. It is very important to keep the curtain up. That is what I mean when I say you have to have a craft.

Changing Experience into Art: Craft

The author's society, the ideology, the mode of life, the morality— these are the foundation for every realistic work of art. Having learned the general concept of the period, you must apply that knowledge directly to your specific text. Transfer your attention from a general concept to a particular example of the distinctive expression of the period in your play. This is the process an actor needs.

The externals—the circumstances and the past—are words. They are mostly in sentences, sometimes in monologues. But there is a difference between finding the plot and ideas of the play and

finding the deep, inner human life of the characters hidden beneath
the words. The words belong a million percent to the writer. They
are so intimate. They have been in bed with him. They are not your
words. They are his. In order to get to his words, you have to have
craft.

Grasping your character's past life is the first step to owning the
part. From his place, culture, and background comes your ability to
live in his circumstances truthfully and put life into them—to "activate" the facts. For an actor, the life of the imagination is much
more agreeable and interesting than factual life. To activate the
immediate and wider circumstances, he must be able to say, "I live
there! I am in it!"

To arrive at that point, he can get some—but by no means all—
of what he needs from the director. The director's task is to reveal
content; the actor's, to absorb it. The director must open up all the
actor's potentialities and arouse his individual initiative by helping
him penetrate deeply into the author's train of thought. In realism,
the playwrights began to say to the director, "You must start taking
away the conventions." Rehearsals are not lessons in method. They
are the process from which the actor takes the author's thoughts and
turns them into living human images.

The director analyzes from a director's point of view. He should
know many things, equip himself from many fields. His job
includes having political knowledge of the problems in society. The
Moscow Art Theater dedicated itself to the service of society. A
director of worth dedicates his soul to develop great great works of
art—ideas of freedom, justice, and love of people and of country.
The director cannot begin to work on the play without knowing the
idea—the basic theme—and neither can you. Broaden your own
understanding of the theme. Do everything in your power to make
this basic idea exciting, colorful, and strong.

You must decide as an actor that you have chosen your profession because it gives you the opportunity to communicate ideas that
are important and necessary to your audience. To do so through the
ideas that are on the stage, that you dramatize, and through your
characterization to educate the audience, to make them better, finer,
wiser, more useful members of society. The audience is concerned
with the author's idea and with your presenting, interpreting it as
artists, as actors. The idea should always be vital and important to

the audience, and it is necessary for you to create it truly. You must keep the idea alive and be inspired by it in each performance. That is the only way to retain youthfulness in performance.

The director, if he's a good one, knows these things. So should the stage designer, the lighting designer, the actor—all the people of the theater who must know how to interpret the play. The author knows, the director knows, the scenic artist knows, the costumer knows—the only person who doesn't seem to think it's his business to know is the actor.

The director can't ask you, "Did you study a year with Stella Adler? Do you know how to handle a realistic play?" He can't supervise you. The director has a right to be demanding. He expects you to come in and do it, and you can't come in and do it without craft.

The actor must know as much as the designer and costumer know. You have to know everything yourself—to get even from the sets a deeper understanding of the play and of the part. All aspects of production have been taken away from the actor. The actor has been directed at. The great guy is the director—he "knows." He knows something, but he shouldn't know more than you know. You should not trust anyone that much. Don't leave it to the director. He could come out with some craziness. Often he comes out with very little that is the meat of the actor's needs.

If I were you, I would not wait for a director. He is going to ask you to do things that you can do on your own. You should be able to figure out what to do. It is extremely important to know that you can do something without having somebody tell you, "That's your entrance."

As an actress in realism, I like to use the stage. I don't like lines as much as I like the stage. In this realistic style you have a sense of ensemble acting—star quality is not needed. Anybody "special" on the stage takes away from the feeling of these people being familiar. The audience should say "That is exactly like my sister," or "That could be my aunt," instead of "That queen doesn't look like anybody in *my* family."

Begin immediately to transform every feature of the character to yourself—voice, walk, gestures, the listening, the thinking. You come to the theater thinking that people always seem to be in a living room or bedroom or kitchen talking the way you do. It was not that way at all. There were great formalities of speech. There was a

tremendous love of voice, like that of Gielgud. The audience adored
it. Gielgud still speaks that way. It is almost impossible for him not
to have the tremolo in his voice. He is the last of that school. He
worked like hell to try and simplify it, but he could not, because he
fell in love with it. Once you are in love with something, it belongs
to you forever. There is one love affair you cannot break up, and that
is the love affair an actor has with himself.

You assume an "intimate" voice is the voice you should use?
What you assume has to be taken out of you so you can assume
something else. Mr. Ibsen wanted to say something on the stage
which would make the actor without a crown, without robes, and
without poetic language say things that have never been bigger.

The language is prose. You could no longer use a voice that did
not resemble the voice of the average person in real life. You could
no longer drop it every time you start a new thought or sentence.
What makes you think you can do that? You stop at every comma
and period. It's a habit you got into in public school. *Talk,* dear.
Keep it up. Don't stop the action.

The truth of a realistic character must be in you. It is not something you "act." It is something you experience. You don't have to
do this with Shakespeare. You can't. It's too verbal, too embroidered. He never just says, "Be merciful." He says it ten thousand
ways: "The quality of mercy is not strain'd, it droppeth as the gentle
rain. . . ." He goes on until I know what mercy is because he talks so
much. The modern play says, "Please—have mercy!" That's all. "Be
merciful." The acting is different. It is less embroidered. It is *less.*

The Elizabethan style, among other things, has poetry. The style
of realism has just one thing: truthfulness. That is the premise from
which you act in a modern play. The author says, "What I'm saying
is the most important thing I, as an artist, can say. I can tell you the
truth through the captain and his life. His truth. That is what God
put me here to do. He didn't put me in Shakespeare's time. In my
modern life I know this captain and have written the truth of him.
That truth is what makes me a writer, and that same truth is what
makes you an actor."

Where does the character lie? It lies in your speech, in your
movement, in what you do with the chair, where you sit. Would
Petra—Dr. Stockmann's daughter, the teacher—sit on the couch or
near a table where there were books she could glance through? If

you were playing Petra and the director told you to sit down, would you say, "Could I have my father's medical journals to pick up?" So she would be near them when Hovstad mentions the article and she replies that she hasn't read it yet?

You only want to do what *you* do in the play. You think that is all that is important. Maybe at the Actors Studio they do it that way, or in Russia, where they do it slower because they have a lot of time. Not me. I'll pick up the kid brother because I know enough about Petra to know she loves kids. I'll know what she is. I don't want to bother with what she isn't. I don't bother with what won't function for me. I'm not going to live as long as the people at the Actors Studio. I'm going to die sooner. I don't have enough time.

The character also lies in his costumes and props. Pay close attention to what they give you. Tremendously strong impressions are made by costume: Nora's black shawl signals funerals and death. Her party dress is illusion. In the party dress, she is in her make-believe world of the doll. As she prepares to leave the house to die, she puts on her black shawl and his black evening coat. The black says suicide—without Nora having to say one word of self-revelation.

The actor is the most important person on the stage. He is expected to have a profound relationship to everything he does and every object he touches or uses. All the eyeglasses and handkerchiefs and fans, the shoes he wears. Shoes define the walk of the period and give you the movement. Small things like glasses or a magazine keep the actor's hands occupied and at the same time keep the audience's attention occupied on period detail. This is very good for the actor's physical behavior on the stage. The objects should have an influence on his action.

There are many traps in theatrical conventions. The actor in realism should say, "I am not burdened by being a king or queen and having to speak fancy English or iambic pentameter. But I have other burdens. Let me see where they can trap me." Actors feel very special about their costumes and props. The prop man gives us a lot of presents. In accepting them, use them with the understanding that modern theater was created so that you could make a text sound reasonably familiar, and that you are responsible for giving that familiarity a special quality—the quality of truth. Familiarity itself isn't good enough. The author says, "I give you the familiarity so you can create the character's reality and speech, but I put on you the burden of creating the inner truth in yourself." It is much easier to think, "Oh, I have all these presents and I can do whatever I want with them." But he put upon you the burden of asking, "Is what I do with it true or just theatrical?"

What do I do in a realistic play to reveal my mood or make the play advance? Ibsen builds his characters by the small points. If Nora tips extravagantly, the *reason* she is so extravagant opens up the whole problem of money and its effect on her and the other characters. Nora must hide macaroons. She is passive. The wife is dominated by the husband. It will help you enormously to observe what other characters say about yours. That is always a key for you. In Chekhov, your whole character can be explained by somebody coming in and saying, "Madame Arkadina is this or that." Everybody has an opinion about you. Watch what the other characters say about you.

Every actor is more suited to play some characters than others. Sometimes you are completely unsuited to play a character. That makes you an actor. Brando is completely unsuited to play practically everything he plays. Each part he plays is a side of Brando. Stop thinking of yourself as having some profile which is good for one part and bad for another. Don't do that to yourself. I played a little Jewish secretary who scuffled around. Nobody criticized me; they said I was a very good secretary. I also played Gwen Valentine and this and that and the other. Do not type yourself. The man who types you does not know anything about you. He doesn't know anything about himself, so how is he going to know anything about you? He is going to make a bad guess. You are a large, complex miracle and you are able to push or pull yourself into different shapes.

This morning I am mean—rotten mean, horribly mean. This afternoon I'm an angel and I won't let those baby seals be killed in Alaska. Every animal is my child—every bird, every flower, every leaf! I have this whole other leaf side—very sexual. Oh, boy! They do not go together. Neither do yours.

But I was asked to join the Ibsen Society and give a definitive opinion at a round-table discussion on Goethe's *Faust.* Nobody else understands it, so I am going to go and chair it. I've had enough experience to do that, and to play a few parts. If there are enough sides of me, there are enough sides to you.

Goethe says if an experience does not help you, it kills you. If it does not kill you, you'll be fine. Before Ibsen, the actor didn't have to *experience* the part. Now he does. He has to know not only all the external facts and circumstances and the literary aspects but what's hidden under them, going beneath the words and reflecting on the spiritual materials to reach the psychological levels of the part.

The thing that must happen inside the actor is to experience it. If he doesn't experience it, he does not understand it. Only the experience changes the circumstances into art, into truth. Anything that is not experienced by you can only be half-true. As people, we live with half-experiences. What the actor does is to develop the *full* experience. If he takes it in and fully experiences it, then he is an actor. If he does not, he has not used his histrionic abilities. That is craft.

Craft has been part of the society for millions of years. If you are a carpenter, you have inside you the faith that the table you make will function, that it will stand up. You come along later and say, "I would like to carve that table, to add to it." So who made the table? The carpenter made the table and you made the table. The carpenter's name is Cellini, but I am no longer interested in that rare person Cellini. I am more interested in the *craftsman*—you.

The writer gives you the bare outlines. He can never convey the experience. Your contribution is the ability to take life in and convey its truth. That is Mr. Ibsen's definition of truth for the artist. Your talent is in your craft.

Craft is what finally transforms the dead factors into living ones—from "theatrical" to human, artifice to art—through that secret ingredient: the actor's imagination.

Changing Experience into Art: Imagination

One lives facts every day in reality. One can live facts imaginatively in the theater. What you must use to bring the life of another person into yourself is your imagination—visual images, living creatures and human faces, the landscape and objects, melodies and voices. Everything. The author tells you what the present is. You have to create the past imaginatively for yourself. In your choice is your talent.

Take things that affect you. If they don't—shop. Why does Nora leave the door open? The tree is too big. Not just that the door is left open—what is it open *for?* The tree has to come in. Don't bring in anything in the present that doesn't have a past. Don't play the props, the lines; don't act. You create the tree and the door. This is the joy. The imaginative aspect in acting is closer and more inspiring to the actor than the factual aspect.

Go from passive to active imagination by visualizing the people and the scenes. Constantly play a game called What Characters Do in the Room. Go to a private house of 1890 in your mind: put the house together, see it, go from room to room, go over it until it becomes second nature to you. Once you know that house, change it—make a new one!

Cultivate your ability to see the people who live in the house— the maid, the cook, the scullery boy. Go to the kitchen, watch them move. How do they celebrate Christmas in Norway?

Go from being a passive observer to having the characters right beside you through *inner image*—your active imagination. Every physical action has an inner action, and every inner action has a physical action that expresses its psychological nature. The unity between these two must be organic action on the stage. Your actions must be defined by the ideas of the play, its characters, and the given circumstances.

Become the main active person in those circumstances. Put yourself *in* them. Ask, "What would I do in the circumstances?" Define the difference between your behavior and the character's, find all the justifications of the character's actions, and then go on from there to act *from yourself,* without thinking where your personal action ends and the character's begins.

When you read the play, select those sentences that pertain to your character—that reveal your character. Go to personal relationships. What is her relationship to her father, her sweetheart, the servants? This is primary for you. Ask yourself, "What is right about me and what do I lack for this character?" Develop the inner qualities you have that are right for the play and fight all the personal traits that are contrary to it. If your character is sensitive and sentimental, find out what she needs to do, what you need to do, to stimulate sentimentality in yourself.

Use your emotion to get your character's psychology as well as your own. An actor must have at his command all the inner qualities which he is trying to develop in the character of his part. The moment he needs to cry, he must cry. If he must remain cold and indifferent, he must do so. There is in every gifted actor the seed of every human feeling and sensation.

The inner technique of the actor is as important as diction, voice placement, and breath control. It gives to plastic movement as much or more significance. The inner rhythm is a necessary control of the actor's behavior on stage. It comes to him as a result of his correct state in the character. The circumstances must be understood and perfectly justified by you. They will feed you if you have correct action. Deal spontaneously in the circumstances from the action. Do that a thousand times. See what the action makes you do—don't plan ahead. In order to achieve the emotion you want, the character's biography must be as familiar as your own, and you must constantly supplement his biography with new facts even after the play is running.

Define the nature of the character's every feeling—egoism, self-pity, whatever it might be. Once you define it, you must search for actions that arouse that feeling. This is the bait that the feeling will rise to. If he is an ordinary man, the most important element in his feeling is possession. If he is suffering, he is trying to draw sympathy from those around him.

After having caught the feeling, the actor must learn to control it. It is the actor that controls the feeling, not the feeling that controls the actor. For example, the General has the problem of making the guests enjoy themselves. Each character has a personal reason for coming in, for being there. You say you just want to have a good time? That is too general. You want to meet somebody who is important for a business matter. You want to find out about the scandal last night. You are in love and come to secretly observe the girl you love. You are flirting because you want to prove you are the life of the party. Whatever your reason is, know it and make it *clear.*

It is essential to keep the idea of the play alive. That is why the dramatist wrote it, and that is why you are directing or acting it. It gives you the opportunity, through the ideas and your characterization, to educate your audience, to make them more intelligent. This is your own important contribution in a difficult time when the theater is used mostly for amusement. The idea should always be of utter importance. The audience that comes to hear a play today wants to see an interpretation of it, and it is necessary for you to do that.

It is easy to convey the plot—that is not the work. Find in the text and in each situation what is hidden and organic to the life of the character. That is what you are after.

Finale: Christmas in Norway

Meet and create these people, these characters. Analyze them and learn their psychology. Answer all the questions: Who am I? How old am I? What is my profession? Who are the members of my family? What is my disposition? Where do I live? You must draw the play of your apartment and furnish the rooms. How did I spend yesterday? How did I spend today until this evening?

Take the case of Nixon, for example. Say, you have to play him or one of his henchmen in a play. Analyze. What is the nature of conspiracy? It is a gradual accumulation of actions and events. To execute that action you must know the life of the period—its chaos and distress, the structure of the government. You must know the place, where the head of state lives, how old he is. To know the person who occupies the throne, *you must visualize him.*

Ibsen is more important than Nixon. I want to take you on one last journey from theory to practice. I want to take you through the opening scene of *A Doll's House*—the Christmas scene. I want you to get some intimate ideas of how to go about creating that scene, that world, and those tremendously important characters, Nora and Torvald.

How do people celebrate?

Let us go into it in detail.

Compare how Nora and Torvald celebrate to how *you* do. See the differences in things, like Christmas, that relate to you. You have to use your imagination to figure out the mood and atmosphere of this brilliant Christmas scene of Ibsen's.

The style is realistic. You will have to say, "I wonder what Christmas was like a hundred years ago in a small, provincial town in Norway." The mood is festive. The celebration starts with things happening offstage—sleigh bells, for instance—to create the mood. If you don't have them, imagine them. The sleigh bells are ringing, the snow is falling, the children are shrieking with joy, throwing snowballs—see all that excitement from the outside coming in. The lighting is evening, the stove is burning. When you come in, you don't come in with lines, but with that excitement, that laughter. He can't get the tree up, the maid comes because she has heard the noise. Nora comes in full of laughter. The whole action of the scene is to celebrate.

How do you celebrate? Nora comes in with a basket, a hat, coat, scarf, and gloves, all the ribbons, decorations. She comes in with the presents and throws them down. Think of it as being your own life. The aim is to understand the life and, through your craft, to become part of and convey that life.

The facts of the play show you the way: Nora, the banker's wife, enters in a good mood. She has been shopping for Christmas. It is a very special season in middle-class family life. In traditional Christianity, Christmas was for recognizing the birth of the Messiah. But when the church became rich and powerful, agnostics and free thinkers started to question it. Celebrate the ritual, not the spiritual aspect. Read Dickens's *A Christmas Carol.* Get pictures of nineteenth-century Christmas. Then contribute your own blood memories of Christmas. Ibsen gives you the middle-class attitude toward Christmas—the woman is in charge of the Christmas spirit. Keep the rhythm of Christmas going.

Ibsen picks Christmas as the earthy part of Christianity that best celebrates the togetherness of family life. Christmas is an exchange of affections through togetherness and *things.* Ibsen wants family life in the most giving time, when the home is most sparkling with candles, presents, and the joy of life.

There are three actions. The first action is for Nora to come home. The second action is the action of celebrating, with all her packages. The third action is his—to admonish her, tell her not to waste money, with all the bills and realism of the real world.

The very first line of the play, when the maid opens the door and Nora enters from shopping, is, "Hide the Christmas tree away, Helena—the children mustn't see it until it's decorated!" We have from that a key to building the character of Nora: she is playful, she likes games. She has chosen in this bleak life to lift things up by her temperament. Her temperament is different from Torvald's and the one which is normal in Norway. She has developed a playfulness, a joyfulness. So when she says, "Hide the Christmas tree, Helena!" she is playing a game with the children. It's her way. If she has a treat for them, when they go to sleep they find a cookie in bed. There is a lot of screeching and laughing. You see the kids in bed with the cookie, laughing, and she's in bed with them. She plays with them, gives the older one money for the little ones—to walk down the street to the pastry shop for macaroons. She has a little purse with coins in it for the children and herself. Let her have that in her pocket, not in her pocketbook. That's where she keeps the money for the children. Her dress always has a pocket where she has money and candy. Nora always has something to nibble. This time it's a pocketful of macaroons. Give her things that make her suck her fingers—baby habits. Another of her habits can be that one lock of hair keeps falling down. There's a barrette, but she is always tucking it back in.

So she says, "Hide the Christmas tree away, Helena," and then she'll come in and scream—so we have some exuberance when the kids come out. They jump on her neck, she twists them around, they fall down, she plays with them under the table. Do a lot of things with her that are not vertical—things she does on her knees. Make her someone who is pliant enough not just to stand up straight—more pliable on stage than just vertical.

Go to Nora's decorations. Let's get them from the garret where they keep the sleighs and old trunks and Christmas things. Go and look up old Christmas decorations—Norway is close to Russia, and they have the same kind of decorative quality. Some were made out of paper, some were Fabergé crosses, little Russian dolls, Scandinavian dolls, Laplander dolls. Bring something from your investiga-

tion so when she says, "The children must not see it until I've decorated it," the line has to do with something you know and are really
going to put on the tree. Don't go to *your* Christmas things first. It
must pass through your imagination second, not first. Otherwise,
the actor's experience has no value. You have to have the joy of your
Christmas things, selected by you, but in *their* circumstances. Your
rule is, "The truth of art is the truth of the circumstances that you
are in, not your circumstances." That's Pushkin. Use your complete
imagination so the Christmas tree has a validity in you.

So Nora comes in with the tree, playful and scattered, puts down
the presents, then notices the porter and says, "Oh, how much?" She
didn't ask beforehand—that is part of her scattered quality. Half a
crown? Easy. She takes out a whole crown and tells him to keep the
change. She overtips. Her not bothering to change the money is justified by her character. It's not written. The text is a skeleton for the
histrionic art. It is not in the text to do it. It is said in such a way
that you must pick up on it yourself. The past is what you act. The
present comes out of the past, which you must have with you all the
time.

You have to get Nora's carelessness. She throws her coat and
scarf and pocketbook down on the bay window. The maid is helping
her with the packages, and it's a game—"Don't let the children
hear!" Nora unwraps the packages because the paper is expensive—
from the best store—and Torvald mustn't see it. She is taking the
paper to throw it in the fire when she sees the porter—"Oh, you
need money?"—and runs to find her pocketbook. It's not there.
Where is it? The maid took it and the macaroons are out and she has
to hide them. She is very clever about where she hides her macaroons
and her cash—it's a whole thing she has with her circumstances. She
has things for Torvald, for the children, all these packages to put
around. She's giggling, she's delighted. She has hiding places like a
squirrel. She has squirrel places, not logic. The actor has to have
secrets that aren't in the text. Maybe she goes to the bookcase and
hides the macaroons behind Shakespeare because that's a book no
one will take out and look behind. The staging belongs to the
actress. It is not put down. There are only four words in the text, but
they are filled with holiday things that she can do. She is very busy
with her mixed-up life and her disorganization and with being

"scatterbrained" when she hears, "Is that you, my little lark, twitter-ing out there?"

She has been bustling about, shopping, being part of the crowd and that stimulating thing that happens outside—that not caring at Christmastime how late you get home. She comes in from the excitement of weather, Christmas, all the packages. She comes home to more haphazardness of having to put everything away, comb her hair, change her shoes, go up to see the children, ask the servants if there are dinner guests, set out the candles, hide the presents. She always has a lot to do. Ibsen doesn't say "bustling" unless he means it. From her bustling, you get that busyness animals have. A bird eats the seed and comes back for more, he never stays quiet and just eats. Crazy little bird flying around—that is very much her movement in the house. One thing reminds her of another she has to do—and now Torvald hears her and enters.

"Is that my little lark twittering out there?" he says. It's time for more action to take place. Torvald now comes in with the third action—to admonish her. He immediately says, "You *bought* things?" For the man, the whole bloody business is always "I'm keeping you, I'm supporting you. You should be grateful to me."

"Money" is the most serious word in any language. You have to get to what "bought" means—to get her indifference to money and his seriousness. She doesn't just buy chairs and blankets. She buys flowers and exotic fruits. Get some of her extravagance in buying expensive children's clothes. Get "bought" from his point of view. Take four objects in the house and find out what their relation is to money. Every object is bought or inherited in the middle class, even the etchings. The couch is heavy—a European family doesn't buy new furniture. There is nothing modern in 1870; it was all made long before. Ibsen shows you they have leatherbound books, but they don't really use them. When you are into money, banking, and law, you don't need the classics or the history of the French Revolu-tion. You *have* them in middle-class life, but you don't *need* them.

When they take a walk and she says, "Let's buy it all," he says, "How many apples, pears, pineapples can you eat?" She says, "I can't eat more than one," and he says, "Let's buy one." He doesn't react pleasurably to the glittering of a biscuit box. She does. We have to get the difference of their response to their life. If she says, "Let's go

skating," he says, "I have to get up in the morning." He has reasonableness from which he approaches the miracle of life. This is the
center of his character—he is "reasonable" about things that are supposed to make you respond. He responds with his reasonableness to
her exuberance.

What is it that they do buy? They buy wood for the fire, fruit for
the table. The tablecloth is something Nora bought—it should not
blend with the books. Give her something in the house that belongs
to *her.* If you give her heavy brocade cloth that matches the books,
that home is not going to speak to you. If you see her hat and the
Christmas presents, then you say, "That's Nora." Put something gay
and Christmassy in the order.

The action backstage for Torvald has not been Christmassy. He
has just written out a dozen checks for the rent, the chemist, the
children's dentist, the gas, the wood, the insurance. He has been
studying the insurance contract, and he's not pleased with it. It is a
difficult policy. There's no compensation for accidents under any circumstances. He has all this business and is studying this thing when
she comes in. She is in her action, and he is in his.

"Is that my little lark, who caused all these bills? Has my little
spendthrift been frittering away the money?" It is good for her to be
busy with her little life, but he is responsible for her, and she won't
have a cent if he dies. She is busy with the candles and the flowers—
completely into celebrating and trimming the house. There is no
transition when he brings up money. His tone is playful—but never
as playful as it seems in the text, because he is also really saying, "Do
not disturb." The tone he brings in is not Christmassy. She doesn't
like that tone.

But she's smart. She reasons with him. She is running after him,
saying, "We can fritter a little because we are going to make a lot of
money soon." He is up against this bird-brained thinking. She is
watching him circulate and pick things up. She reasons in her way
and he is listening to her and walking around until he finds his place
on the stage. The stage is full of presents, a tree—all this costs
money. He picks up something she bought: "Is this necessary?" She
says, "Oh, you'll be making a lot of money, Torvald. This year we
can really let ourselves go—the first year we don't have to economize." As he does things, she uses her mixed-up logic on him. But
let it come out of what *he* is doing. If you just use the lines, you're in

trouble. She can play a great deal with her things—the presents, the Christmas cards that have arrived—things she can toy with while he says, "Christmas, hmmm . . . I see," in his chair.

Torvald must have his area. Each character has his area on the stage. Torvald's has to do with a place where he can sit and it's easy for him to have a glass of port. He likes comfort. He might go over and fix the fire. Give him a solid area where he can have his decanter, his cigar box made out of the best silver—all those things around him that are not around her.

He says, "After the New Year, yes, but it will be a whole quarter before the money comes in." She says, "We can borrow some"— good logic. Remember, the center of a man is to reason. He believes in being logical. But Nora's nature says, "I don't want to be serious. My father wasn't serious and everybody has made me not serious and enjoyed me the way I am—I'll go on this way." She isn't Medea— she has no problems. The children are fine, everything is fine. She forged a check. It didn't matter. She went to Capri, had a great time, danced the tarantella. What does she have to worry about? Things are working out for her.

He goes to the table and grabs her by both arms and says, "Nora, suppose I borrowed fifty pounds today"—he puts her in a chair— "and a slate fell on my head and killed me." She says, "Oh, let's not talk about that." She jumps up and he catches her by the arm and puts her back again. She's in his grip. She is in the chair and he is over her as he admonishes her: "But suppose that happened." She gets up and thinks, and he lets her think. She is away from him as she says, "I shouldn't care. . . ." If she says that right away, there is no fun—she hasn't done anything with the line. She has to get *away* from him.

"What about the people I borrowed from?" He is still trying to reason with her. She is now center stage and says, "They're strangers." Now she is stage left and he is center stage as he says, "That's just like a woman." He goes over to the library and takes out a book. She wants to see which one it is—didn't expect him to take out a book. She is wondering what he's going to do next. He goes back around to center stage with the book. She is leaning over the chair like a squirrel. He reads, "Neither a borrower nor a lender be. . . ." He is Moses with the tablets. She is leaning over the chair as he is giving her the Ten Commandments. She is on the verge of hysterical giggling, listening with a frown. The staging must be interesting in order for the actors to act.

She says, "All right, Torvald, just as you like." She wants to get back to her Christmas, and the only way is by giving in. He watches her as she moves away in her orbit. She leaves him the forestage and the book, the library and the presents. She goes upstage, with her back to him. He goes around a chair to get her because she is deflated, but she runs away to the fireplace. It's "I don't want to play anymore." She moves away from his orbit, creates her separateness. She won't look at him when he says, "Ah, your wings are drooping." He is so straight. I like his tone. She moves away. He has to deal with her somehow, and there is no way to deal with her. Have her run away, run into a corner. She is hunched over at the windowsill, looking at the snow. "I don't like that tone. I don't want Christmas to be like that." She's tragic all of a sudden.

It's a real exchange. She has to react to the melody of admonishment. She's got him cornered, because he simply cannot understand her mind. How he can win?

He has a good wallet. Like a child, she wants to get the wallet, and he picks it up high. There is a whole play with the wallet. Take a long time. He lowers the wallet and she runs to him and he takes out some money and gives it to her—"ten shillings, twenty, a pound . . ." She counts it exuberantly and says, "Thank you!" He takes out more money and she says "Thank you!" again. Every time she says "Thank you," he gives her more and she grabs it—three or four times. It's like giving a pet one piece of meat after another. The playfulness has to be there. There's dancing with it. She is playing her tricks. Give her a lot of horizontal qualities, jumping on a chair, celebrating. Usually, as she does these tricks, he is in his chair watching her performance. If she just says, "Thank you, Torvald, that will go a long way," we don't have her character, nor do we have the play, nor do we have the seduction of money over a woman. It must be a seduction. The way you play a whore. If you give her more money, she gets lively; if you give her less money, she starts to button up.

There is a real playing around—she won't let him go. It's a game between them. He sees a box on the mantel and says "What's there?" going to it. She says, "I bought the boy a sword, a horse, and a trumpet"—male victory objects, generation after generation. Ibsen is painting the conqueror: the woman gives the man a horse, a trumpet, and a sword and says, "You go out and play the game of winning in the world." The girl gets little baby things—"they break so easily." She is going to have a cradle. What could be smaller in the world than a cradle? In a realistic play you can't just say "a trumpet, a cradle." Ibsen packs all the meaning into ordinary words. He says you will get the truth in this kind of language, no longer in poetry because you are middle-class and it doesn't work.

She is showing him everything and he is watching everything from his chair, watching this enchanting squirrel play with her baby squirrel's presents. He says, "What would you like for yourself?" She says, "Oh, I don't want anything." He takes her by the hand and leads her to a stool and puts her on his lap and says, "Yes, you do." The baby is on his lap and she begins, "Well, if you really want to give me something . . ." Now, you have the real sexuality between them. She wants money—but it's not that simple. It's a real whore's business of seducing him.

She's on his lap and says, "Torvald, please. . . ." It's a real sexual thing. He laughs and teases her, and she gets up—leaves him at the most sensual point: "Not so easy, brother." It's a real interplay with a real woman who gives herself and then retreats. He is lost for a moment. "I'll give you the money, but don't spend it on unnecessary things. . . ." He is back in that thing of yielding. Torvald has a masculinity in this scene, which he has and lets go of. He must have the masculinity—she loves him because of it. She likes the play between them, likes being dominated, likes being taken care of, likes having babies with him. Now, he will give her what she wants.

He is again center stage and she is again on his lap. "It's incredible how much I have to spend to get some pleasure out of this dame." That's his reasoning. "Incredible, how expensive this little skylark is." You have to get that tone for him. When he gets that tone, she says, "I save as much as I can."

Now you get the real discussion: she's saying, "Look, Torvald, under my conditions you would cut your throat. Given my condition, I save as much as I can." It's the first time we get a sense of her saying, "You don't know—you're not fair to me."

In Ibsen, be very careful of every line—what it means, what is being said. Everything has a beginning and grows: the money, the love, the sex. It is so worked out. "I do the best I can." She says it in such a way that he laughs at her seriousness—"Look at you, trying to be serious! 'As much as you can' is nothing!" She says, "We squirrels have expenses, Torvald—you can't imagine." It is Ibsen saying that a man and a woman are unable to know what is going on inside each other.

He laughs and says, "You are an odd little soul." But as he laughs and she really faces him, he sees for the first time what he doesn't see fully until the last act: "You are like your father, always on the lookout for all the money you can get your hands on, and as soon as you get it, it slips through your fingers. There's a side of you that I don't know and that I don't want to know."

It's a very strong indictment of her. It makes for the big misunderstanding: Torvald wants Nora to be sensible with money. She goes to the stool near him and starts the game again. When he says "spendthrift," she jumps up. He is now inspired with his sharp mind. He takes the whole stage. Nora is happy that he doesn't know he owes all his "big thinking" to her. They are really separated. He takes a cigarette and a glass of port: "Did you remember to invite Dr. Rank?" He is busy around the table where he functions. "I've ordered some very good wine." Nora is busy decorating and fussing, while he is busy speaking about money and security. This shows you how the outside life—and Nora's life—affects Christmas.

Outside, the snow is falling. The house begins to shine with light as she goes from one candle to the next. Build it so that the fireplace is burning brightly and Nora is the one who brings the brightness into the home. Don't have her in dark clothes. Put her in something cheerful with fun in it. Everything about her has to have the cheerfulness and merriment of what she brings to that home when he says, "Bought? Have you been wasting money again?"

Nora is tremendously flexible, also manipulative, stubborn, exuberant—all the things you find in a child. A child has those colors. She was kept young, unequipped to mature. Do not do anything "mature" for her. Torvald is mature. Don't put anything childish in Torvald. As long as Nora does her tricks for him, she is safe. Nora says, "You might give me money, Torvald. Only just as much as you can afford, then one of these days I will buy something with it." He says, "Well, out with it! What do you want?" Every time she wants to say something, she manipulates her thoughts. When did she start doing this? When did you? Do you manipulate? Bring it back to you.

Build that Nora is trying to control something. And so is Torvald: "Nora, you can't think how I am looking forward to this evening. I have ordered some good wine." In all Ibsen plays there is a great deal of humor. Women don't know wine. Torvald goes into areas where he can be important without paying a price—the pretensions in their lives. The man holds forth. He announces, "I've ordered the wine." He wants power in areas that make him ludicrous. If the woman doesn't play along, she gets into difficulties. Torvald is looking forward to this evening.

He says, "We'll have a wonderful Christmas together—not like when you worked." The three weeks he spent without her were dull, he says. She didn't find it dull. For the first time, she was earning money. When you begin to make money, you free yourself as a person. You want the freedom of money to be able to say, "I live with you but I don't need your money as much as I need you." It's a statement on modern economic life—an effort on the woman's part to free herself a little from the man's grip.

"It was the dullest three weeks I ever spent," he says. Nora says, "I didn't find it dull." What did he do? His briefs. He has the fantasy they are together. Later, she says they have been married nine years and never sat down and talked to each other. It's a middle-class illusion that they are together. Ibsen makes clear the way people live. What is it about work that Nora didn't find dull? The joy of discovery, of creation, of doing. She came away with something. She embroidered and people bought it and liked it and the creating interested her.

But she can't tell him outright that she enjoyed it. She is always manipulating to repress and keep from expressing something inside herself. The main thing in her life for Torvald—and for herself—is to please him.

Nora enters the play singing, gay and lively—a happy woman and happy mother, with a Christmas tree and presents and the love of her children. At the curtain of the first act, she is still clinging to the belief that the danger of corrupting her children is no more real than the legal danger of her forgery. "Contaminate my children? Poison my home? Never—it can't be true." But her face is pale with terror. She is fighting against death—the disgrace and destruction of her doll's house, plus moral disaster for her children if she continues as their mother. The joy has gone out of her family life.

At the start of act one, Ibsen brought the Christmas tree into the center of the stage, but as the curtain goes up on act two, we can see from the set alone that Nora no longer hopes to succeed. She is terrified now. The family, the unit, and the gaiety are all spoiled. She will not—she dares not—play with her children now. The Christmas tree has been pushed into the corner, stripped of its ornaments. The candles are burned out. What a fine theatrical symbol this Christmas tree is—of dejection, of sadness, of the loss of hope.

I do not work with you in the techniques of acting. I work with you on the basis that you have some craft and that it is healthy. You can't go to a play without craft, unless you only go to it with the purpose of a critic. Some people are terribly interested in the critic's point of view. I am not. The actor should not be, either. The actor must know what the purpose is: you can't lie in a modern play.

When Nora walked out, the whole world heard the bang.

AUGUST
STRINDBERG

SIX

FATHER KNOWS ABYSS

Strindberg on the Page

IBSEN SAID, "For God's sake, don't get married if you are nervous. You'll leave Scarsdale three years later—'I've got this house, let me out!'"

Strindberg came along and said something else.

The professionalized woman was new. There weren't many actresses in those days; there was little chance for them to be. The eighty years since then have made a big difference in your temperament and in how you feel about family life. I hope everybody gets married and has lots of children and goes to California and has a big career and does commercials, travels all over the world and is a great success on television and is able to come back and study a little Ibsen and Strindberg with me.

Each playwright writes in a style through which he makes a statement in his own time. The playwright needs for you to know that. You have to know a lot about the author.

Strindberg is talking about such a monumental change in the society that it might make civilization go under. You get it in the play and symbol of *The Father:* "I am the father and you cannot change that dominant need in me. I am the father—father of the country, father in the home life, God is the father over man." If you monkey around with that, you are monkeying around with something very big. In this play, the mother kills the father. She is able to do that not because she is wicked but because the social situation has developed in such a way that she can undermine him for her own needs.

Strindberg comes twenty years after Ibsen and deals with the whole European breakdown of the "rules." Strindberg gives you the woman who hasn't had enough time to equal the man in development but who still says, "I'm smarter than you." She has the lower-class servant mentality even though she is middle-class. She does not have the man's aristocratic point of view. She is climbing to take over. She is in that moment of "I want something, even though I don't know what it is"—compelled by the historical moment to want more than her capacities permit her. In order to get it she will lie, steal—do anything. Strindberg plays lead to violence.

Strindberg is the psychological dramatist. He is an antifeminist, although in *Dance of Death* the man is the villain. That's the base of Hellman's *Little Foxes,* too. O'Neill is a big follower of his in *Strange Interlude.* Once you start dealing with a Strindberg theme, you are dragged into the deepest abyss, from which you cannot emerge. Know your playwright.

With Strindberg, you get exceptional situations which made him the most influential playwright of his time. He was taken over by Williams, O'Neill, Odets, everybody. What Strindberg was getting at was so forceful that all modern playwrights called him the source. Ibsen was a source, too. But when O'Neill got his Nobel Prize, he said he owed the prize to Strindberg. Shaw put up the money needed to translate Strindberg.

If you play the piano, you know Mozart. Know who was your father when you play a play. Know where it all comes from.

The works of August Strindberg (1849–1912) are highly autobiographical. He was born into a poor class. He had a stepmother and slept in a room with five other children. His stepmother was a working-class servingwoman, his father a bankrupt "gentleman." His early life was full of poverty, deprivation, and insult. He went to school and was treated terribly, was thrown out, and then had to go back and teach in that same school. He became a middle-class intellectual painter and musician (piano, guitar) as well as writer. He lived a lot in France and was an escapist. At first a socialist, he became aristocratic by developing his mind. But the aristocracy of mind was killed off by the aristocracy of money. You must analyze Strindberg's life to understand his works—his naturalism and misogyny and the dualism in his characters. He wrote fifty-five volumes of plays and novels. He had one of the most self-tortured lives in the world and wrote very autobiographically.

Strindberg was an atheist and a moralist. He was highly neurotic and had two nervous breakdowns. He hated whom he loved and saw enemies in the people who were close to him. He was driven to great anxiety by a hostile society. He had three bad marriages and was terribly hurt and was institutionalized twice. His great inner turbulent suffering gave him a certain attitude of kindness in the end. He had a desire to live like a married man and have children, but he didn't want to be disturbed. He saw the woman as a madonna/virgin but also as a corrupted prostitute. He wanted his wife to be sensuous and virginal, motherly and submissive, housekeeper and soul mate, all at the same time. Unlike Ibsen, he had a sexual passion that never stopped. *Like* Ibsen, on the other hand, he believed man was responsible for himself and for his fellow man. He made great demands on life for happiness, success, peace of mind, and the world's respect. He was a torn man. He had a divided self.

Strindberg is considered more modern than any other writer. He seems more contemporary than Ibsen or Chekhov. "Modern" can be defined as the immediate crisis in one's soul. Strindberg saw that the world was fragmented. All the rules for personal life and community life were broken. He understood and predicted the forces that would break in our lives.

With his first play he was a success. He broke in on two plays, *The Father* (1887) and *Miss Julie* (1888). He deals with the drama of man, not individual drama. His characters are representative of their sex and class. The Captain in *The Father* is without a first name—he stands for all fathers, very strong, but with the weaknesses of a feminine side. Jean in *Miss Julie* is dominating and has no weakness. Strindberg understands Jean's drives. Strindberg, for his entire career, searched for the truth of man. He was part of his society and went through many phases—atheism, hypocrisy of practicing Christianity, the loss of faith. Loss of faith is accompanied by pain, through which one must reach out for some sort of security. Strindberg reached the painful recognition of alienation from belief in God and tried through his characters to reach some other plane where he could attach himself.

Man wants something higher. He is alone, looking for salvation.

Ibsen vs. Strindberg

Ibsen and Strindberg were both at war with the existing social, political, and religious institutions. Both left their countries and wandered the world. They were alienated from the world even when they were honored and emulated.

In Ibsen, the single person is rebellious. In Strindberg, you can't really rebel. In Ibsen, you don't break the social form. In Strindberg, the social pattern of life is broken. The revolt is a strong, nervous one. It doesn't come through as ideas but as temperament—violent. Inner conflict with Ibsen leads to ideas; with Strindberg it leads to chaos. After Strindberg, all plays are about the inner confusion of man from which he can't emerge. Strindberg rejects God, accepts Him, negates God again and becomes a fatalist.

Most of Ibsen's plays are about women. In *Enemy of the People* you have a daughter, who is a professional, and a mother, who is passive. In Strindberg, you will see why the daughter becomes a professional and why the mother doesn't. Hedda Gabler was two women: one could only live for the man; the other was restless with three men. Ibsen's woman says, "If I can't love—the deepest thing in me—I will kill in myself the need to love anything." Although they were contemporaries, Strindberg was convinced Ibsen was a fervent champion of his hated enemy: emancipated woman. Strindberg saw the cult of feminism infecting Scandinavia like a pestilence: women were trying to undermine the male domination of society. Ibsen and Strindberg both had an uncompromising revolt against modern life, but in different ways.

Ibsen considered woman less corrupt, less able to be corrupted—not exposed to the outside world and by nature more spiritual than man. Strindberg viewed the rise of woman as a sickness in an alienated society—woman grabbing onto life like men. He felt Ibsen's view of woman put down man. Strindberg was revealing his personal feelings about the woman question. Ibsen was indifferent to it except as a symbol of individual freedom.

In Ibsen, there is a conflict of ideas. In Strindberg, there is a conflict of sex.

In Ibsen, people are trapped by society. In Strindberg they are trapped by themselves. Here starts the modern drama: the self-trap from which you cannot emerge. In Ibsen, you want to be successful, you go out into the world, but you can't rear your family. You may be recognized as an honest man, but you cheat. In Strindberg, a man can't evolve from his own difficulties in family life. He brings in the full depth of personal problems that were never brought in before: sex, marriage, the complexities of man and woman. He doesn't care to teach the audience; he shows the reality of the family unit, the male-female sexual relationship and their modern struggle for power.

The trap is loaded with dramatic tension. Miss Julie is trapped by many things. Her mother taught her to ride and to be surrounded with honor, but also to hate men. She can't emerge as herself, doesn't know where she is going. Strindberg uncovered a new problem—how people trap themselves. Ibsen was the start of realism, but modern drama starts with Strindberg and this inner psychological trap. Miss Julie is trapped by her guilt and uncertain identity and inner conflict. She can't face reality. She can't control her sexual drive toward a servant—she feels she has done something wrong, dishonored the family.

Strindberg's is not a discussion that is reasonable. Ibsen's ideas are clear. Strindberg is not clear. No Strindberg character thinks he can get out of the trap.

What is this inner conflict? You love and go out, but are withdrawn. You want to be powerful, yet you are also weak. You want to be married and you want to be free. The dramatic dualism.

The torment of a person's soul is his sexual and social dualism: he has in himself both male and female components, the dominating aristocrat and the submissive proletariat. In *The Father*, the man is both child and lover; the woman, both mother and vampire/

mistress. Everyone in Strindberg is both servile and arrogant. Past romanticism, the fight is normal. Men are both strong and weak. The dualism a man has to live with can't be resolved in himself. He doesn't know how to attack or reach the inner problem. This dualism pertains to both men and women. Men have a feminine side and women have a masculine side. Neither is able to work it out.

All logic, predictability, and order are lost. What is important is the desperate need of the moment. All else is lost in the anguished torment of the moment. Strindberg finds human life to be pitied. He sees nothing behind the door of hope and expectation except the labor of keeping the dirt of life at a distance. The dirt of life is everywhere—in deceit, endless repetition, and unconscious impulses that pull down a thoroughbred into a mongrel, rolling in dirt.

Death is the liberator—a sleep to men and women who are doomed through no fault of their own, hoping one day to be reborn under a sun that doesn't burn, in a home without dust, amid friends without strain, love without law. These are the ideas of earth and life and agony—the limitations of human possibility. Strindberg's plays move from personal anger and bitterness to the hopelessness of universal life.

Ibsen and Shaw tried to answer: What is behind life? Strindberg asked the question without trying to find an answer. He exposes himself as a modern man, alienated, existing between heaven and hell. Strindberg tried to find a truth in a forsaken universe. He hated and wanted to destroy the world—burn it, demoralize it in his search for truth. Strindberg believed that the modern world doesn't care *what* happens but *how* it happens. He wants to know the machinery behind it.

In Strindberg, no progress is made—man is in a trap that will lead him down the drain. In every play, injustice is inherent. Miss Julie is a victim of her parents, Midsummer's Night, her period, etc. Life is so complex.

Strindberg says modern ideas have no quality, no ethics. We have no capacity to think and are in the level of the servant class because of this confusion. Jean steals but assumes the manners of the upper class—repeats and mimics its ideas, but does not assimilate them. Strindberg says that the inner drive and outer behavior of a man like Jean are in conflict. Characters must go from old to new values. Industrialism, Darwinism, Freudianism, communism—society is in transition. He predicted a terrible, destructive vision of life. He is a pessimistic playwright, versus Ibsen's kind of qualified optimism.

Man is fighting to make the cross from broken values to modern values. He finds archetypes everywhere—in the kitchen, in struggling with bank accounts. He deals with household drudgery—disgust of the physical. He writes of people who break under pressure from a dark chaos. We are aware that we are floating, but we would rather float than be dictated to.

We are in the modern theater with modern problems. There are individuals who reflect the problem—the archetype. No man is written as just "him." He represents millions of people who have these problems. Don't think, "I am acting this character alone." He is representing some aspect of the society.

The main issue in many of the plays is man's inability to cope with the new woman who is emerging and has brought confusion into family life. The fight for emancipation changes her and affects the man terribly. Strindberg says one of the two in a marriage must be stronger. That is the basis of the male-female power battle in the family. Somebody is successful, somebody must be destroyed. Their relationship is a struggle between two hostile species who are fatally attracted to each other. A mindless life force drives them to each other. They are vampires who drain each other of their vitality.

Strindberg and Women

Strindberg's historical moment was also the historical moment of transition for women. Originally, society was ruled by a matriarchy. That produced violence between the sexes, which produced a patriarchy. Women's movement against men was a struggle that would bring the downfall of mankind, Strindberg said. Man was up against a lesser kind of human being.

Strindberg was a prophet about what would happen in society between men and women. He questioned the balance between men and women. The Western idea of woman—that she is scatter-brained, childish in relation to the male—still exists. Nora stands for that woman, accepted that pose. She was idealized by the man. By playing the "little" woman, she made the man big.

Laura in *The Father* is the opposite of Nora, and the Captain is the opposite of Torvald. Torvald stands for the wise, monumental father. The male hasn't changed much: if he can't get Nora through the Bible, he will get her through money—the middle-class attitude to woman is buy her, like a whore, keep her "little." The philosophy of both Ibsen and Strindberg is to free yourself. Ibsen said, "But don't leave the home base." Strindberg says emancipated women had no home base.

Laura has no respect for the Captain—for what he does or what he stands for. It is very autobiographical. Strindberg was a most educated man in Greek, Latin, science. A woman doesn't need a man to be that powerful if she doesn't share it. If she isn't living up to her potential, she is going to resent the advantages of the man. It is the end of the era when the woman automatically accepted her traditional role. In 1880, Europe was busy with the emancipation of the new woman. The revolt of women was coming to the surface. It is the beginning of the birth of the individual in finding himself in a society without established rules—the moment of transition between liberated women in competition with men.

Women cannot live by being submerged. Strindberg analyzes the break between the man and woman. He reveals his ambivalence by dividing them into two classes: (1) the older, more motherly women—kind and compassionate—and (2) the emancipated females, whom he calls "the third sex."

Strindberg developed this theory of the third sex—the woman who wants to be liberated from her womanly side, reverse the roles of authority and take over. She has a strong masculine streak. Ibsen's women were not in the social fight; they stay at home. Strindberg's women were not vulnerable, not kind, but caught in their own split.

Strindberg was angry at women, but had a sense of women and needed to love. He was attracted to women for their maternal qualities but hated them for their masculine attitudes and competitiveness. Emancipated women were already out in the world by then, actresses mostly. His first great torrid affair was with Siri Wrangel [von Essen], an army officer's wife. He idolized her aristocratic bearing and ethereal beauty and eventually married her. She became an actress, came to doubt his sanity, and tried to dominate him. His second marriage, to a young journalist, was bitter, too. Not least of the problems in Strindberg's unhappy marriages was his obsessive jealousy.

During his long travels abroad, down and out in Paris, he dabbled in the occult and in drug-induced hallucinations. He could not stem his psychotic feelings. His disorder verged on insanity. Strindberg saw both a comforting mother and a whore in every woman he loved. He tried to make the woman into a mother but, with the incest taboo, accused her of being evil. In feeling she was evil and not being able to sleep with her, he became impotent. His desire for the mother/woman made him weak and passive, even though his intellect loathed and rebelled against that weakness. He wanted both the masculine aggressiveness of an adult and the passive purity of a child.

In Ibsen, the woman is a child, but she believes in the intelligence of the man. In Strindberg, you get a woman who is with a brilliant man but says, "What about me?" She begins to compete with him. Twenty-five years later you don't have the woman in the social situation who says, "He is active and I am passive." You begin to get the competition of the woman in society—this third sex who says, "I can do it as well as you."

In the beginning woman could be very much in love but didn't accept sex. Woman saw the childlike quality in the giant of the man and loved him for this quality. She accepted sex both to please the man and for her own desire for children. But she couldn't accept him as a lover. She was only capable of being a friend when she was a mother, not a lover. The sexual attraction of woman to man is the need to propagate the race. It is not a healthy attraction. That strong desire to propagate the race finally releases the hate woman has for man. The attraction is an evil, destructive one. Sex perpetuates the race, but out of it comes a great deal of hate.

The woman in Strindberg wants the man to be the father and husband and to lean on him. At the same time, she wants to be free. The mother part is kind to the man, his friend. The lover part is his enemy. There is too much contradiction in feelings with both roles.

Hostility between man and woman is a result of the romantic attitude towards love. Their love life is built on romantic traditions, and those traditions are false. They don't work, so you are left with antagonists. Strindberg analyzes the emergence of the woman as a competitor to the male. He believes that when the woman is emancipated she is no longer fit to sacrifice for the family. She can no longer go back to the old mode, it is broken. She becomes ruthless, because her fight for freedom is so strong. In her freedom, she creates an enemy in the man. Strindberg has a great deal of antifeminist in him.

Strindberg is in open hostility against the mate. In this sense he is a Freudian playwright. Strindberg was a bitter man. He says people have a need to hate. He says they are tied to each other through hatred as well as through affection. Modern woman is diabolical in her desire to win over the man. She is by nature stronger, more unscrupulous, more manipulative. In order to achieve her end, she will even deny the man's parenthood. She will do anything to win.

In family life, who is going to take over? Strindberg's experience is that there are no two powers in the home. In the fight for domestic power, somebody is stronger and someone is weaker. The universality in Strindberg is the struggle for power between man and woman, who want and need to destroy each other.

After Strindberg, man is a complex unit by himself. From now on, he is not capable of having a relationship which does not have a fight in it. When he deals with two classes—the aristocracy and the servants—there is a fight between them. In the family fight between the mother and the father, who is going to win? No relationship without conflict. It is not only about family life, but that is the area every writer deals with from now on, after Strindberg, to reveal the society. We know exactly how the father thinks about religion, about morality, about military ethics. We understand how the man or woman functions in the outside world when we see them in the inside world. It is never just about the inside; it is always to reveal the outside society. Every author gives you a man, a woman, a child, a grandmother, a dog for you to understand what is going on in Washington. It is never just for us in New York or Pittsburgh. That is why these writers are in the libraries. They are defining the society through the individual's character.

The mother turned mistress is not compatible in the wife—one or the other, not both. The woman in Ibsen was mostly the mother. It revolted her when she had to turn into the mistress. The Captain didn't understand the dichotomy in Laura—wanted her to be both. (Now men know, but they still want both.) She has the power to put the Captain in an insane asylum. It is an uneven fight. Laura is stronger because of her immorality, lack of honesty, size, dignity. She lacks what makes the man big. Strindberg said that if the woman ever gets to the top the society will be extinguished.

Strindberg wants a higher state of man, but he's not likely to get it. He sees that the individual is in conflict with the crowd, but he is more interested in the psychological problem, the inner problem. The struggle is no longer between man and society. Strindberg gives you the struggle between man and woman. It is a war, a fight to the death—survival of the fittest. It is a primitive struggle. What Strindberg discovered between man and woman was nothing less than war.

Strindberg wasn't alone in this idea.

Schopenhauer said, "The sexual attraction is a diabolical invention of the propagation of the race by the will of the species, ready relentlessly to destroy personal happiness in order to carry out its ends. The satisfaction of this will leave the lover with a detested companion for life."

Nietzsche said human life was based on "a deathly hate [between] the sexes as its fundamental law."

Schopenhauer was a pessimist. Nietzsche ended up as an optimist with his superman theory. Strindberg was a pessimist but, as a follower of Nietzsche, came to the same belief in this idea of the powerful, historical superman, which lifts his plays.

Strindberg is antidemocratic. He didn't want to be taken over by the masses. He was an aristocratic individualist, not by birth but by his military background. Strindberg was not a small man, and neither are his characters. In most of his plays, man is outsized. Strindberg creates the "big man" by separating people into geniuses and mindless followers.

In *The Father*, the Captain is a free thinker, unconventional—doesn't believe in an afterlife or in any newfangled notion of feminine virtues. Much of it is based on Strindberg's own life. He and the Captain both felt they understood women, both had a contempt for Christianity, and both admired masculine virtues. The Captain is an important military officer and a scientist. He knows or thinks he knows how to deal with men. But he's terribly weak with women and recognizes this in himself and becomes angry at himself and the woman. The fight comes out of this split in his own character and in the character of men and women.

Strindberg admired the male strength of will, intellect, and body. He conceived his male characters as supermen who lived beyond the way of the commonplace, the way of ordinary people, the bourgeois morality. The social virtues of love and sympathy that came out of bourgeois conventions he considered feminine and did not respect. Religion with its softer values of pity and compassion was suited only for women, children, and savages.

Strindberg attacks the institutions and emphasizes that in the women's revolt against the tyrannical men, the men are tyrannical because of their weakness, not strength. His position is that society is trying to undervalue and deprive men of their masculinity and transfer it to women. The male position has gone from aggressiveness to possessiveness: The Captain is a strong military man, a scientist, doesn't believe in God—but he ends up in a straitjacket. The man must find a way from his dependency on the woman—but there is no way. Strindberg says it's a lost cause. He took a very negative view of life.

When Nora leaves, it is Ibsen saying that the man is not going to be head of the family anymore. The male psychology itself is still unquestioned. Strindberg carries it further. Now, the male is split. From 1880 on, the most discussed figure in theater and literature is the historical father as leader of society and family life.

That discussion cuts across all class lines. Now, in Strindberg, the working class for the first time is deeply mixed up with another class. This didn't happen in Ibsen. Every Ibsen conflict was in the middle class. The working class was only concerned with how to survive—money and food, not love.

Now the lower classes are no longer capable of staying down. They want what the other classes have. They want property but they leave out the mind. In every power-drive situation, someone is weaker and someone is stronger. The dominating aristocrat and the submissive proletarian, or vice versa—Strindberg felt pity for people, but he didn't respect or love them.

Strindberg was a forerunner of the Soviet "agitprop" plays later that agitated the public to take a political point of view. Know what class the characters come from. The "old warrior" aristocracy is going down. The father is a captain and an intellectual, but he is reduced by a woman—inferior mentally and physically, but with a certain great strength of her own. Laura, the mother, kills the father not because she is wicked but because she doesn't have honor. Honor is the name of the game.

How does Strindberg arrange this? It has to do with class. Ibsen writes about the upper middle class and the servant classes, who are very kind, good people, still. By the time you get to Strindberg, democracy is coming up and the aristocracy is going down. Before, the aristocracy had the ability to create a civilized way of life for the lower classes to be guided by. They needed someone to teach them what is good and bad. Up to now, like the peasants in Russia, they depended on Christ. Now they don't. There is a weakening of the class structure.

Strindberg says, if you have a class—maintain it. If you break it, you go down and it's suicide. There is chaos in the mixture of the classes. Miss Julie kills herself not because she was raped but because she was dishonored. She willingly went to bed with a servant and lost her honor. Miss Julie in the class conflict wants to go down—she is drawn to the kitchen. Jean wants to get up and out of his class. His senses are developed, but inside he is common and he cannot emerge from his vulgar inside.

Strindberg says the lower classes have a great advantage in that they don't occupy themselves with honor. He has sympathy with Julie and likes her class, but he says the future lies with Jean—son of the working class, who educated himself to be a gentleman and developed his senses to be unscrupulous on his way up. He is dislocated, doesn't think of himself as part of the servant class anymore. He is on his way up. He has learned the outside of everything, but the inside is vulgar. He respects Miss Julie because she is high, but sees that she does what a prostitute does—goes to bed with a servant. He has the brutality of a slave.

In Jean, we see the lower-class concept of life: "Get to the first branch." The need to climb. He goes after what is good for him, not what is truthful. He looks for what will give him an advantage. He has the upper hand with Julie because he is a man—virile, sexually strong, senses keen, takes control of the situation. He sees dirt in Julie's upper class—its mixed-up emptiness—but he still wants it and glamorizes it. He wants to achieve what he thinks is its happiness for himself.

Strindberg doesn't think love can exist between different classes. Man lacks the spirituality necessary for love. Julie knows her attraction to Jean is not love—it's sex without love. The servants know a lot more about her than she thinks. If you want to survive, you must be in control of your destiny. Julie has failed by not controlling. Julie wants to go down, cannot stay on top. She has a death wish—a need for self-destruction. Julie believes the servants love her. Not so; they mock her. When Jean gets her into the room, he says he will bolt the door. Julie: "Do you promise?" Jean: "I swear." But he doesn't. Strindberg says a man will say anything to get what he wants under the circumstances. Brutality keeps Jean from having a sense of honor. He should protect his mistress, the head of the house, when the Count isn't there. He is no longer fit to be an honorable servant or part of the household.

Strindberg predicted that the class with honor would go down and the working class would come up. He predicted our society today—classlessness with no honor and a lot of money. You see it in our own mixup between one class and another—the absence of respect in our society: you don't respect the people who wait on you in a restaurant, and they don't respect you.

Servants in Ibsen are very loyal. In Strindberg, they are disassociated, gossipy, alienated from the family. Their attitude is one of hatred, arrogance, relishing the downfall of a mistress like Julie. Someone must dictate terms. The stronger one wins. Survival of the fittest.

Shaw said the upper class was demoralized by money, the middle class vulgarized by money, and the working class brutalized by money. With Strindberg, the lower classes were on a march upward. They gave up integrity for materialism and contributed nothing to the society with their climbing.

From here on, no one trusts the servants.

Strindberg's Characters

Strindberg doesn't write about characters you see every day. His special style doesn't permit that. His plays and his characters are intense. They don't have that surface reality of "Come in and sit down and have coffee." They don't have that superficial quality at all. You immediately understand not to mix up Strindberg with anybody who came before.

He is opposed to simple stage characters—those who can be expressed through physical defects, habitual gestures, or repeated expressions. They are from past and present civilization—torn pieces of human behavior, patched together to make up the human soul itself. All modern characters are complex. Don't simplify them. They have a conflict with one another and also self-conflict. When you play Strindberg, don't try to "work out" the situation—fight with it, struggle with it.

The characters are no longer romanticized. The father is both strong and weak. The Captain is very modern. He is modern about science. Science came into Western culture and restated every single idea—religion, marriage, money, everything. Now the character is in difficulty because there is no tradition he can hang on to which will last. The traditional way of life is lame; it is paralyzed. I remember the first time I looked out the window and saw a dozen lesbians with little children. I accepted it, but I didn't accept it. I was bewildered by it. In seeing that, I had a certain confusion of living without knowing what is right or wrong. Everything is right and everything is wrong. We don't have a right to say that is wrong because there are no guidelines anymore.

The Strindberg technique is new. Each character is complex, and the justification for his actions comes out of the complexities—the social situation, the inner psychological situation, the season, the conflict of classes, the domination in the sexual relationship. You cannot play it logically. You have to analyze the background, not just the lines. People in modern plays bring in a great deal of the past. The characters are created before they come on stage. This is what you have to learn to do from the text. The past is so strong it is impossible to think of acting without it. Bring the authenticity of making it work for you. It is the histrionic duty of the actor to say, I know this character, I know how he walks, how he thinks. I know what he did and how he did it.

There is no way you can take away the difficulty and really resolve it. If you win the argument you go away saying, "I won because I shouted, but he has a point." Everybody carries his truth, has his own conflict. We are in an interesting theater where the characters are always complex. Don't play it on a simple level. Don't come in and think, "I am setting the table." Set your table but think, "If I do this, I won't be able to finish that." Put that in. Put in that there isn't any absolutely "complete" thing you do. In good plays, the character wants to do that, and more, but it's rattling and he can't.

"I want to stay home, but I'll go out. But I shouldn't go out." Keep that duality in you. It's interesting. If you have it in you, the audience is interested in you. One reason Pinter and these modern writers are interesting to people is because you don't know what they are thinking and you are interested. The audience is interested in the thing the actor *doesn't* express. That is part of modern acting. It is not solvable. It's not just an orange. It has a little to do with an orange but also something to do with sex.

Strindberg uses unusual people in unusual situations. That is what makes them so strong. He does not judge his characters. He analyzes them and allows them to reveal themselves through many aspects. You can't play Julie straight. You must have the confusion which is in her. Find the action through the mood. Before, playwrights labeled and fixed a person. No character from now on is fixed. With Strindberg, the character is both "nice" and "dreadful." The community is unsettled. We are no longer in a way of life that is constant. Before, a king was a king; a serf was a serf. Now we don't know. The definition of modern man is not that he lacks character, but that he is multidimensional.

Julie is not of one piece, not like her father or her background. She is not really a man or a woman. She was told to be strong, not to be inferior to men. Julie is mixed up from her mother's influence and her father's weakness. She doesn't know how to define herself. She is not aware of her own limitations. The woman in the new play wants to be independent. But nobody really can achieve independence. That is the struggle, but it is not the accomplishment.

Julie is a woman who expresses herself and is modern in the sense that she wants to be heard—wants power and the symbols of power. This type of woman has degenerated, her qualities as a woman have degenerated, in Strindberg's opinion. His attitude toward her is negative. He is not on her side. He says this type is not good for society—she is the "third sex," produced because a man and woman want children in a sick society, where their roles are not clearly defined. Julie cannot face reality. She falls down. She cannot control her sexual drive for a servant—sex drive with no spiritual value. Jean's attitude is that sex is sex—it *has* no spiritual value. Julie throws herself away on him and his low level—cannot match his strength because he is not divided in himself. Jean's masculinity gives him a brutal strength. She sees she is beaten—"out-maled."

Strindberg says this type of modern woman is fighting a losing battle against nature.

Throughout Strindberg, and particularly in *Miss Julie,* the woman doesn't need love. She needs to get out. She uses the man for what he is worth. She may marry or have a child by him, but she wants to get out. If she stays where she is she is ruined, but if she gets out she is also ruined. It is very pessimistic.

The actor's wealth is in his imagination and in his ability to create a character like this. The actor's wealth is not in his bank account. Until now, no actor made a million dollars. The biggest actors in the world made only a little money. You don't think about acting over two thousand years. You are thinking about a freak thing that happened a few years ago with the movies. Nobody is worth a million dollars.

The modern play is economical in language. The modern play coming out of Europe or America is extremely compressed in its language. It is not like Shaw. England and Shaw have a verbal tradition. Shaw talks so much that it is hard to get to the play. He has such an essay in front of the play. The modern play is based on reality. This reality doesn't need fanciness, doesn't need iambic pentameter. It is not written in verse. It is written in a middle-class speech that comes out of human beings in the Western world. You have to approach the middle class from the point of view of a modern sound. The fact that the speech is condensed doesn't mean it isn't great.

In *Doll's House,* when the husband says, "What are you doing in there?" she answers, "I am taking off my costume." That's all she says. It means, "I am discarding the role I've been playing all these years." In one little sentence. Is it big? Cosmic? Does it take a genius to say in six words what a whole character is doing? That is what modern language can do. It may be familiar but it contains much more than the words appear to be.

It is familiar but not the vernacular—not the way *we* talk. Not street talk. Pay attention to that. If the language has quality, so does the deportment. People who speak well also behave well. People who don't speak well also don't behave so good. "Well, I mean, shit"—you don't say that. You don't say "Screw it!" in Ibsen and Strindberg. There is a sense of orderliness. Laura's hair is orderly, her behavior is orderly, the way she wears her clothes is orderly. That is unbreakable in the society. Up to 1930, people didn't go out into the street unless they were dressed properly. You'll never understand that. Men didn't go out without collars and ties. The breaking down, the doing what you want, being on your own, living how you want, eating the way you want, having your own rules, broke all the forms. Now, the only form is at a wedding.

There is an educated aspect to the language of Strindberg. It gives the impression his characters are educated. Don't leave that out. You went to parochial school, you were trained in the military, you went to the university. You get a sense that you are in a tradition. We don't get that in our country. You cannot play Laura without understanding language. She has to be able to speak. She has to teach her child. She comes from an educated family.

The dialogue of these characters is not in "ordinary" speech. It gets below the surface reality. They are intoxicated with their own words. The rhythm of the argument is often illogical. Expressed through such dialogue is the irregularity of the mind functioning. They speak about one thing, but their minds are elsewhere. There is a big contrast between the inner thought and the speech. In conversation, their minds jump and the dialogue wanders. But you must watch out, because everything that is said in the beginning is picked up and made fuller later. You often reiterate the same things with a new or different inner implication. What you say is not necessarily what you think. You say one thing but mean another. Strindberg's search for truth gives you very few answers. Both the audience and the characters are uncertain of the ending.

The problems in Strindberg are not hidden; they are out in the open. Which does not mean they are resolved. In the school of naturalism, you see but cannot overcome the problems: heredity, incest, alcoholism, mental illness, sexual drives, homosexuality, sudden vulgarity by wealth—all those things that reveal the trap of life without emerging into some higher thing. It opens them up as if you were in a hospital.

But the problems of modern man are so tangled up that nothing can be put right. Everything must be annihilated. War should be made on all religious and social and political institutions. Strindberg looked for God in vain and in great pain. It is very modern that when you are in trouble you can't go to God or to the family and there is no rest. A godless world traps you, money traps you, society traps you, women's lib traps you. Everything is split apart.

You must face Strindberg's plays and characters from the unsettledness of the society.

SEVEN

SIX CHARACTERS
IN SEARCH OF AN ACTOR

Strindberg on the Boards

EVERY MODERN CHARACTER is in difficulty. That is why he is in the play. Always see how the character is involved with conflict. No character goes out happily ever after. You have to ask in every play, What is this character up against? What is he bothered by? A lot of what he is bothered by is not what he is saying in the play. A man I hadn't seen in ten years called me up recently and talked a lot and a long time about nothing. What he wanted to say was, "I'm lost." He couldn't say what was wrong, so he said something else.

What you are really thinking, you can't say. It happens all the time. People are in trouble and a lot is guessed at or shown. A lot is completely covered over. One of the great things in modern acting is that you are covered over. You do something with it. We'll see how it works.

In order for you to understand your moment in the theater you have to understand in depth that there is nothing on the stage anymore that is theatrical. We can't depend on that. You can't speak theatrically. The nature of the society changed and you became a person. You have a voice and I have a voice. Chekhov said, "Don't give me Bernhardt. I don't want her. I don't need the golden voice, I need people."

You have to find out how to create people. You find out through the playwright. Strindberg will tell you what he wants from these characters. He writes in a style which needs you. In a novel you can say, "The car went straight and then turned in where the hedges were, and they got out and walked up and she opened the door. . . ." That explains what happened to the car and the people in the car. In a play you don't get that kind of descriptive help.

You have to create the character on your own. You have a girl called Emma in *The Father.* That's nice, a girl called Emma. I have Mary in the office and Tara and I know Gladys—but I don't know Emma. I don't know who she is. I know only the playwright's idea that women now are not now the charming virgins we had before. He shows you an example with Laura. Her brother says, "Watch out for Laura, she is not good." A girl doesn't have to be pure from Strindberg on. A brother doesn't have to like a sister. A sister doesn't have to like a father. The characters have relationships which are not romanticized. It's an enormous gift. It is rare to play a nice girl anymore. Ann in *Man and Superman* is a killer. In the third act, her mother says, "Ann plots and schemes—I never liked her, and she never liked me." This is the graduation to Strindberg, the painting of the woman in a realistic way.

You can learn how to treat realistic characters from three sets of people in two great plays, *The Father* and *Miss Julie.* Once you know these six people, you can create them and others on stage. Nora and Torvald in *Doll's House* represented the revolt of the woman against the tyrannical male. Laura and the Captain in *The Father* represent the revolt of the male against the tyrannical female. You must understand their similarities and differences, in and beneath the texts.

You must see how even a simple prop like a lamp conveys totally different realities. The lamp in *Doll's House* is Ibsen's symbol of enlightenment; it illuminates and reveals. In *The Father,* it is Strindberg's instrument of aggression. See the difference in settings: *Doll's House* is as tangible and solid as the real world. *The Father* is more like an African jungle with two wild animals at each other until one of them falls. See such things, and remember that an actor must be able not only to understand but to execute the text.

Work with the play. It will make your life more interesting and your brain more aware of what it is to act. The approach is not "Here's the text and I'm going to say it, I'm going to feel it." It doesn't work that way. It takes an author a long time to write a play and pick the words. The thing he invests in building a modern play is not in the words. It is somewhere else.

You have to make an investigation: Where am I? Who is she? I had to do a scene the other day, and the moment I got the text I started reading the lines aloud, "Oh, hello—" when it dawned on me, "My God, I'm doing exactly what I tell them not to do." The temptation is so great to go to the words. The words "I feel so good!" have nothing to do with how *you* feel. The words alone are not good enough for you. I will show you something better.

The words are external—a telegraph, a lightning rod that you must do something with. You think that the words are important only if they are being *said* in some nice way. You are completely filled with language that carries you through life without your really being there. You don't have to be there when you say, "Once more into the breach, dear friends!" In your life, you would say, "There's a catastrophe here! The enemy is coming and our men are wounded and, for God's sake, they can't escape. C'mon, boys, c'mon!" You would not say, "Once more into the breach." You would say "C'mon!" twice. That is you. Shakespeare doesn't need you. He needs the words.

With Shakespeare, it doesn't matter about you so much. If you're pretty, you can say, "The quality of mercy is not strain'd." Shakespeare doesn't need such great acting—his words carry you. He doesn't trust you, you see. The modern theater starts with giving up a lot, and what it gives up first is a ruling class. If you have a king with a queen and somebody wants to take the kingdom away—that kind of part can't really be played anymore. We don't have a King Lear. We don't grow them like that anymore. Authors don't write much for kings now because they don't exist very much. The king of Sweden is a bore. He won't let people take his land—he's no fool. But he is really a middle-class king. When he comes out of the palace, he is wearing the same clothes as everybody else.

A Shakespeare play doesn't need you. A modern play does.

I. Nojd and Emma

[Synopsis of *The Father*: The Captain is a great army officer and a brilliant scientific thinker. At the outset, he is talking with the Pastor, his brother-in-law, about a nagging minor matter: Corporal Nojd, his protégé, has impregnated Emma, a scullery maid. An even more nagging and major problem is his wife, Laura, their struggle over their daughter, and Laura's interference in his work. She intercepts his mail and plants seeds of suspicion about who fathered the girl. As the battle escalates, his great brain and impeccable honor prove no match for her assault on his fatal psychological weakness.

—B.P.]

What the modern play gives you, first of all, is a place. The first thing you must ask is, "Where am I saying this?" Most of us don't care. We say, "I enter from here and then I'm free. I'm where I need to be"—wherever the hell that is—"and now I can do what I want." In *The Father,* the Captain comes in and says, "I've been to the post office." It has taken him five hours to go to the post office—two and a half to go, two and a half to get back. So when he comes in and says "I've been to the post office," it is not like *my* saying it. When the Captain says it, it means something else—to drive five hours in the middle of the night in the sleigh.

Understand that "I've just been to the post office" has nothing to do with the words. Approach the text to get as much as possible out of what's happening, starting with the place. London in 1885 is one play, Stockholm in 1885 is another, and if it's Russia or America, you have four different plays, not because of the words but because of the place. Make yourself aware of the time and place right away. Leave the words and go to the larger circumstances surrounding the words.

The play won't tell you much about the larger circumstances. It will tell you it's summer or winter. If there is no sun, and eight months of the year you are in darkness. That is very good for you to know. You have to locate yourself historically in time—1885 Sweden, one hundred miles from the capital in a country which did not develop roads. You use sleds. Be prepared for both indoors and outdoors.

You will have to say, "How do I face this outdoors?" Today we all wear these insulated jackets outdoors. They didn't wear them in 1885, because they didn't have them. The clothing industry was no more developed than the roads—your choice of clothes is more rural. The wool industry makes coats, but they don't make millions of them. 1885. Sweden. Winter. Work on the outside before you go inside.

The author says the play takes place in a room. But he gives you very little to work on in that room. It is a captain's room—guns around. There are guns and a military quality in the room. There is no sofa. If your mind thinks "I'll sit down," the question is immediately, "Where will I sit in a room like this?" We sit on sofas, we don't have guns around. Completely forget *you.* I've never been in a room where there were no sofas. To me, it's very interesting that the center of life and the living room in this play has nothing of a woman in it. It's not in the lines. But the place will talk to you if you let it.

In *The Father,* you are in a traditional home made into a fort. A man surrounded with guns is not the same man who has two couches. The circumstances will lead you to the action. In this place, I would say, a woman would feel uncomfortable. A woman doesn't like to feel uncomfortable. Laura wants *him* to feel uncomfortable. It is her house, her curtains, her pillows. She just about ruined his estate, but he had to give in to her—otherwise she would have become hysterical.

The outside is darkness and ice and a hundred miles from a post office. The inside is a place where the Captain has made a fort for himself which is his life. In the tenth minute you have arrived at the center of the play. In order for him to survive he had to build a fort, and that is what the play is about. Sorry, but the words won't give you a goddamn clue to this. It is the outside place and inside place which will give it to you.

A fort is for battling. There is an army around the Captain, but he is not getting the respect that he wants. He says, "I have jurisdiction over our child," and she says, "That won't help you—I will get the child even if I have to kill." The motive for killing is there and it is very strong. The strongest motive in a woman is not to give up the child. I don't know why—I wish she would just go and have a fine life of her own and see the kid once in a while. But she has to operate in this armed camp in such a way that she can get what he wants.

Each situation gives you the truth of where it takes place. Chicago is different from Boston. Say, "I will never again do a play without knowing if it's Boston with a tea party or whether it is Boston with the new acting company that is there now."

So the immediate circumstance is the living room. The larger circumstance is a provincial town outside Stockholm in 1885. These circumstances will lead you to a plot, which must be well understood by you. The Captain is chastising one of the soldiers in front of the minister because he has impregnated a servant girl. You discover the plot as it comes to you; it doesn't develop right away. Maybe first he talks about something else. Instead of thinking, "How will I say that?" or "I like that, I feel that"—take it easy. I would wait.

There are things that are so interesting if you wait. If you wait as long as I do, you really find things. I didn't realize it was so dark, black. But I also didn't realize how pleasurable these little places can be, with the gurgling water and walking and skating on it when it freezes over. I didn't realize that until I studied. I got a few books on the Vikings. The play becomes absolutely clear if you know. Some inquiry has to be made by you about the country and how it functions. What kind of government does it have? I know how I function in my society. I go to a church. I used to have to go to school. I bank at a certain place. I know where the doctor is. If I get a ticket, I go to the traffic court. This is what surrounds me.

When we play "today," we are at ease because we know what surrounds us. You are not at ease in a play if you don't know what surrounds you. Make some inquiries. The Captain belongs to the military system of that moment. Are you part of a system that can draft you? You are ignorant of it. Take it seriously. A soldier could be conscripted for many, many months.

Pay attention to the class you are in. The Captain is a Swedish army officer. As the play opens, he is speaking to a pastor, his wife's brother. Are you a teacher, a doctor, a pastor, a soldier, a porter? The middle class in Sweden one hundred years ago with its professions is not us. I must know I'm playing a captain in a professional class within the middle class. There is royalty, aristocracy, the middle class, and the working class. We are in no class in America. That is why we have our kinds of plays where we don't know who is who. In my own life, I don't know who is who. You don't have a clue today. Understand the class in its time, not your time. In this play there are several classes. The orderly is one class. Nojd is the military class. The Captain is in the intellectual middle class and the Pastor is part of the clergy. These four classes are there together. The wife is middle-class. The nurse is of an older generation. Everyone has a different religion.

That is very interesting to me. Strindberg talks about each one's religion. I don't think I've heard anyone talk about religion in America. You will have to think about what religion you have. If it's active or passive. One of the few things that mustn't happen in America is an argument over religion. It is so forced on us to be a slave of what we think that nobody says, "What? You won't go to your father's funeral because you don't believe? You won't say a prayer?" You say you're a free thinker and an atheist, but at death suddenly you say, "Oh, please, forgive me if I've hurt you." It goes very deeply. You don't fool around with a thing that has given you throughout life some kind of form. If an airplane crashes, you don't say, "I hope she isn't killed." You say, "Oh God, please God, don't take her from me, I beg you." You revert to some kind of religion.

There were four different kinds of religions in Sweden, and they were important. The Swedes opened it up. Religion is a very forceful part of Strindberg. Laura, the Captain, the Pastor deal with profound aspects of religion. The Captain is fighting to modernize himself. He is a Christian, yet he knows every philosophy. Religion is at the very center of the play. It is not as middle-class as *Doll's House*. Every man in Ibsen wants power. The desire for power substitutes religion in Ibsen. Strindberg deals with it differently.

Try to understand how the Pastor uses the stage differently from the Captain. Each character has a place where he lives. Say, "I live very differently from the maid or my mother or father or my boyfriend." Everybody has his own way to live in a room. Strindberg is writing about a father who has to put it all together. He sees in the servant society no leadership. They cannot lead themselves, so they run to the church a little, then they fornicate. They go to church and steal a little from the house. They are not able to formulate a center for themselves.

We have to see how the church now, at the end of the nineteenth century, functions in a home with the father, who is no longer religious; with Nojd, who is semireligious. We have to see this new setup. A man is not much led by a clergyman anymore.

My parents were very interested in me. They were artists. They had a theater and there were a lot of kids and nurses and all. They were in an artistic circle. When I was twelve, my father said to me, "I'd like you to play Portia, so when you grow up you must study law." We didn't get involved with the thinking of the artist. We got involved with the thinking of the scientist or the man who was building armies for patriotic reasons—men with the qualities the Captain has, which make the civilized man.

Corporal Nojd is in the army, working-class—paid by the army. I'm fooling around with generalizations about Nojd now. Ask about each character, which class? How does he relate to the society? Nojd has a boss. Nojd is the person who is being bossed. There is no boss who doesn't have problems with the class that is coming up, in the army or the factory or the civil service. The worker resents the need to conform to the boss. In the society is a democratization. But this doesn't always bring order. Nojd is in the army for discipline. It is a very important discipline, like the discipline of a doctor or teacher. There are values in the army's discipline, otherwise it couldn't attract a man of the Captain's caliber—the discipline which can hold up the society and not let it go down.

That is us too. Our children have to go to school, learn a profession, not use marijuana. If they use marijuana, they go on to something worse. This break in the society can't be controlled. It has gone so far that it is almost impossible for the President of the United States to have a normal son. That father-son thing is difficult and will be difficult from now on. Mother-daughter is difficult, too.

So the army's discipline is supposed to guarantee the society a certain security. It doesn't work if a soldier can say, "I'll do it my way." Nojd says he'll do it his way. He is part of the church but also of the working class. The church isn't taken seriously. This is a generalization given to you by Strindberg not because he wants it to be but because it's the truth. The working class is not particularly loyal to anybody. Nojd, as a matter of fact, is in a very good position in relation to the Captain. Nojd feels a part of this family. The Captain is also the father. Nojd is his child and he is bad. It is paternalism. The Captain says, "I told you you have to behave. She's a woman, there's danger in pregnancy, you have a certain responsibility." He feels intensely. That is what makes him the father. You can only be a father if you have a child and are beginning to have bad children. He can mark Nojd AWOL, have him discharged, punished, take away his privileges, put him in solitary confinement—anything. But he doesn't, because he has a soft spot for this young man who is seventeen, part of his household.

In the army, they are stationed here and there. What do soldiers do? All through history they rape and create bastards and take over the women. This is the tradition. One of the things soldiers do is create kids. It is not a new thing. The Captain knows this—he knows this guy. He did it himself, slept with girls who offered themselves. He did that, but he grew up. He changed. We have here a captain who is capable of control. He got married and had a child. He evolved.

Nojd is young and virile. He can satisfy himself when he wants, and he doesn't want anything else. His relationship to the Captain is impertinent. "Listen, you were a guy and I am a guy. I have to have a little sex, for Christ's sake. I can't marry the girl, you know that." A man like the Captain you can be impertinent to, but he is the strong influence. The Captain is strong. Nojd is tied emotionally to the Captain because the Captain is tied emotionally to him. This is still the nineteenth century with the relationship of the top to the bottom. Nojd doesn't want a boss, but the Captain is the boss and Nojd can't do anything about it. It is a moment in society where the class is not settled down. There is still paternalism, but the working class is learning to fight the boss. Understand that there is no character anymore who is not willing to fight for another way.

Nojd uses women for his appetite. He uses life for his appetites. Nojd's sexuality is what he holds on to. This is what gets him ahead from the cultured masculine point of view that is really dark, elemental, primitive. We, too, still use this side of ourselves. We do what we want. It is a graduated sense of Nojd's antagonism toward the Captain. We have inherited that. What Strindberg said has advanced to you and our own society. The younger generation is against the police, and the police are against them. It is all in turmoil. The standards are broken.

Nojd's relationship to the house is that he breaks the rules and is being punished for breaking the rules. He is the bad boy, and the bad boy is the beloved of every family. I realized that with my own father figures in the theater, like Stanislavsky, like my father, like Reinhardt. Their paternalism made the actors serve them. A real father figure is not great unless he loves the people who work for him.

Nojd might stop impregnating girls, cheating at cards, getting drunk for the Captain. But this bad boy won't stop because of the church. The church is too old to be identified with. Nojd's mischief hurts the father. The Pastor sees this and says to the Captain, "If you don't believe in God, you'll get nervous. I tell you, calm down! You have an individualistic view, you're functioning alone with your own belief, and you're going to collapse." Strindberg puts a person there who watches the Captain but doesn't really care much about Nojd or really the Captain either. The church doesn't take on the immediate impact of what life really is. The church doesn't take it personally.

Build Nojd, too, from the pride the Captain has for him and the pain he gives him. He has seen and admired Nojd. He has seen him lead and ride and jump and the way he leads the entire cavalry to do the jump, how he goes first. The Captain thinks this first-class and has been watching him with great joy. He has seen him break in horses that nobody could break in, watched the charm of Nojd as he rides in the corral and is thrown. He sees Nojd loving and kissing the horse that threw him, jumping back on and being thrown again. He loves Nojd—loves his fearlessness and the fact that he is physical and big and a man. But when he comes in to be reprimanded, the Captain doesn't think he is a man, he thinks he's a child—and has no way to deal with him. If you build him that way, it will give you an opening of how to build the scene. It is complicated.

The Captain tells the Pastor, "He is up to his tricks again. He's up to tricks not only with the girl but with me." A real son-of-a-bitch. The Captain gets worked up. He is with his own thoughts—the *past*. He has this whole past to think about. From now on, no line in a modern play does not have the past in it. He has a disturbing report about Nojd: "You have been with a girl called Emma. Women have a responsibility to their way of life, to themselves. You have influenced them away from their responsibility. Every woman knows she mustn't have a bastard." The Captain's point of view has honor. "You have come in with your sexuality and injured this girl. I want you to know that when you do things like that, my daughter hears about it. My daughter is influenced by you and the way you talk to Emma, put her on your lap, how you treat Emma. You can't do that."

Who is Emma? I have to find Emma. Emma has lost all direction. She is young and full, with her hair turned back, and she is in the kitchen. She does kitchen work, but she has one thing she does better than anyone else. Men know she is there because of that, and because she lets them know.

I want to open up her class of people: who demoralizes them and what their impulses are and the fact that they have no place to go or change—nobody cares. She has lost the sense of what her body is really for. She likes the sense that her body is for fornicating. She enjoys that sense of herself. She doesn't enjoy the morality over her when she gets pregnant and somebody says, "You little whore." So she goes to what she likes. She is primitive enough to say, "I do not think it's so bad. I haven't gotten pregnant yet. I've been doing this for a long time." This new girl is a child without direction. There is nobody there that she wants to copy. She goes to church, but there is no influence there. She is belligerent, like Nojd. Everybody tells them they can't do what they like most to do. What people like most is drink, eat, get fat, fornicate.

My father told the audience, "I try to bring you plays which help you to understand your life. I cannot do that if you don't want it, but if I follow you, you'll take me to the whorehouse." That is what the theater was meant to be. People in the theater wanted to give the audience values. If you took the audience's values, it was a whorehouse. That is what we have on television, a whorehouse.

You see the platform: the Captain and the church don't seem to be in control anymore. There is no sense of virtue in the people Emma is working for. Laura is in the kitchen undermining the Captain. Emma sees what she does. Don't make young Emma innocent. She has an idea of "I am leading my life the way I want to lead it. I want to go to the dance. I want to go to the barn with Nojd. It's not just something *he* wants. *I* want it too." Their generation doesn't want the old rules—"Your mother didn't do this; she and your aunts were all virgins." They want to go to some uncertain future which will give them all the advantages of now.

They don't want the certainty of the past. They want the insecurity of the present.

In this historical moment of transition, religion has been pushed off the map by modern thinking and science. So I've evolved from monkeys? The rituals of the church kept people in line for two thousand years. Now it's going.

Everything has changed. The music has changed from classical to romantic. We are going toward twelve-tone music, from melodious to dissonant. Painting, poetry, drama changed. If all the arts changed, then certainly so did the church. How is a pastor going to talk to a thug? What does his profession have to do with this future ignoramus?

The father desperately wants help from the Pastor in correcting his "son," Nojd. They keep passing the buck.

"Why didn't you say something to him?" he says to the Pastor to begin the scene. "Why don't you haul him over the coals?" You get Strindberg's idea that the Captain represents the male at the most crucial moment of civilization in two thousand years, when Darwin said we were just a species of animal, when Marxism was doing away with class structure. When man had only himself to go to and realized he was caught in a bind.

The Pastor has to respond. Go to the thinking of the clergy. "How am I going to approach a man who is taught to kill? If he is taught to kill, of course he is going to do what he wants sexually. Killing and sex go together. He is trained to use his muscle and brain to kill. Do you think the church can influence him?" The Pastor knows a man trained to kill is going to be indulgent in his private life. What can religion do?

The Captain is saying, "He will never be a man by his own rules. He has no discipline. You have dominated every man for two thousand years. Why don't you give him a talking to? What good are you if you can't hold on to one man, for Christ's sake?" The excitement of this first scene is not the words. It is the idea that a man who leads without leadership is going down. The whole thing in this scene is that the Captain has failed. He cannot control his woman, he can't control the army, he can't control or use the church. He is looking for a way to survive.

The Captain says, "Once in a while you are called upon to take God into your hands and present it to the soldiers. Could you do that for me? Could you act as a pastor for once?" His attitude to the Pastor is, "You have been monkeying around too long. I don't get it, myself. I had a terrible time finding my own values. I don't depend on anybody anymore. Could you try?"

The attitude of the Pastor is that it won't do any good. People will go their own way. They will finally come back to the church because they believe in the church. They don't believe in the Captain because he is temporary. The Captain is too interested in the emotions of life and not the control of life.

From the church's point of view, what the Captain wants is weak. He doesn't know how to use his power to dominate other people when confronted. He says, "I cannot control Nojd or his way of life. He is too strong for me. He is working-class. He is physical, sexual. I cannot control this animal." The Pastor sees animal, man, and church. That is the trinity in the play.

The Pastor tells the Captain, "You are playing a losing game. You need God to frighten people. It's your fault. You with your modern scientific thinking did it. You took two thousand years away. The common people need the discipline of the church. Society is going down." The Pastor thinks he spoke very well.

The Captain thinks what he said was terrible. Settle for giving the child to an orphanage? "Why didn't you talk about religion? You just muttered stupidities. You should have told Nojd, a child is the future." They don't agree.

The words ooze out of how each character thinks. Find out from the characters. Don't talk except from thinking. Olivier rejected a million-dollar movie part because he wanted to go into the Old Vic for twenty-five dollars a week instead. He didn't want to be a vaude-villian anymore. He hired himself out into the thinking field. He said, "Yes, I can sing a little and dance a little, but I mostly want to think." That is what keeps the actor in full growth. Gielgud did Lear three times. The actor thinks himself into the part. If he doesn't think himself into it, he is going to do the words or himself and it doesn't make very good theater.

Whenever you begin a new section, go over that large problem that the author had to face in order to tell the truth. In order to tell the truth in this period, artificial behavior had to go. The authors took the moments in the characters' lives where they were needing to analyze. You have people unmasked on the stage. This was tremendously interesting and new.

Read the scene and underline the facts. In the first line we get a fact: the Captain says Nojd has been up to something. The next fact is that Nojd went to the dance at Gabriel's and took Emma to the barn. The characters are in the barn and before the barn. I'm sorry, but all this has to be created by you. The Pastor says, "It would be hard on the girl if she's pregnant." That is a fact. It makes you go into the social situation of that girl. If she has a baby, she won't remain in service; she'll have to go to the poorhouse. The child will be given away so she can continue working. The servant girl who is pregnant is going to have to face a lot that you have to supply her with.

Oh, did anybody notice that Emma doesn't even appear on stage? What, am I crazy? All this about a character who never appears, who you'll never play? I am crazy for your acting. For the fact is that she is important and you must know her, even if you and the audience don't see her.

Go deeply into the social situation of that girl. This is the work the author did, but he left it out because it could not be included in the style. Get behind the situation that produces the words. That is what gives you the chance to go to your artistic imagination. If you know a servant girl has no money, that men sleep around with ser-vant girls in Sweden and that there is no way for this girl to avoid that, then the actor with his artistic imagination can honestly say, "She is going to have a hard time." It doesn't make any sense to say that or to act in a modern play unless the truth of the situation behind the words is in you. The situation behind the words gives you the ability to say the words. If you don't use that creative background to know what that girl is, you have no right to talk about her.

Until now, you have not been made to do that.

II. Laura and the Captain

The past hangs over the play. The conflict starts right from the beginning. *The Father* is constructed like *Ghosts.* The actual start of the play is years before, when the marriage started. There are three ideas: the male-female struggle for power and control; the two-sided chaos within the man; and that suspicion and thinking without doing can destroy you.

In the antagonism and drive for power between a man and woman, the woman is up against the overpowering position of the man. Her drive is unique, threatening not only the man but the society of the whole West. The man has an aristocracy of mind and honor which is not ruthless. In *The Father,* the woman wins because she is more ruthless.

Strindberg paints Laura in very harsh colors. Pygmy woman, who will bring an age of barbarism. She is part of a great historical struggle. Laura takes the club away from man, becomes Hercules. The reversal. They are not fighting with the same weapons. Her superior weapon is that she can lie. It is part of her nature not to have honesty or integrity. Strindberg says she didn't have time to join the world of science, so in order to do so right away she has to lie, steal, cheat. The brute strength of the man falls before the insidious weakness of the woman. Clytemnestra kills Agamemnon without any conscience. But when Orestes has to kill, he can't do it.

The Captain and his wife are in a battle they can't control. Man has given up the need to be a Christian and the security of the afterlife. He no longer has a sense of continuity, except the one he gets from having a child. He depends on that continuity for himself—

the power to create and raise a child. This idea has the bigness of *King Lear, Hamlet,* and *Macbeth.*

The father wants to give his daughter values with which to be strong. He has postponed his own important work in science to support the family and rear her. He has one thing above all: continuity through the child. But he would have no rights over her if it turned out that she isn't really his child. If that were taken away, how could he go on? It would mean suicide for him.

The father has been the center of the world for a long time. He represents that purpose through the ages—that ability of man on earth to create civilization. He has that role. It has been handed down from father to son. Up to now he has understood his ethical role as responsibility to community, family, to what he feels is his truth. His truth has come from judging his society.

But this father judges in the way people now judge modern society. The way we judge the presidency, the Senate. We no longer just accept that a man is a senator. In the society now people say, "How is he really leading his life? And I have to lead my own life. I can't lead my father's or mother's life. I can't do what they did or what they tell me to do." There is a way of breaking from the father and mother now, and once you break from that, you must then put something else together.

This is new.

When the Doctor asks Laura, "Has the Captain shown any symptoms of instability, any lack of will power?" she can honestly answer yes. Strindberg says that, because the religion and politics we have believed in are all mixed up, man accuses himself. He doesn't say, "I can fix it." Ibsen says that. Ibsen's man says, "Change the system. If the reservoir is polluted, tell people it is polluted and get the crooks to jail." But Strindberg's father has many things around him which are unclear to him. "I don't know why my wife is rejecting that part of me which makes me want to live. I wanted to live because I wanted to love; I was lonely and I wanted to join somebody else so we would be together and less lonely." This is being denied him. He as a powerful man realizes that man needs to love and join a woman in order to have something tangible in a mixed-up society. What is tangible and forever is continuity through the child. This is very powerful. If it weren't, we wouldn't have so many bar mitzvahs and christenings. With Strindberg, you have to play a man who is ambitious but bigger than ambition—capable of loving and of functioning. If that is taken away, he is in the dark. All through the play, we see that the father is being injured in his need to balance love with life.

The Captain handles the Doctor very brilliantly at first. He asks where he would like to stay. The Doctor says that is up to him. The Captain says, "It is not up to me, it is what *you* would like best." He says, "I would like best what you would like best." The Captain says, "Look, I don't care where you stay, I have no feelings about you—make up your mind, you have to decide which is more comfortable."

In the Captain, you don't have a man whose will is broken. You have a man whose will is very healthy.

But as the Doctor says, "If he loses his will . . . The will, Madam, is the backbone of the mind. If it is injured, the mind falls to pieces."

The Doctor says, "A sick man can be made to believe anything. He is highly susceptible to suggestion." The Captain is like Othello, who was also the strongest man. "Your wife lost her handkerchief? Oh, I saw that Cassio has it." Why does he have it? "Well, I saw them talking. . . ." He is finished.

The will is very strong in an Ibsen person. In a Strindberg person, the will is very weak. People are easily destroyed in a society where God doesn't hold them together and the father and mother are in competition. You have to be very strong or come from a lower class to survive.

The first scene between the Captain and Laura shows you this is war. It is killing. Don't read it off the cuff, because the cheapest thing is temperament. Temperament is not terribly interesting until the talent comes in. Laura interrupts him. To have somebody come in while he is counting disturbs him. She doesn't knock, she just walks right in. In her doing that, he is cruel with her. He presumes she has come for money. "You've come for money?" From this you get that Laura is not in charge; the man is in control of the economics. But there is something wrong in a house when the man says, "Where are the bills?" He should know where they are. The impression is that she takes care of some of these things. There is an unusualness.

She reacts to that. This is the first time he has asked her for the bills. He wants to look them over. It's a shock to her. The man supported the household, but the woman ran it in 1880 to a large extent. In this particular thing, they don't behave the normal way. He treats her like a servant. He is rough with her about this money business, military.

Something has gone wrong, not with the money but with the ethic. The father leads the society aristocratically by making the decisions on how they function, how their daughter should be educated. That is why he is called the Father. His ethics are strong. His attitude towards getting into debt is strong. He is a symbol of authority. No debts. No affairs. If you marry, you have rights over the child and the education. The woman is supported and gives up certain rights. I am astounded at that. No father can take away a child from the mother today. But in this period, marriage has those rules. You get the sense that Strindberg is on the side of this man. He and this modern woman have a real conflict. It is not she's right and he's wrong; they are two people emerging in themselves differently, and the marriage cannot hold it.

The Captain is in a constant state of trying to make himself clear. He is a talented man who has to support a family—child, servants, and all. If a man obligates himself to that, he has to sacrifice. Most men do sacrifice. They alter their way of life in order to marry and raise a family. Women often don't understand that men do this. They think it's natural—"What's the matter? Go to work. You want to write poetry? That's for girls or lesbians."

He says, "I have more than my share to take care of. I not only have to deal with what life I have, but with my wife. I have to accept her." All through, the Captain has a deep need to be a part of this marriage, to merge with this woman. You are not torn asunder until death do you part, and all that. It is stuff made up by the clergy, but it is the deepest need of life to make this wigwam work. The father's attitude to marriage has a certain honor. It is the *Pastor* who says, "You don't know what I know about women. You love a woman who doesn't have any love."

The Captain has the ability to say what is going on inside him. Hamlet was the only person who said "Who am I?" Otherwise, that hasn't happened before. A man never displayed his inner weakness. He is the Captain and the master but also has the helplessness of the modern man. This is a revelation. Play both sides. The modern character is capable of betraying his inner self. He had to become insecure to get that close to himself. The insides are convulsed enough to come out with some truths.

In act two, they are discussing the education of the child. Should she go to church—be confirmed? Should you teach her to go into a thing that is obsolete? It is not the greatest thing to make a girl into a Christian, Jew, Islamic. Where women are under religious jurisdiction, there is a strong putdown. The Captain says it has to do with the whole way men and women, fathers and mothers, are going to influence the future. "I have against me the inferior thinking of women. The child is going to be surrounded by women, and their thinking now is insane. The insanity of my mother-in-law, who believes dead spirits are talking to her and says this to my child. She is crazy because she couldn't love. She made a slave of my wife."

The mother-in-law is his born enemy, but instead of saying it, he has to "talk out" the fact. This is your job. "She has made my wife take out of my child's room every book except the Bible. My mother-in-law has encouraged the maid to become a sneak thief because of her inferior mind and curiosity about my life. She has told my daughter things about me which make me repulsive to my daughter. She says a man who wears a uniform is a killer and likes to beat people. My wife, when she sees me in my uniform, wants me to take it off. She has infiltrated every aspect of our lives, trying to keep her daughter for herself and obliterating me as the husband." This is the mother-in-law.

You have to understand what the mother-in-law did to him. Whenever he had colleagues in the house she would come in and say, "It's time to go." She would sabotage him. She would make Laura laugh at the way he spoke. You must experience everything by going behind the words. If Laura mimics him and his quiet speech, it hurts him. Always take what affects you. Don't load yourself with fiction. Know what you are talking about, feel it, experience it. If you don't take the experience of it, you are getting more fiction. It is the author's job to take the fiction and make it extremely human. It is your job to defictionalize the fiction by experiencing it. In modern theater, your talent lies in your choice. Your choice is what makes you create the experience of the words through your thinking. What you take, you add to your experiencing the text. This can't be arrived at unless you know why the playwright wrote the play in that moment of history—the predicament of man without firm rules.

He is at a loss against religion and the depravity of man. Man has always been depraved, but the human experience has been to lift himself up to being a man of spirit and truth. You know that about the Captain and about religion in his life. Now, he is being dragged into the underworld. That is what the play is about.

Everybody here is in conflict. Look for this conflict. The main thing is to be able to lift the play out from under by experiencing what they are thinking about and then saying it. Add to the text. For example:

He says, "This child—the entire youth now—is subject to becoming liars and fools. My mother-in-law wants my child to think dead people come down and talk to her. This girl is facing the falsity of a crazy woman who invented something she needed for her own selfishness. The horror of this woman. This is insanity. All these women talking to the dead and to their own God. This one is in the Salvation Army, the other one is a Methodist. . . ." The Captain sees that religion is in the hands of imbeciles. The Captain is explaining this to the Pastor. He says, these women will really ruin it all.

He is hurt by his wife in this menagerie of crazy women. He says it is like walking into a tiger's den—this immature, feminine thinking. Their hate of men. I feel like going in there with a club. But they would tear me to pieces. Their hate is in the open.

Laura wants the child to become an artist. What does Laura really want? What does she think art is? It will keep her close to the house; she'll be able to supervise her. She'll frame the pictures and put these bad pictures in everybody's room. "Artist" means sacrifice, not having anything to do except express a great hunger to say something through art. That is not what Laura wants. Like her own mother, she wants the girl at home or traveling with her wherever she goes.

Strindberg is giving you the new influences of women over the child. The breakdown. When the woman moves away from just loving and helping the child and wanders into something she doesn't quite know, she will take on a fanatic quality. That is what they do.

Women are not educated enough. They do not go to the university and become physicists or doctors. They go where they can go. One goes to fornicating and the other goes into the Salvation Army.

This child is tossed around in a sea of people who want to influence her. The mother is supposed to be the one who loves, and the father is the one who influences. It is the father who has created the world, philosophy, science.

Today, the father in our terms is Kramer, who gives the child ice cream and toys.* He takes him to the toilet three times in the picture. That is the symbol of the father for the Western world now. Not one minute in that movie did he say, "I can't be a father, I've forgotten how to learn. I spent all my life in business without any growth. I don't know what to tell him except, 'Have more ice cream.' I have not been prepared. I have nothing to tell him." It would have been a better picture. The father has lost his place except through money and toys.

Strindberg's father wants to give his child a chance to be free, so she can teach school or, if she marries, so she can help herself and her children. The play is about the changing values in a society going down. He says, "I have the right by heritage to put her someplace where she won't be destroyed"—to be a father in the large sense of giving her a way of life. We have lost that. This is the big protest: don't lose the father who has been created for hundreds and hundreds of years.

The whole thing has size. I wouldn't use familiar things. We won't get the strength of him by bringing him down, making him familiar. Avoid that. Strindberg is tense and the play is tense and there is tension coming out of the society. If the play tells you that he is a force, a big man, my advice is not to make him like you. My advice is to go to the Harvard Club and look at men, look at pictures of that generation and see that they didn't sit on a chair sloppily. A man's chair was meant to stay from one generation to another. There is nothing disposable. Everything, every glass, had a heaviness, an authority of knowing it would be handed down. The same with the morality.

---

*Adler is referring to the contemporary hit film *Kramer vs. Kramer* (1979), directed by Robert Benton, in which mom Meryl Streep leaves hapless dad Dustin Hoffman to fend for himself and their son, while they battle for legal custody of him.

Work with pictures. See what an army man looks like. See, in that generation, he has something that was still regal. Still big. So does Willy in *Death of a Salesman,* but this father is different. He is an army man. Go to the body immediately. Look at people and see what you can take for yourself. Nojd's body is different from the Pastor's. The gestures are different. Build the Captain as an attractive man that women like, and who likes women. Don't ever leave sex out of a good playwright. Don't play for ideas alone. These people are aware of their opportunities to love and have children—build dynasties. It's not "Let's see, where should we go?" They are not orphans in the storm, like we are. The storm has broken there, but they are still not orphans. They still have style, still have form.

I want to know how he sits, walks, opens a door, how he reads—does he put glasses on? I would unencumber him. He is too big. Don't diminish him with weak eyes. Let him have strong, penetrating eyes, penetrating understanding. His power of accounting tells him, "Something is wrong, somebody is doing something wrong. And I am responsible. I should have known."

There was a time in the theater when a director came and directed and built the play, and then somebody else came in and told the actor, "Don't do it that way, take it from me, I'm the producer." Then the director came in the next day and said, "What happened? What is this?" He was undermined. This is the Captain's situation. It has a great deal of tension and nervous energy, and it doesn't know where to go because he doesn't know where the crime is. There is a crime in those first few words, in his accounting. Something has gone wrong with the entire estate and the way it is run. These are the impressions.

It is factual and it is big.

The Western idea of woman is that she is weak, childish. That scatterbrained quality of the female in relation to the male—that "You do it for me"—still exists. Nora stands for that woman. Laura is the opposite of Nora, and the Captain is the opposite of Torvald.

[In Strindberg, the man has a soul and so does the woman. The souls of these two different individuals are in conflict from the depths of themselves. Their souls are tormenting themselves and each other. Strindberg brought this out and is a genius in understanding that.]

Laura is a new breed. He doesn't create her suddenly. He builds her through other people to make you understand her character, the willfulness of this Laura. She is willful from childhood up. If you think about yourself or others, you will see the willfulness starts very early. As a kid in school, she wants to do what she wants to do. She has this will which makes her belligerent with men. She is trying to break out. In the modern plays, if you see a woman unhappy or uncomfortable, it is because she has to break out. She has to get it some way or other, sometimes through love, sometimes through giving up love.

We are giving birth to this new woman. She isn't quite out of the womb. She is three-quarters out. She fights with the man because she doesn't want to be destroyed. Laura is not a villain, she is modern. With all her modern problems, she still believes in religion. She needs that flirting with mystery, with going somewhere safer. She gets hysterical when it is attacked. Science has attacked everything. We take it for granted now, but then, it meant something dreadful was happening in the home. [The Captain is with books and science and meteors, and she thinks he is crazy because she doesn't understand a microscope. Here is a grown-up, powerful man looking through a hole at slides. What is he doing? It is worse than mysticism. Understand from her point of view, he is a lunatic, out of his mind. He has brought something foreign into that established way of life. It would drive certain people crazy. That is the way this man affects the people around him. The majority is very much against him.]

You are in a suburb a hundred miles from Stockholm, the center of education. Education in Sweden is strong, but not for women. They have only recently got the privileges of working as a teacher or in the post office. They don't have the vote. Men are dealing with women who are aggressive. They burst out with this playwright. The woman is the center in the conflict.

Laura's first appearance with the Captain is in a room which makes for tension. The mood, the atmosphere, of the play has tension. Everyone who comes in is on a lower level than he is. That is a difficult thing for him. The life in his home is full of God, mystery, dead people coming down and conversing at the table. It's crazy to him, the atmosphere here.

Laura enters, convulsed with her own problem. She is living with a man who makes absolutely no sense to her. She wants out. She is feminine. He married a beautiful woman who was romantic for ten minutes. What he didn't know was that she was modern. He didn't understand that. One of the keys is, don't marry out of your class. Don't, if you are religious, marry somebody who is not religious. Don't marry somebody who wants to be the boss if you want to be the boss. Know what's against the partnership. Don't do what Mrs. Harris did. She waited fourteen years for a man who was organically incapable of being faithful. You have to know. If you don't, you wind up like Mrs. Harris.* She is an archetype of a lady who just didn't see the truth. A psychoanalyst in two hours would have told her, "Look, tootsie—out!"

The misalliance. Look for it in the conflict in plays. See where the marriage is toppling, from what point of view. He is stronger than you. You don't like that. He is more educated than you. You don't like it. He's a scientist and he wants his world. You want him to be with you. It is horrible to be with any man who has his own life. Why shouldn't he wait until you're ready and have his world with you?

Do you understand the difference in their temperaments? He has this turmoil around him, this anger, and she is watching him. Read the scene now and work from the point of view of the woman. Understand the man in order to fight him. Understand how the other character thinks. Understand that the women want their freedom. She is angry. She has been angry a long time but she didn't show it. Don't put it on just a personal plane. Life marches slowly, and we are discovering the deep-rooted cosmic anger she has in her.

Laura comes in and sees this man doing his large gestures. He is

*Jean Harris, headmistress of the posh Madeira School for Girls, shot and killed her ex-lover Dr. Herman Tarnower, celebrated author of *The Scarsdale Diet*, in 1980 after waiting more than a decade for him and then being cruelly jilted.

talking to himself and she waits and watches this great man, this captain, this man of knowledge, with his own world. He is central, she is trivial. If a man did that to me I would kill him. She's mad. She watches this performance—the performance of a lunatic. "Who the hell does he think he is?" She thinks how disgusting it is that a man of such size should indulge himself as he does. People laugh when he goes away and imitate the way he talks. They are right to do so because he is pompous.

She sees him as oversized, conceited. Always ask yourself how your partner sees you. Don't depend on the language. Being close to a person creates jealousy and anguish. Husbands are jealous of wives, wives are jealous of husbands.

Laura doesn't need such a big man. She needs one closer to herself so they can go to church together and play dominoes. She doesn't need a man who is known all over the world for his articles on meteors. It must be terrible. She stays in the back and he doesn't feel or see her. She has to play humble. "I'm playing it the way you want me to be. I don't mean to interrupt you—do you mind?" He catches that she is playing a part. There are two or three times when she actually bows to him. "Am I disturbing you? Am I, the little woman, allowed to open my little mouth and say something to make you realize how important it is?" Know what she is thinking. When I played the part, I didn't know what I was doing. I just played, swam around.

She is role-playing the sweet little girl. He sees this and acts pretty tough with her. "What do you want? I have work to do here. You need money?" That is how you talk to a servant. "You need change? I'll give it to you later." He doesn't look at her. You have to know a great deal of background in order to know why he treats her that way.

There is always one thing in a human being that shouldn't be touched—one point. It may be his saying, "I don't want you to betray me." If she doesn't respect his work, that is fatal. She doesn't respect what is closest to him—what he is creating, his meteor work. His books have been taken away. She has warned him that if his books and microscopes and things are in any part of the house where the child is, she will destroy them. The source of his absolute indignation is that she is undermining his work. Build that she is against what she thinks is the stupidity of his mind that is running things there.

"Housekeeping money? Do what you want. I need to get rid of you, I have to work. Leave the bills here and I'll go through them." She might go over and pick up some of his papers: "You want me to account for things to you? Is that what you expect?" You have to see how this woman is walking through his life, demeaning him by picking up what is his and putting it down. Very feminine. Very pretty.

If a playwright gives you a desk, paper, chairs, armaments, he wants you to understand that they will help you to act. Ask, "What can help me?" I would have her see that he has just signed this and that paper. She picks one up casually but in her mind she is saying, "Mr. Authority—a man who knows how to treat soldiers but doesn't understand anything about a wife who hates him. I don't sleep with you. I don't listen to you. I have nothing to do with you. I have my child, my mind, my thought." But she has to hide it.

In act two, the Captain says, "Come in and let's talk. I know you were eavesdropping." That gives you a hint at her immoral character. A person who eavesdrops is pretty low. He says, "This evening, I went to the post office and from the mail I fetched it is clear to me that you have been intercepting my correspondence."

She takes his letters. Her whole operation is to destroy him, but she does it without the sense that she is doing it.

That is the moral situation of this new woman, the third sex. Strindberg says she has no principles.

Laura says, "I acted from the best of intentions. You were neglecting your military duties for this other work." That is not the way a wife speaks. That is the way a mother speaks to a child. "You've been doing something wrong—you haven't been doing your homework." The Captain is known all over the Western world, but she says, "You're being bad, I had to interfere."

The Captain says, "You know very well that one day I shall win more distinction in this field than in the army. What you want is to stop me winning laurels of any kind, because this would stress your own inferiority."

It is very clear about her lesser ability, her inferior mind. She is crooked, takes letters, and listens at doors. This is not the woman he married. He married a lovely wife who turned into a competitor. He shows you that she is in competition with him, doesn't want his mind to be bigger than hers. She doesn't *have* a mind.

When Nora forged a check, she was not socially responsible, because the woman was not part of the outside world. Twenty years later, the woman wants to fight the man, she wants to get out and know the world. Laura knows exactly what the money situation is—insurance, pensions, the estate.

[Laura is feeling her way through in the society, but she doesn't yet know herself or the society well enough. She is living with a brilliant man but she is stupid.]

For a long time the antagonism of male and female was covered over. It is no longer covered over. Move over, I want to get there. Who is stronger in the family, who is the boss, who wears the pants? All this, in a vulgar way. Man is still fighting this invasion. Strindberg fought it. He didn't win, but he fought it. Women don't have the morality yet. They cheat and say, "I want all your money if I'm married to you. Even if you die, I want to be supported." That is the mentality of most women, including mine. "I want a divorce— you tell that bastard . . ." Woman is more emotionally than intellectually equipped. She is not built like a man, where the mind controls the passion. He has been trained to do that for two thousand years.

Laura is not yet trained.

Ibsen's Torvald plays games with Nora. The Captain doesn't. He did at first, but then he stopped playing because he saw he was losing his sense of honor and that Laura was only pretending to love him.

Nora wants to share Christmas with Torvald. Laura doesn't want to share. Nora sleeps with Torvald, believes in him—idealizes him. Laura has stopped all that. She doesn't love the Captain, has stopped being his wife. She has the capacity to say what is truthful in marriage. Nora lies in her marriage; when she finds out the truth, she leaves him. Laura wants the *man* to get out.

Either way, you can't love a man if you can't tell him the truth.

Men and women fight with different weapons. You see it in the way Laura talks "weakly" to men. She says to the Doctor, "Yes, we have been fortunate not to have any serious illnesses, but all the same things are not quite as they should be."

That is opaque. She doesn't say, "I'm not sick, but my husband is." She says, "Things are not quite as they should be"—a very feminine way to talk to a man. Because it is so oblique, the Doctor weakens. Laura undoes the masculine clarity. A woman learns how to operate a man. It's quite a challenge to learn how to talk to a man.

Laura: "You don't believe what I am telling you?"

Doctor: "I am convinced, madam, that you believe what you are telling me."

He doesn't say she lies; he says she has decided what she says is the truth. That is a very keen observation by Strindberg. No woman is a liar. She believes the lie, so it is no longer a lie. It is all pretty unconscious—the way she speaks without responsibility. From line to line she makes up a whole play she doesn't believe in. Don't play her as a villain.

Doctor: "May we not postpone this conversation until I have had the honor of meeting the Captain?"

His sense of honor is immediately clear—not to talk about someone who isn't there and can't defend himself. Another woman would say, "You are quite right, I'll wait." But Laura doesn't. Her sense of honor is crippled. If one partner has honor and the other doesn't, you have two unequal forces. The person without honor has more force.

Honor has to do with integrity. From the start, which is very brilliant in Strindberg, you see it is missing in the culture of the generation coming up. It is being tripped up by a more democratic way of life. Instead of marrying a girl, pay her off and let her go have an abortion.

Laura doesn't know all this, but the Captain does. He said, "I loved you until you made me compromise so deeply that I had to rescue myself and become a scientist." He rescued himself from all her things that weren't open and aboveboard. Her way of life was too compromised. From then on, somebody is going to be victimized. Somebody is going to say, "Never mind the standard. I'm going to climb." In *Miss Julie,* the servant climbs because he has nothing. Miss Julie doesn't have to climb; she has everything. Everybody I know wants to get somewhere else.

The emphasis in Strindberg is on psychological difficulties in dealing with life and each other: it is possible for one to plant a suspicion and drive the other to insanity. A crowd, a nation can be completely remodeled by an individual's power of suggestion—Hitler, Mao, Joe McCarthy.

[The Captain loses his mind. Suspicion destroys him. He doesn't know if it's the work of outside enemies or his own mind. A mother will commit any crime to win control of a child. But the play is not about a domestic fight. It is about an historical struggle of enormous intensity: man's masculinity at stake.

Once the Captain throws the lamp—uses violence against his wife—he is lost. His manliness has been degraded. He has been defeated by a third sex. When Laura denies that he is the father, the Captain is finished. All he can do is go to his fate with courage. When Laura wins in the end, she is devastated. Something happened that she didn't exactly want to or expect. She breaks down. Even if you win, you lose.]

III. Julie and Jean

[Synopsis of *Miss Julie*: It is Midsummer's Eve, that one wild night of the year when upper and lower classes mix. Julie bursts into the kitchen of the family estate, hot and amorous from the revelry. To the servants' shock, she makes shameless sexual advances to Jean, the dangerously handsome and ambitious footman. After token resistance, he "gives in" to her, and she to him. Her naïve belief that it's "love"— that he will take her away from it all, from the emptiness of her life—is soon brutally disabused by him. What little honor and self-identity she possessed before is destroyed. So is Miss Julie herself.

—B.P.]

In *Miss Julie* the play and Miss Julie the character, there are two battles going on: the inner one (heredity, sexual drives) and the social one (for power, amid the mixup of the classes). Julie is going through problems too difficult for her to resolve herself. She is an aristocrat who finds herself in the kitchen because of loneliness.

Why does a countess leave the upstairs and come down to the kitchen for a servant? From enormous loneliness. From an inner despair.

The opening is strong: you immediately know something is going on when Jean says, "Miss Julie is crazy tonight." It is Midsummer's Eve. He's in the kitchen with Kristine, his fellow servant and girlfriend. Actors, watch out! Strindberg always gives you material in the opening scene that is picked up and made fuller later in the play.

Don't be foolish and overlook this wonderful character Kristine—a simple, straightforward woman who belongs to her class and doesn't want any confusion about it. She knows who she is.

When Julie gets involved with Jean, she becomes common—worse than lower-class—in Kristine's eyes. She loses form. From now on, Jean and Kristine both think about her in a common way, and they have a right to. They talk about her intimately. Kristine is so disgusted by Julie's behavior she says she's going to give notice—she doesn't want to serve this family anymore. Kristine says Julie is acting crazy because she is having her period; she was overexcited when she asked Jean to dance with her. Kristine tries to refocus Jean, bring him back to reality. Jean is embracing Kristine when Julie enters and sees she is in competition with her servant. She puts herself on an equal level: "I won't steal your sweetheart." Julie asks if Jean is her fiancé. No, it's just an affair. Kristine sees that is what Julie wants, too. Kristine knows the situation—a roundabout way of telling Julie, "I have your number." The lower class knows its place, but Julie doesn't allow them that. The broken class relationship makes for confusion.

Kristine is in the groove. She does what she needs to do for herself. She either sleeps with a man or she sleeps like a log. Why does Kristine feel it's so bad that Julie stayed up all night? It is the collapse of Kristine's world if Miss Julie stayed up all night and drank, the collapse of an ideal. It's a moment she doesn't want to face. "Don't tell me that." You need to respect the people that you work for.

It's such a creative moment if you find it—to lose your world. I know the moment from the Group when Franchot Tone said he was leaving and signing for Hollywood. "What do you mean? Oh, my God!" I wouldn't face it, didn't know what to do—how to face the collapse of that world, of the theater. The whole structure was going to collapse.*

Put it back into the play. That is creative breakdown. To find how Kristine's world collapses, *personalize* what it is in her situation that collapses. They were intimate, they have had that life together, the kitchen together. Now they will have nothing. There's no Group anymore, no place where people work together. Everybody is going to suffer—not just me. Everything is going to suffer with the collapse of an ideal. Strindberg shows you that both worlds collapse. But look how strong Kristine is. She'll get another position. She has taken it in hand. Is the build of that scene clear to you? You can't fail in a part if you know how to break it down.

So the action takes place in the kitchen. The servants are talking about Miss Julie, the countess—the first time servants deride the master in a play. The attitude toward Julie is one of hate. The servant class hates the upper class, gossips about them, takes pleasure in bringing the upper class down. The two classes are spiritual enemies now.

Push the abnormal situation, not the words: Julie is doing something not suited for her class. She is dancing with the servants. Strindberg paints them as cheap, vulgar, angry towards the upper class. Julie is abandoned, alone, whirling from one person to

---

*The Group Theatre, founded in 1931 by Harold Clurman, Cheryl Crawford, and Lee Strasberg, was a breakaway organization from the Theatre Guild. It was the first to present the works of Clifford Odets (*Waiting for Lefty,* 1935; *Golden Boy,* 1937), among others, to the public. Among its luminaries were Stella and Luther Adler, John Garfield, Elia Kazan, and Franchot Tone, who provided much of the Group's early backing through the money he made in his popular Hollywood film appearances—a fortune compared with the salaries paid to New York stage performers. He went back and forth between the coasts until he finally decided to "go Hollywood" permanently, when the Group lost not only Tone's name and prestige but his financial backing. Adler was not exaggerating the blow or the "collapse": the Group disbanded soon, in 1940.

another. The servants are laughing at her and her superiority. There is a brutality in their attitude to her.

Julie's mother gave her her attitude toward men: disgust, alienation.

"My natural sympathies were with my father," she says, "yet I took my mother's side. I learned from her to hate and distrust the whole male sex. I swore to her I'd never become the slave of any man." Julie doesn't go with her father. She has no road, no direction. She is trying to find a place, but her place is historically being broken down.

She has a strong sex drive toward Jean—a haughty will to conquer. She is stronger than most men. But Jean is not weak, and it is hard for Julie to exert power over him. She is out of control emotionally because of her sexual desire. Jean is one of the new breed of servants who steal food and liquor, who have no conscience. He has been quick to learn the new democratic game. He likes it. He is ambitious.

Kristine says, "She always has been crazy since the engagement was broken off." Julie lost her fiancé, lost her security. She is running wild because she lost her base.

Julie tried to train her fiancé with a whip—one side of her has the need to dominate a man—but she failed. She lacks the maternal quality that was so important to Strindberg. She is boldly attracted to the male—that masculine side of her—and asks him to take his uniform off. The pantomime scene is Strindberg's technique for bringing in the Midsummer's Night vulgarity and sexuality. Sexuality without romance.

Jean, with his own powerful sexuality, immediately traps her. He gets something in his eye. She tells him to hold still. He puts his arm around her, she slaps his hand. She touches his muscles, says he is trembling, teases him. She is in control, gets the man out of control—she is playing the man. He grabs her and she slaps his face. "How dare you!" Suddenly he doesn't know who he is. He wants to go back to his work. She says no. Julie's character is ruthlessly tyrannical.

But she also confides in Jean, tells him about her dream: she is dragged down in her dreams. You begin to get a woman who is dealing with her inside, not the outside. People are now revealing their insides. This is very new in drama. Julie has inherited great pride. In the beginning, she is tactless, cruel, heartless, self-indulgent, torn by contrasting feelings—vain but with a wish to degrade herself. Her sexual force reaches out for satisfaction, but she wants love too—the brutality of the man attracts her. Miss Julie is in conflict with herself. The destructive force in her reaches out to those who will destroy her. She will destroy the entire lineage—she inherited too many weaknesses. Even so, the audience is touched by her, has a sympathy toward her. You must play Julie with psychological weakness, anger, and strength.

In the beginning, Jean comes in carrying his riding boots and spurs—a symbol of authority and control. He is not in control. The count, Julie's father, is in control. Jean is just a servant. But he has the outward symbols and makes use of them.

Jean is immaculate. He sees that Julie's fingernails are dirty, a symbol of her falling. She neglects the outside symbols. He respects her position, but although he is part of the family, he thinks about them with no love or dignity. Jean reacts to Julie's entrance into the kitchen like an aristocrat. Julie should understand but doesn't. Jean has good manners but steals. He is the new lower-class man, with a low moral standard. Julie treats him as an equal. The moment you go into the kitchen, you *become* the kitchen. The working class is not salt-of-the-earth anymore. Strindberg's is a scientific, not a social, analysis: ruthless commonness, sexual strength is the future of man.

Jean is running Julie down. But he also looks down on his own class, doesn't want to identify with them, either.

Jean is many-sided. He lies and manipulates from the kitchen. He is exposed to more things than Julie. He dresses well, goes out riding; he is more colorful than she is. He could be played by the young Alfred Lunt—a man of the world. He has this quick adaptability. In his scene with Kristine, he looks like hell, he's been up all night, but he's sharp enough to want to find out if *she* knows what happened. Did she sleep through it all? What does Kristine know? His character is cagey. I would not make one movement of his direct—he's in and out, slippery. He's putting on his valet's coat and looking in the mirror while he says, "Were you asleep?" Always doing one thing and managing something else. When she says she slept like a log, that's a big relief for him.

You cannot play him gauche or awkward.

Jean has a constant desire to climb out of his class. He wants money, power, and status. He looks for what will give him an advantage—talks ideas that he doesn't understand. The lower classes attach themselves to ideas without depth. They have a slave mentality by inheritance, a constant fear of those above. Jean is divided. He admires and yet hates the upper class at the same time. He has what it takes to survive—not sensitized by honor, not vulnerable. The separation between him and Julie is very sudden. Jean recognizes that she is like her mother. Julie wants to be in the barn but also to give orders. On the other hand, she says "Tonight we're all the same." She is split.

Julie has the dream of people who didn't need money—they already had it. The aristocratic mind is high up, but her society with all its art and beauty is going down. In the new era, our values are money values. Julie sees the servant class around her rising. Strindberg says these lower classes are slime and scum. They bring greed, abandonment of values. Materialism makes people sink.

Jean is on the ground with darkness around him, primitive. He wants to get to the top where the sun is shining and rob the golden eggs.

Jean is the middle-class future—dominant, without honor, his modern values based on the moral degeneracy of material success. Strindberg says Jean's ruthlessness is necessary to conquer a woman. Strindberg is on the side of the climber. He understands the ruthless class. His feminine side sympathizes with Julie, but her weakness— the Christianity crutch, the values of sympathy and compassion— must give way to Jean's survival-of-the-fittest brutality.

Man and woman are born enemies. Sexual forces determine their fate. Jean reaches up and Julie goes down. But even if Jean wins, he loses, because he too is trapped. He is trapped by his own character.

Finale: Julie, Blanche, and Poetic Naturalism

Julie and Jean are like Blanche DuBois and Stanley Kowalski in *A Streetcar Named Desire*. Blanche and Southern society are going down, just as Miss Julie and her class are dragged down. Blanche's name means "pure white of the woods." She has been with a thousand men, but Tennessee says that she is pure. She *is* pure. One side of Blanche is an extreme realist—practical, down to earth. The other side thinks of poetry, music, love, flowers. Blanche talks down to the working-class man. She is both an aristocrat and a whore. She has to die. You have to play both sides of her character. *Streetcar Named Desire* is opaque. It is not writing that should be clear. You don't know *Streetcar Named Desire*. It is not so realistic. It is poetic, even though the language is not poetry.

When you take away poetic speech and give people human speech, that is naturalism. When the scenery helps the actor to create realities, that is naturalism. When the actors behave humanly, that is naturalism. Naturalistic plays show you that life is sorrowful and cannot be fixed—*Miss Julie, Streetcar, The Lower Depths, Anna Christie*—the hopelessness and drabness of these slice-of-life situations, of the natural state and what life does to a person. Tennessee's characters can't emerge; they're doomed. He and O'Neill are pessimistic; Odets in *The Big Knife* is pessimistic; Anouilh is very angry and pessimistic; Lillian Hellman has it—every playwright after the war.

It is naturalistic because there is no horizon, no way out. You are trapped through yourself. Darwin showed that you're not in the hands of a super force. Very disturbing. There is no more ideal; the whole world is going to pieces. They don't evolutionize—there is no way to help these people, no road for them to take.

When Jean asks Julie if she loved her father, she says, "Infinitely, but I must have hated him as well." That is deeply Strindbergian. You don't really know what you feel about things because you feel double.

Strindberg characters, so involved with themselves, do not end up except in the mire, going down into the bowels of the earth where they are drowned. You never feel that something worthwhile will rise out of the ashes. The trap sucks you in and never lets you out. Strindberg is the first Freudian playwright. The complexity of the inner man carries his plays. Strindberg watched people and said the sexes have a battle to the death. He analyzed their behavior rather than their social performances. Everybody gets pulled down in this enormous conflict. He says man is in greater pain than ever before; man is in eternal pain. Ibsen gives you the sense that there is some hope, that society if it gets better may free you. Strindberg says that the longer it goes on, the more miserable it will get. The Strindbergian character is the person who says, "I'm sinking, I'm sinking." Until Strindberg there is no play where a woman says, "I'm sinking, going down, losing myself, come with me, you're a servant, kiss my feet, do you love me?, I depend on you, you dirty skunk."

Who is there to blame for what happens? What is there to do?

In realism, the better the playwright, the harder the solution. If the people seem real, if they pertain to you, if you understand the class, if they speak humanly, if the problems are large—you're in realism. Hamlet is not understandable, but Hedda is. Laura is. Blanche is. A discussion about them takes place in the audience. Realism needed a new actor who could play it. It needed Stanislavsky and the Group Theatre who could stage it. It was revolutionary. It was concerned with the problems of its day and time, not of remote kingdoms. It was aimed at making the audience see the truth.

ANTON CHEKHOV

EIGHT

RUSSIAN REVOLUTIONS

Chekhov and Stanislavsky

CHEKHOV SAYS that beauty brings a sense of loss; that the possibility of happiness is too far removed. Life can give you a little, but beauty has a way of disturbing you because you can't have it all. It isn't easy to define this kind of unhappiness, but he explores it in the plays. Chekhov has no theory of life to explain things like Shaw or Ibsen or Strindberg. But he is perhaps the greatest author in the understanding of human beings. He understands that the human life is lived inwardly. Chekhov in Russia is considered greater even than Tolstoy. I would say that he is my favorite author.

He criticized himself right down to the depths. He said, "I'm a cheat, I'm a liar, I don't love anybody, I'm a lousy writer." He is constantly battling with his apathy and need for self-approval. You meet characters in *The Seagull* who have that apathy but who have the ambition to fight through, the will to struggle for something better. The individual he admires most is the one who at least *tries*. In Chekhov you get an understanding of the man or woman who makes an effort. It can be a weak effort—there is a kind of fragility in it—but they make it. "I'm going to work, I'm going to change my life." It doesn't have to be strong, it doesn't have to be large, if even for a moment they can see, "I have to push myself ahead a little bit."

There is great weakness in Chekhov's people. He doesn't have a lofty sense of man, in his time, with dignity. "What difference does it make? I'm defeated. To hell with it. Give me a drink." Most men of his society have given in. Chekhov has a feeling that the great past of the Russian intellectual is over. He says, "I am living in a moment where I have to sell things to support my brother and sister." He himself writes stories to sell, and then he writes a play to sell, and then he says, "I have to write and sell more."

Ibsen says society has to be changed, it is corrupted by false values. Strindberg teaches you something else. Chekhov doesn't believe in a philosophy, doesn't believe in God. Uncle Vanya doesn't believe in anything. If you believe in communism, it is better than believing in nothing. But Chekhov has no thesis. That is one of the things that makes his characters dissatisfied with their lives. He doesn't have a world view that you discuss when leaving the theater.

Chekhov was preoccupied with studying man despite the fact that life had lost its bigger meaning, which made him able to smile at certain things instead of scream. He is interested in man. Most audiences find this close to their heart—the fact that he is close to the inner meanings of human emotions. He sees the world for beauty but does not think it is full of great significance. That is lost and he knows it. It is our loss, but we can't help it. He felt no obligation to explain life, but to put it down as he saw it truthfully. He was able to see what other writers before him had seen but did not understand. He put it down for the world to understand: man as he functions as an individual, with the suffering inside.

Chekhov stopped preaching at an early age and became an observer. His understanding of life brought out the empathy he felt for people and you feel as actors when you do the play. The compassion Chekhov brings out universally is why he is so much more played than other writers. Chekhov is an artist you understand if you think of him as a man whose art is expressed best with no words, like painting or music. You feel Chekhov the way you feel music or realize a painting. It is not the words, it is something without words that comes through to us, because it is on a human level. The experience is inside. He presented the life around him as it was lived physically and inwardly. The times were turbulent, and Chekhov chose to show with truth and precision the hopeless longing that one felt in one's heart.

Uncle Vanya makes no point. Chekhov said a play need not make a point. At its best, it might suggest one. He wanted to provoke a mood rather than communicate an idea. He reached that part of the soul which is touched by the arts that speak without words. He studies man in a world full of beauty and wonder and sorrow. The real theme of Chekhov is the destruction of beauty in the world, which is always very sad.

What makes Chekhov different from any other writer? Why did an entirely new system of performance have to be worked out because of him?

The introduction of Konstantin Stanislavsky into Chekhov's life and plays was an intrusion on the whole realistic theater. You cannot work with plays anymore unless you do it. From now on, you must come with a complete understanding of what the character is experiencing. You cannot come onstage and look for the experience on the set. You can only come on after you have injected into the character his essence that you find from the external things.

In Chekhov, minds don't mesh. One character does not know the other. That is Chekhov. He puts people together who don't understand what is going on in each other.

Once I was taking a walk in Venice on a very hot day—men with their shirts off, working-class. I saw a man walking in front of me, sweating. I said, "Gee, from the back of him, I would have said he was Stravinsky." I slowed up and looked when I passed. "Jesus, that *is* Stravinsky!" It didn't occur to me he could ever look like that. It doesn't occur to you that a guy in a sweaty shirt is Stravinsky.

That's how Nina feels about Trigorin in *The Seagull.*

I am trying to tell you that from the beginning in every relationship there is a superficial misunderstanding as well as a misunderstanding in great depth. Never do two people understand each other on the same plane. In modern acting, don't come in and expect the set or the lines to give you the play. They will not give you the play in Chekhov.

You have to come in with a past for your character. You have to match up with what doesn't mesh. You have to bring what's in you to the lines. You must know how Chekhov builds a character, a relationship, a scene.

Chekhov couldn't have done it without Stanislavsky because he is the kind of a writer who puts so much into the past of the character that unless the actor knows how to understand that past he can't get the present or know what's going on on the stage. Each character comes in with his former life. You can't come on and expect the stage to feed you without knowing your past.

Trigorin in *The Seagull,* for example, is modeled very much on Chekhov, who wrote, wrote, wrote. He wrote hundreds of stories. He wrote five hundred jokes a week in the beginning because he had to make money in the joke papers. One time Chekhov was sitting with a very unimportant journalist named Potapenko and he noticed an ashtray. He said, "Tell you what, see that ashtray? Tomorrow there will be a story about it." And there was.

The reason most actors can't play Chekhov is because they think, "These people are Russian, they are different, they are strange." But Chekhov creates them and the play in such a way that makes it possible for you not to follow so much the plot as the people themselves. Read the play to see what the differences between these people are. Their actions are human. People live *life,* not a play. We live, "I went there and now I'm here at a class and then I'm going home and out to dinner." It is not a play. We don't live a play, we live a scene at a time.

So Chekhov doesn't write a play where this scene connects with that one, and that scene connects with the next. He writes this scene and it is perfectly disconnected from the next scene. If you can understand that, you can understand Chekhov.

It is worth understanding.

Chekhov lived into 1905, when the first tremendous revolution was put down. The political ferment was all around—enormous socialist and anarchist and nihilist political movements. Tsar Alexander was assassinated. There was a complete police state. The serfs had been freed in 1863, but they made them pay for their land and there was no money to pay and so there was chaos.

In Stanislavsky's and Nemirovich-Danchenko's realistic production method, the first priority is that the director and the actor must understand the social situation of the time of Chekhov's plays. What was it? The Communists, left-wing social democrats, right-wing radicals—all kinds of radicalism is in full swing. In twelve years you have the Bolshevik revolution. It is incredible. We are dealing with a moment when the revolution is right there.

The key word is "transition"—from one way of life to another. If you can't make it, you go under. Many people went under when the revolution came along. You think you can play Chekhov without understanding this social situation? But you don't. You have to be told or you have to get it on your own.

Get it on your own. *Read.*

Oh, well, I'll tell you, because I want you to love me. Isn't it awful that I am begging for your love? On second thought, I take it back. Don't love me. I don't give a goddamn whether you love me or not. I give a goddamn about the plays.

I was so absolutely committed to the plays and the period that there were always twenty books about Chekhov and Tolstoy on my bed. There I was in bed with Tolstoy and Chekhov and all this history. I said, "I can't see anybody for two weeks. I can't answer the telephone." It's crazy. When you are working on a playwright the social situation is so strong that it gets you.

Chekhov is very close to today because everything is in such flux. Tolstoy and the kings and queens and Count Nekhlyudov—all that is gone. It is a changeover into the middle class. *The Cherry Orchard* is the middle-class buy-up of the land. In *The Three Sisters* they have nothing left, only one old nanny. There is a change coming.

This aristocratic class is not democratized. When someone comes in from the outside who doesn't fit, like Natasha in *Three Sisters,* it is a shock, it is like thunder to them. It is like being at a lecture Einstein is giving and having some kid say, "What the hell are you talking about?" You can't have that.

Chekhov doesn't deal with anybody's mind that he doesn't respect. He doesn't deal with the working class or the peasant class. He can't deal with the mind of the working class because they *have* no mind. If you work ten hours a day in a factory, your mind is not to be relied on. This might be very disillusioning.

I wasn't a Communist myself, but I was awful close. My generation was very much a part of class structure and we wanted much more for the worker. But we didn't want him to become the President. We didn't think it would go that far. Terrible actor, that Reagan. I better not talk about politics. I have already testified in Washington. I was on the blacklist of those big senators who were saying, "You are betraying this country." Chekhov's people all have a point of view because they are in a political moment. We are in a political moment, too. We go down and have tea, but we know that money is being raised for the next war. All right. I better not talk politically anymore.

But this is why I say Chekhov is so close to us. The social situation pushes the character down psychologically into an understanding that he is a failure. In every play there is a teacher. Now, every teacher in every play gets ten rubles a month, which means about five dollars a month to live on. Medvedenko in *The Seagull* says, "I make so little money and you don't love me because you look down on me—I am a teacher and I am poor." If a man wants to get married and can't economically, he is injured, his soul is injured, his position in life is injured. As a teacher he is looked down upon. He has no respect for himself.

Does he want a revolution or not? Does he want the church or to get rid of the church? Does he want children to have free education? Should the peasants be freed or not be freed?

The play always takes place in a social situation. The playwright says, "Here's the situation: the cherry orchard is being taken over by this new crowd who is going to buy it from you and chop it up." This new crowd is the materialistic middle class that wants things. They have absolutely no use for orchard blossoms. That's us, too. That is what happened to America. Shaw said the middle class became vulgarized and the lower class became brutalized. So the takeover is about the lower and middle classes raising themselves. When the revolution really *did* come along, the middle-class materialists gave over the orchards, the forests, and everything else to Lenin—and they were eradicated.

You have to know this.

In Chekhov, the people are disregards, left floating because they are upper-class or military-class and are not used to working. How do the historical moment and the transition affect that class? Transition, revolution, property taken away. The author doesn't give you that; he can't. This is why it is important to get what the partnership of Nemirovich-Danchenko and Stanislavsky does—their procedure not to be static as to the staging. It cannot be static anymore. The actor has three-fourths more to do than Chekhov put into the play. You will see what Chekhov put in and then I will show you what Stanislavsky put in. Then you will know the technique of realism.

Now, to know it is not really to be able to do it. To be able to do it you must have a very, very good technique. Read the book *Last Rehearsals with Stanislavsky* by Toporkov. Read what he did to these actors. He killed them. He told a big star from St. Petersburg, "It's terrible! I don't want that kind of acting!" When the actor saw *The Seagull,* he said, "I don't want it, either. I want to act the way they do in *The Seagull.*" So he left his big position. Many actors did that, to get in with Stanislavsky. Finally, Stanislavsky took him in and turned him into his best character actor. That is something we don't have here—not Strasberg, nobody. I do it best. At least I will admit to you that it is all Stanislavsky, whereas Strasberg said it was all Strasberg. The ego was so great.

The genius of Stanislavsky and Nemirovich-Danchenko was to understand the literary side and, although they did not go away from Chekhov's words and indications of what to do, to be independent of those demands. They said, "We will do what you want, but we will give it what will create the truth." Realism is after the truth—of middle-class or communist or working-class life.

To get the truth they said, "We have to add to it." They understood that they had to add the social moment and make each actor understand his relationship to that moment. Both the director and the actor had to understand the author's character and what was going on in the character's mind and feelings. That is what you call the psychological approach.

I don't like words like that. If you say "psychological" to me, I don't know what you are talking about.

But every character has a unique way of thinking and feeling about life. Without that, you don't have a character, you have *you.*

Something great is going on in Washington today, getting so many more Democrats in. What is going on in this social moment? It's a Republican government. What's going on with so many Democratic victories? I don't know, but I know they must be upset. If we went into communism in the next two or three years, would we understand?

The bottom line in these periods is pain. Transition is pain. In *The Cherry Orchard* they laugh on top of pain. But always in transition there is a bottom line of agony and pain.

Chekhov says Russia has lost the security and connection with the past. Security comes in a situation like England's. The queen is there and you and her son have the security of knowing, "When my mother dies I will be the king." The English are better off in that sense. Here, the President walks out of a hotel and he is shot on the street and he says, "Honey, I forgot to duck." Brezhnev and the Russians say, "A man walks out on the street and is shot? The President? And his wife brings him jelly beans to the hospital on television? It is crazy."

We have lost track of the past, too. We don't know what it is to have a Roosevelt up there anymore. When a country is in transition, something rotten is going on. It means unhappiness with the state of affairs, and people are affected by it.

Tolstoy says, "The peasant has to remain a peasant. The peasant has to stay religious, has to belong to God, has to have his mysticism." Chekhov didn't like that. He said a peasant is not very different from Tolstoy or the tsar. He is a man. He needs some money. He's not with Tolstoy anymore. He's a headwaiter somewhere in Moscow. He doesn't want to be a peasant anymore. He is pushing to get further up because the old society is going, and where is he going to be left?

God and Tolstoy and the aristocracy are gone. The people are left to themselves.

The big posture is gone. We are not heroic. We are just leftovers from an age when men were strong, women fragile.

He says, "Perhaps there will be a better world." But he doesn't really know. He is not a prophet. He can't tell. Some of his characters say, "I hope so." Others say, "It is finished."

You are part of this. Those thirty-five years between Chekhov and Tolstoy really took centuries to come about. The changes are tremendous for these people. They are very mixed up because in those last thirty-five years the world changed more than it did in the entire past. Everything is broken. Society has left people without values, so they have to find their own, pick them up wherever they can. Science says, "You had it up to the third dimension—now we have the fourth, so throw out all the other dimensions." Einstein in one sentence changed it altogether. We had fifty years of Freud; now he is finished. Developmental psychology takes his place.

Those changes are what Chekhov recognizes. He says you can

pity people and recognize poverty, but you don't have the strength to say, "I am not going to be a victim of materialism." Everybody says, "Where's the money and how can we get it?"

Chekhov sees all the people around him, brought up and worn out by their weaknesses. The wastefulness of their lives goes on. It doesn't add up to anything. There is no security.

My security as a person, as an actress, didn't come from me; it came from my parents and how I was brought up. I didn't doubt for a minute that I was going to act, because the background was secure.

Security does not come from struggling alone. It comes from being handed down, like in England. "You are an Englishman. This is your king." That kind of traditional handing down. "As an Englishman, you do not do that." But that has evaporated.

Chekhov feels the artist works hard to make it easier for people to live. He says science and art have helped, but that most of it is lost because most people are swine. He says, "My heart is with them but they are swine. I understand their swinishness and I am sorry, but I am not writing well if I am just helping these swine to believe in their world." Very much like the movie industry with all its cowboys and adventures helps people believe that junk is the truth.

Chekhov was writing for an audience all over Europe. He said, "I don't know, maybe the ideas I put into my stories are helping them to be pigs. I don't know whether I should write. I don't know that it is helpful." Unless art helps people to civilize themselves, it is worthless. He is torn. It's what good actors feel when they go to Hollywood. "I don't know what I am doing. I'm certainly not helping the world by doing this lousy film or that lousy TV series. I know it won't do anything to help society or show the truth."

If you are in a sitcom, you are not going to think—or in the theater, for that matter, unless the plays create in you the kind of thoughts that Chekhov created. What is important in your work— and what saved me—is that through Chekhov and Strindberg and O'Neill and Tennessee Williams you can understand the world. The problems they put into the plays make you think as a person. You take those thoughts and words in the character and think them through for yourself, and that is how you begin to *become*.

Nora says in *A Doll's House,* "I don't owe anything to my children or my husband. My first duty is to me, and so I am going away to find out how to live." That changed the world. One sentence of Ibsen made the world realize that you are responsible for yourself. She doesn't have to lie or be a whore or be at the disposal of ideas that she doesn't think through. Don't you believe in religion? She says, "I don't know. Maybe I do, maybe I don't. I have to go and find out." The actor likewise must say, "I have to find out what I believe in when I do plays."

You will find out in Chekhov.

Chekhov said, "I don't care about changing the world." He was not a Communist, not a Socialist, not a Social Democrat. He belonged to no intellectual club. He was scientific. Science plunges you forward, makes you examine. He went to medical school, he knew the problems, knew the revolution was coming. He got money from his writings and built houses. Poor people and sick people went to Odessa. They said, "If we get down there, Chekhov will put us up—he'll take care of us." I think it was like going to Christ. He had six brothers and sisters, and he supported them. Chekhov was an architect as well as a doctor. He knew that if you do something it has a structure.

There was such a split between him and Tolstoy, even though they palled around together. Tolstoy came from great family distinction and wealth. But Chekhov the intellectual broke down the barrier of who was an aristocrat and who wasn't in that social moment. He said every man was an individual and had to get attention as an individual. His own individuality was what made him a great writer.

When you approach a Chekhov play, look for the individuality in each character. Don't say, "Oh, yeah, Vanya's an uncle." Vanya is an example of a Chekhovian twist unlike anybody else. He is a man who is very socially minded. "We have to change the world for the workers and the peasants—equality." He was so willing to change everything, but to individuals he behaved like a pig.

Tolstoy would have said, "He wants to change the world, therefore he's a good man." Chekhov says, "He's not a good man at all. He's a pest. He can't change the world. If he would just be pleasant and show up when he's supposed to it would be better." That takes away a lot of the heaviness in the plays.

Nowadays in America, intellect has been traded in for a better car, a better pool, better tiles, better kitchen—you must *really* have a good kitchen. In Chekhov's Russia, you could put on a good play because you had an intellectual audience. Even the working class was lively. It caught on. Chekhov bridged that moment. He said, "I don't need the belief in God, and neither do the peasants." He didn't believe in peasant wisdom and all such myths. He was a doctor. There was no longer this big business with God. In one of his short stories, a mother teaches her daughter to go out and "for Christ's sake, send us some money so we can get to the next town!"

The three sisters have to work because they need money.

But the whole class is still intellectually sharp—every member can talk to you about Greek philosophy, about who is a good writer and who isn't. They know literature, they are cultured, they are not broken. They are not draggy, even though it was a miserable moment. There was a general collapse in the society, no money for schooling. Chekhov built five schools himself in different towns in order to give the children some place to learn. Nobody reimbursed him; he didn't expect it.

Here today, they build hospitals to make money off the sick people. Open a place for poor people to go in the winter—but make sure you get a percentage out of it. We think like thugs. In this class, they didn't think that way. They said, "You want to build houses and tear down the cherry trees? You can't do that." Rather than tear down the cherry trees, they left.

Chekhov understands that every man needs to know why he is living and is puzzled about the rules—where have they gone? Who should we look up to? Tolstoy is gone. Turgenev is too delicate and trimmed, like having drinks at the Plaza. I like Turgenev a lot, God forgive me, but he's a little too classy. Chekhov doesn't like that. He says everybody knows the problems and that the society is going to change. Here, everybody knows Mr. Reagan is not really interested in how many poor people will die on the street this winter. We are living in a rotten time, too. Chekhov says you are spiritually going downhill. He said, "I know my words won't do anything." So he built cottages for poor people himself, and his sister who was a nurse treated thousands of people with cholera. Never asked a penny for it.

He is saying, "You're getting old and if your clothes don't look so pretty on you anymore it's because you are not pretty inside."

People were clinging to him. In a way, I find that most people in my social life cling to me like that, hold on. They need me to say, "You can do it, too." When I embrace them I feel that I am embracing children. They are fifty or sixty, and their way of life has permitted them not to use their strengths.

What Chekhov wants to develop is the thing he developed in himself: "I am sorry for you because I am sorry for me, too, and terribly against myself. I am constantly asking, 'Am I good? Is this right?'" Whether you're a doctor or professor or lawyer, you must not settle down into "I've made it." That is very much us, too, isn't it? We must push forward.

As a scientist, he reveals everything through his characters. Every character makes it quite clear what his problem is. Don't make them difficult. The play is very clear what Konstantin's problems are, what the uncle's and Nina's problems are. It is interesting to know that there is something rotten in the state of Denmark. The society has lost touch with tsarism. It is going into revolution.

People are revolting against something. Their demoralization happens because of the social conditions, like it happens to you and me.

Chekhov's father owned a small grocery store, didn't give him "breeding." But there is no reason to be a slob even if you come from a generation of peasants.

He is tough on weakness. He says, "Don't be a slob, don't be weak, don't be apathetic. Don't let the apathy get you down to the point that you have no self-respect. Make a fight. You must work at it constantly, day and night. You must never stop reading, studying, exercising your will, every hour is precious." Chekhov says that in this moment the only thing you can save is a little art, a little music, a little painting, a little writing, a little landscape, a little bit of what the world still has to offer.

As the stomach gets fuller the soul gets sicker, and by fifty you don't need the landscape, you don't even *see* the landscape. You are worn out inside. It was a predicament of life then, and it still is.

We finish with Chekhov's idea that most people are forced to lead empty lives because materialism kills the soul. Those who have a thinking mind—able to think—are a privileged minority.

*   *   *

We are in the same jam that Chekhov's characters are in. It's a small jam, but we can't get out of it. Most of the people in Chekhov are small, not heroic. You must realize how close you are to his moment in history. In every Chekhov play, someone says, "I guess we all have to go to work now..." "The money is gone..." "The cherry orchard has to go..." You are not in Tolstoy-land any more. You are with a class that had the best of everything but now has to do something different. That is pretty close to us. You can't go back, and the transition is hard on people.

Chekhov wrote commercially, and then he wrote for himself and his own soul, and then he wrote commercially again. He never settled which way to go, how to compromise.

It is like going to the movies and coming back to Broadway and then going back to the movies. He is constantly unsettled, and so he doesn't let his characters settle their problems either. The ones who are successful are just as unhappy as the ones who fail. The people who fail feel, "I was not meant to fail. I could have been somebody. What happened? Why am I not somebody?" He writes about men who can't pull through. They are not big enough. In his time, men got smaller in their thinking. You don't see the heroic father anymore. He is gone. I don't know where he is. Maybe he's playing tennis now. But he's gone.

A friend of mine is a big European businessman. I said, "Is your business like mine, where I don't rest for a minute? Every day I am full of anxiety because of Chekhov." He said, "That's it for me, too—twelve hours a day devoted to what Reagan is doing to me." The economy is changing, it is doing this, doing that.

So what does he do? When he has a day off, he goes out to the country or walks on the beach. It is not very heroic. It is reduced. In another moment, as a European he would have been part of the struggle against Nazism or against war. He would have been in something. But he is nothing now. He takes a walk.

When a revolution is coming and everything is impermanent, something happens to the will. "The hell with it, let it go, for God's sake. What is the struggle for?" Certain people try to fight it through. I, for instance, am a fighter. I said, "I'm not going to wait in Hollywood for somebody to give me a part—that's not my style. I can't wait around. If nobody else is going to do Chekhov, well, I will. Somebody has to do it."

A lot of Chekhov's characters look forward, and the looking forward gives them a kind of anguish. The *not* looking forward gives them a kind of peace, of quiet acceptance. They either go forward into life or accept the fact that there is nothing to go forward to. The three sisters accept the static situation. Their hopes were there, they *wanted* to leave, but the greater part of them made them passive. They don't emerge from their impossible situation. The struggle to emerge puts you into the brutal reality. Chekhov's realistic approach is about the brutality of life. The poetic quality of dreaming about getting out gives you the poetry but also the passivity.

Chekhov characters are essentially without trimmings. In that sense, Russians are more like Americans than the English. They are honest, almost babyish, without affectation, unclothed. They're not unclothed the way we are—careless, rude. They are aesthetically refined to the end. There is no vulgarity in their speech, conduct, or relationships to each other. They are pure but passive, without much hope under the strict tsarist regime that edited their lives—locked in. They gave up not because they were lazy or stupid. They were just worn out by trying. If somebody in Chekhov says, "To be or not to be," somebody else answers, "That is the question." Chekhov's audience understood and identified. They had the same problems as the people on stage. They all recognized Shakespeare; we all recognize Johnny Carson. That's the difference. When I leave a Chekhov play, I feel I have been with part of my family.

You cannot play Chekhov to an audience that wanders in; the audience must identify. Therefore, you must identify with the techniques of realistic acting that came about through the art and genius of Stanislavsky. The theaters were cheap government-controlled places that did cheap plays. There was no expression for the good actor. So the actors organized a theater which could say something. That is what Stanislavsky did and the kind of plays he produced, to open up the social conditions of Russia.

Chekhov's world is an old world and a strange one. In thinking about Chekhov you can't think in a contemporary way. He is situated in a place far away—one hundred years ago, but more like two hundred—in a provincial town. Russia has too much provincial history to change because of communism or anything else. You go twenty minutes out of Moscow and you have thatched huts and medieval roads. It's not like going to Pittsburgh. It is a vast country that cannot be industrialized. It is far away and terribly small. No cars, only horses. Little choo-choo trains go by now and then, but they don't stop where these people live; you have to travel miles to a train stop, through snow and difficulty.

When the trains go by, they whistle. That brings out memories in people.

Everything with Chekhov has a lot to do with memory—with people who think of how it used to be when they were children and played in the garden and swung on the swings. Nostalgia is in the atmosphere, and because of that people smile a lot. People smile because a lot of things that used to exist don't exist anymore, they're just memories. People smile because of the impossibility of getting out. The audience joined the character in this understanding when he said, "I am stuck, I want to go to the city but I can't, it's a terrible fate." In Chekhov plays there is a lot of talk about fate. That is part of the inborn passivity. "It is my fate to stay here." In *The Seagull*, Nina says, "Odds or evens? Shall I go and become an actress or not?" It puts your life in the hands of other people. It is a tendency of that particular generation to think of fate.

The modern, postcommunist point of view is that Chekhovian characters are kind of comedy people. I remember a splendid, first-class critic, when we were working together on the last speech of *Uncle Vanya,* said to the actress to laugh at that point and I said, "No!" Certain important critics think the plays are comedies and can only be approached from a postwar situation—that the last speech in *Uncle Vanya* is comic. I don't think you will find many laughs in it. Smiles, but not laughter. Chekhov says it is not about tragedy but the constant heartbreak of daily life. He understood something about daily life—the constant disappointment of wasted talent and stifled ambition, of not achieving what you want to.

That to Chekhov was the heartbreak.

There is more drama in an old man sitting in the park on Seventy-second Street doing nothing than in a melodrama. In the last act of *The Seagull,* Masha is humming and knows that Nina has tried to commit suicide, left her baby, left everything. She knows Konstantin has killed himself, but she goes on humming, because that disguises it for her for a little bit. The heartbreak of life is that you sit and say, "I'll have another cup of tea, my foot's asleep, let's have lunch, but what am I living for?" That is more heartbreaking than saying, "I'm so tragic."

In Chekhov, people are heartbroken all day long and live quite normally. They live without hope and without a future, but they have the ability to live in a closed circle and accept their fate. They are closed in with each other. The everyday tragic fate of life is with them. They walk around within this situation, accepting it. There is no theater for them to go to, no movies. They substitute something else for that: talking to one another, revealing themselves, communicating with one another directly or indirectly.

In our unfeminine (and therefore unmasculine) age today, women are not women, they are "females." But they were still women and men then, and very much alerted to the need to express their love. All Chekhov is full of love.

Chekhov's characters are always strongly imprinted in your mind. They don't go away because of your sense of identification with them. You are a very good audience for Chekhov because they didn't believe in their government or the time they lived in, and neither do you. They let things go, wandering around in that kind of hopeless atmosphere. You can't throw out the tsar and we can't throw out dirty politics. But in some way, people hope.

Nina in *The Seagull* is typical of Chekhov's understanding that you go from the dream world of hoping you'll have romance and life will be poetic, and you descend into the abyss of life, take your chances, go out and struggle, you get hit, your child dies, your man leaves you, you work like hell, and somehow you emerge. Most people do not. The three sisters do not emerge, but they accept their situation. They have a strength, they want to live. That is what drives them, a dynamic duality. They try to overcome the unbearable impasse. Chekhov says it is not their fault that Russian life kills the best and interferes with their free action. It is not their fault this happens to them. They don't disapprove of one another. They don't say, "If only you would get out of my way, I could go on." Even if you hurt them, they don't attack you. It takes out the vulgarity.

Playwrights always write about the historical moment, and the Russian historical moment was that you had no place to go. The only one to get out in *The Cherry Orchard* is the middleman, who sells the orchard. We are now the middlemen, too—the agents who make deals.

We came out of a working class into the business class. They came out of a brutal peasant class. Chekhov writes a great deal about the savagery of the peasant class. The people who come out of that are fighters but with no culture, surrounded by ignorance. The fighters in Chekhov are brutal people who come out of the working class and make deals. Lopakhin is nice, but he sells the cherry orchard. The others can't. The decadence of Russian nature at the end of the nineteenth century wouldn't let them.

The Seagull is about personal life, home life, the intimate joys and sorrows, the good and bad fortune. They are a touching, moving group of people. You feel close to them because it is intimate. The author loves their good and understands their bad. That is what is special about Chekhov: he does really understand. He has patience with them. He is a doctor. He doesn't judge them. You get a sense of loving, that he can't say Arkadina is a terrible mother. You feel that Chekhov understands her better than anyone in the world, understands what she is up against, her compulsion to act, her relationship to Konstantin.

The inner element in Chekhov is delicate but not sick. It is disturbed, sometimes futile, but without the neurotic self-destruction of Strindberg. Strindberg's people destroy each other and themselves. Not Chekhov's. His people want to live, really want to go on. They are in a trap, but in a way they are heroes: if you can live within that trap, something heroic comes out.

Once in California I visited a women's prison where all the inmates were killers. Everyone was there for life. But they were all getting their high-school diplomas or their bachelor's or master's or studying law. They'd never get out, but they were finding themselves through their minds for the first time.

It gave me a sense that if I was in jail for life, it would be all right, because I have a hundred years' worth of reading to do. It would be great. I wouldn't be disturbed by anybody.

In Chekhov you don't fight your way out, you don't rally the crowd. Nor do you do what Strindberg does—you don't eat each other up. Chekhov's people are unmasked, and their nakedness called for an acting method that didn't exist yet.

He does it very delicately, very poetically. The characters open up to each other. He puts them in a bad spot and they are struggling to solve it to the best of their ability. He is sorry, he wants the audience to be sorry for them. The audience doesn't know what can be done about it either. There is no solution.

Older people know there is no solution. But Chekhov writes about young people who know there is no solution, and they meet it. It is like watching a flower fade. What can you do? You can't do anything about it. You don't revive it, you don't give it a hypodermic needle. You just let it die. That's an image of Chekhov's characters in their situation. Life is sad. It takes the anger out. They don't hope too much. They have to have a lot of courage. Chekhov puts them through hell. He understood and reveals their ineffectualness, just as Ibsen reveals his middle class and Strindberg reveals his mixing of upper and lower classes. Chekhov characters live on atmosphere and have an ability to accept the outer and the inner circumstances. The larger circumstances are living in a provincial town and the inner circumstance is living without money, without getting out, without love and without the means with which to express love.

A Chekhov character's inner movement keeps him going, an inner thinking all the time. This interests the audience. It is a secret, and it must belong so strongly to the actor that it creates an inner movement in him, too. Arkadina and Nina and Treplev and Masha are in a constant state of suspense. Something inside them is moving, giving them an inner action. If the audience comes away saying there was no action, it means it was badly played. At first glance, nothing seems to be happening. "I am in mourning for my life." But these inner actions give his plays a sense of poetry and involve you in them.

There was not a technique for Chekhov before. The whole Stanislavsky technique was created for this. It has to be dynamically played from inside. In Chekhov it is always the character that speaks, not the personality. Chekhov says you are responsible for the different colors in the characters. He is constantly challenging the actor for inner characterization—inner characterization is always complex.

He makes no judgments about these characters. He lets them vacillate. There is no idea of "God's in his heaven and the Pope is coming to visit!" When the Pope was in New York I said, "We are all Catholics—even me!" He was here for two days, the whole atmosphere was Catholic, and then he went away and we are the same old bums.

So the characters contradict themselves. Treplev in the beginning says there should only be pure art and in the end he says, "What the hell 'pure.'" Look for the contradiction, see what is changeable in them. Don't come in without recognizing the different colors. No Chekhov character resolves his lack of peace. Chekhov says, "You must be at war with yourself and not let your soulful self die out. I don't care if you are a murderer, you must save yourself. You must become educated."

We have a certain kind of intellectual tourism. "I have an opinion. I've read Proust—I didn't study him, I just read him. He's the greatest." Yesterday I was having dinner with a famous actress and she said, "I think Pinter is great." I said to this great star, "Do you really think he's great?" She said, "I certainly do." She didn't say, "Well, people say he's great but I don't really know. Sometimes he's great and sometimes he's not." She just gave this touristic opinion.

If you go to your next-door neighbor and all he cares about is the stock market and the *Wall Street Journal,* you are not going to become a cultivated person.

You must find your equals and associate with people who are not set on just making money. Chekhov gives you a sense of what it is to be cultured, an outline for living. You do not neglect your old mother, you see that your brother goes to school. But don't lie, because it reduces you. Two people are debased by lies: the person you are lying to and yourself. He is creating his own tradition. He can't find it anymore in the society, so he is making his own.

Chekhov's philosophy is never to let go—always to keep his mind open and keep himself clear about what is going on around him. I must say that. I am very Chekhovian. I am now going to study developmental psychology. I am very much on that kick. I am going to get a teacher in and learn about it.

I am a student by nature. I am a scholar as well as an actress. This side of me has made for a great deal of progress in my life. I hope it does in yours. You must be constantly interested in something that stimulates your mind, whether it's acting or science or piano. (Now I'll go home and worry because I said I was so wonderful.)

Material needs eat up the human being. The instinct to satisfy the flesh is fundamental, but so is an instinct in all men to satisfy the spirit. That's where God came in. Man created religion for himself to nurture his spirit. Now, that is gone. Now, you have to nurture yourself. Chekhov says we put the handcuffs on ourselves and then say, "I am not free. I have to go and build a house in Malibu." The money puts handcuffs on you so your spirit doesn't grow. That is what is the matter with us all. The middle class has lost the art of growing.

Chekhov gives you no answer, and sometimes you get angry that you don't find the answer yourself.

There is a great deal of self-deception in his characters.

He exposes his characters' emotional and mental weaknesses, the sloppiness of their minds. It is good to trace this in those characters—and in yourself.

The three sisters desperately want to go to Moscow. It is a symbol. In one play, it is the seagull. In another, it's Moscow—the symbol of happiness. Many years ago when I was living in France, near Vichy, I said, "I have to see snow!" There was no money, but I got some and went to the Alps. I had to go there to see snow. There is a thing in people that makes them say, "If I don't go, I'll die—I must!" Emigrés have this when they go to another country. Moscow has nothing to do with reality but with something that needs to be restored in their souls. "I have to go—I'm going to see the Palladio if it kills me." It has no sense. It is a wish of the soul to expand.

I can't give you everything. I can only tell you what I've experienced and try to give you a framework for Chekhov. Always ask, "What is the Chekhovian thing happening here?" Don't say, "She's enthralled." That's how she *feels*. Find the Chekhovian situation. I want not what you feel, but what is Chekhov.

Chekhov is intimate, but if you use his language that way you will kill him and yourself. They are not talking about important things.

"There will be a storm tonight. Have some snuff." "No, thank you, I don't want any." It is not an intimate *tone*. It is still formal in this society. I was brought up in the theater and I never heard anybody call my father anything but "Mr. Adler." That formality remained in the theater. Keep that formality in Chekhov. Don't make it a stock company, or down in the Village.

Speaking is very important. So is silence. Yesterday a BBC man came to interview me and as we started he said, "We have to have a moment of quiet because we have to register absolute silence." There were about twenty people, and there was silence for two minutes. During it, I realized that speech was invented to avoid this absolute void—for animals and man to fill up that void with sound. It was only two minutes, but it seemed like a thousand. Talking is really to fill the silence of life.

Words are symbols for things which have to be experienced first before you can understand what they mean. The woman who said "I think Pinter is a great playwright" didn't experience Pinter enough to say that. That is the fundamental thing Chekhov needed Stanislavsky for. The actor could no longer say words which were not experienced by him. It isn't Shakespeare. It is impossible to speak in a Chekhov play unless you experience what you are talking about. Otherwise, you are faking it. In your choice is your talent— what you respond to. If it's not in your experience, don't take it. Take something else.

Remember that Russians are not American. They have a lot of resilience and a very energetic language. That is a thing you don't have, which is unfortunate. You just say "Goodbye" [*quickly*], but if you say "Do svidanya . . ." [*slowly, savoring*]—that is energy, even if you're sick in bed when you say it. Your own language is not energetic. It's dead. The English have done something to it. They can energize it, but you normally don't. You can't do Chekhov that way.

His language must have energy. Irene Worth once, as I passed her dressing room, screamed, "STELLA!" I said, "Yes, yes? What is it, Irene?" She said, "STELLA—CAN THEY HEAR ME?" I mean, it was *booming*. She had developed in life and theater this wonderful voice. Irene in a room, no one could top—no American, anyway. She had an energy that made her into a great actress.

Your lack of energy has destroyed your acting.

There is nobody in the entire Moscow Art Theater who can be in movies, but they are people who, through their acting, are radiant. It is not the same old theater of "stardom." Stardom is finished with Chekhov. He wanted everybody in the ensemble to be stars; he didn't want a single "star." The English repertory theater is an ensemble made up of stars. Chekhov said, "I don't want special people on the stage. I don't want Bernhardt. I don't want special voices. I want *people.*"

The producers of the Moscow Art Theater were inspired by a new artistic principle that Stanislavsky called "inner realism," which can be used very well in all realistic plays. Stanislavsky said you cannot do realism without *inner* realism. You can't play Chekhov with the artistic principles of Ibsen or Strindberg.

With Chekhov came the birth of Stanislavsky's and Nemirovich-Danchenko's production method. The realistic plan and principle of the play means you have to map out each scene, each character, each idea. There are several ideas in *The Seagull,* close to those of Zola, but how are we going to execute them? They didn't know how until this principle of inner realism was created. The author provided the characters and the indirect action and a few instructions like "She gets up" or "He sits down," but he didn't give them everything else. That required a close collaboration between the author and the director's psychological insights into the characters. Understand what is added. Stanislavsky adds what makes it actable for the actors. He added the candy and the sugared buns and the waltzing and the sunshine.

The doctors in *Seagull* and *Three Sisters,* for example, are observers of life—patient and understanding. So when you have a doctor, don't play him as though he were a lawyer or botanist. Chekhov's scientific principles led him to precise detailing. He watched the way a person moved his head, and Stanislavsky picks up on that and gives him his own gestures. You like to use *your* gestures. This you can't do anymore. You must use the gestures of the class and the character. When I was with some movie stars once, I sat forward but everyone else was sitting back in their recliner-chair things. They said, "Don't you ever lean back?" I said, "No, never." They said, "Why?" I said, "Because I know the anatomy of a chair." A chair is not a couch. It has a back, and I am perfectly "there" with the back. I was there on a chair, not on a couch, but of course if somebody comes over, I lean toward the person—I am fluid on it. I don't sit on it in some fixed way. But they said they didn't need to learn about that. They're movie stars—why would they have to learn those things?

But a couch is not a chair, a chair is not a couch, and a stool is not a hammock. If you don't learn that, you'll be *you* all the time— boring as hell in life and on stage. Stanislavsky realized that. How Nina sits on the floor is different from how Masha sits on the floor. Stanislavsky made that difference. He put Nina on certain pillows and Masha on something else. I'm so anxious for you to understand that, and to see the development of the *doing,* not the development of the *words.*

It was difficult for Chekhov to find what he wanted for the audience. He didn't just say, "I'm going to write plays." He was close to the theater and he had a lot of trouble. Chekhov and Stanislavsky had to develop a way of work, because Stanislavsky was a very stubborn man and felt he knew more about the theater. In one play, he had two birds singing backstage: he taught one bird to follow the other, so it was a duet. Chekhov said, "You don't need so many birds." He didn't want it. Too many animals, too many dogs barking. Stanislavsky liked all that, and within the style, what he did was fantastic—with the lighting, with the trees, the foliage, the birds, the singing.

People in Chekhov sing. There is a great deal of choral singing and humming in Russia. That was so before communism and it is still there. They sit around and do it with or without a guitar. Three Russians together always harmonize. So in the opening of the second act of *The Seagull,* instead of the crickets in the first act, Stanislavsky put in the birds. He had two actors who could imitate birds and he told them to whistle. But when he heard them, he said, "They're not real." He said, "One bird sings and asks a question, then the other bird must answer the question." He wanted the people imitating birds offstage to speak to each other, to create a thing with the birds that would be lively and interesting. It had to be truthful. No lies.

The same for the interiors, which he worked out in detail. They had to provide a realistic background with an observation of the tiniest details so that each character could use them. It doesn't say in the play that Arkadina throws Dorn an apple when he's on the floor. It doesn't say that she hands him the rotten side of the apple and takes a bite of the good side. The actor has to do that, knowing her character. If Masha throws him the apple, it's different from the way Arkadina throws him the apple.

Stanislavsky provides things that belong to each character individually. One thing he does with Masha is give her nuts to crack. It is a dirty business, digging stuff out and eating the bits, and it gets all over your hands. He gives her snuff, too. He creates for each person the props that go with him. Arkadina drinks her tea differently from Masha. As she is drinking it, she is waltzing around saying, "Look at my figure," holding the cup. "Look how beautiful I am from this side. Don't I look young?" Chekhov wrote it, but Stanislavsky had to create it.

He put the concept of the writer into acting terms. Without the actor, literature can not be put on the stage. In movies the clouds or the storm can do it, the automobiles can do it, the street does it. But in a play you can't show a street, you show a scene. It's a different technique, and it is owned by the actor. If the director understands the character he will say, "Don't take that piece of pastry, take the little one. That is according to the character." Maybe it is your instinct to take the other piece, but it's not the character's instinct. It's the little things. Sitting on a couch is not like sitting on a chair or on pillows with rugs over them. By elaborating the props for each character to use in his own ways, you add to inner realism. This was Stanislavsky's contribution to the modern theater. No author in realism can do away with him.

When Stanislavsky did a play with a hundred people on the stage, they all had to write a background of who they were: peasants, neighbors, what their work and family was. They were not allowed to come on the stage unless they were motivated by that background.

They come in to do some peasant dancing? So the youngsters practiced the peasant dancing while the older people sang some of the old songs and they talked about how to dress for it. Do you understand? He didn't let anybody come on stage unless that person had a complete background.

They were responsible for every object in its minutest detail.

When I went and saw the Pope, I couldn't take my eyes off the costume. If you don't think that was done by the greatest designer in the world, you're crazy. Everything about it was the greatest—the starched lace peeking out beneath the tunic, the linens and ribbons and sashes and most exquisite materials, all meant to make you understand "That's the Pope!" Like you'd understand "That's a king." He wears a crown and he sits on a throne. If you have a crown, you're a king, and when you walk, people step aside.

If you're not interested in that, it's okay with me—but it's impossible to act without it.

Do you understand that you neglect the outside? I'm telling you, the details of the character as you learn it on the stage can make you into a great star like it made Marlon in movies. But if you don't have the theater training, the movies are not going to make you into a star—a star, maybe, but not a great actor. Marlon is a great actor who could become a great movie star and go back and be a great actor.

Every movie part he plays is greater than the one before. The last one was a capitalist. He says, "You got too much chlorine there." He looks at a frog. Marlon, putting in his own life, says, "That frog is going to die. Who put the chlorine in?" He is the capitalist examining the man who takes care of the pool.

Once I said to him, "Marlon, they told me you shot a rabbit," and he said, "Me? I'd rather die than hurt anything alive." I know this about him. Animals are much more important to him than people. What I'm saying is that his understanding of acting and character is translated into movies. Yours should be too.

Stanislavsky understood Chekhov, who loved the theater but didn't love Stanislavsky very much because he bothered him. Stanislavsky said, "Look, without me you'll fail, because I can add something. The director will lead the character into the audience's hands so you will be understood." I worked with him, and it was the greatest experience. What he wanted was so big.

From Stanislavsky on, you had to have the autocrat director.

The author's ideas had to go through the director to get the relationship and the character—the director had to understand it first. His colleague Nemirovich-Danchenko said Stanislavsky's innovations were the greatest addition to the drama since its inception.

What he and Stanislavsky did with staging is the autocratic ability to make the play live. You cannot play Chekhov without Stanislavsky, because you will just go to the lines. The director used to just say, "Go here, go there," and the actors did it. That is the vertical way. The other way to present a play is that the director tells the actors what the play is about. Everything goes to everybody through the director. Even the set designer goes through him.

You have in Russia still these authoritarian directors. We don't. Strasberg tried. But he was not equipped to understand as much as he thought he understood.

The tradition of character acting is still very strong in Russia. The audience identified actors by the characters they portrayed and the skill with which they played them. They did not follow the actor's personality, only the variety of parts he played. They knew the actors by their portrayals. My father came out of that school— "You must see Adler as Shylock," "You must see him in *The Living Corpse*!" People went to see the actor portray the character. Chekhov inherited this tradition of writing for characters. The uncle is a character, the doctor is a character, all played by character actors—not personality actors—in different roles.

You must characterize in Chekhov; the character speaks, not you as a person. He wanted to take out the music between the curtains, which was a tradition there. "Don't bring in anything to the theater which doesn't make the play clearer." His great objection to having music between the curtains was that it didn't make the play clearer. He wanted nothing on the stage which did not help to make the play clearer.

The reason Chekhov objected to Bernhardt was because she always played herself. She played heroines and made them into unusual women with an unusual voice, as she was herself. He didn't want that. Once I went with Max Reinhardt to see *Three Sisters* with Katharine Cornell, Judith Anderson, and Ruth Gordon. It was an opera! They were such special people. I told Reinhardt that they *sang Three Sisters*. I walked out in the middle—they were the three witches from *Macbeth*!

In Chekhov, opposite to Shakespeare or Shaw, the audience must say, "Olga is just like my sister" or "Masha is just like my cousin." Everybody must be related to that unspecial quality you have in

Chekhov, which brought about realistic acting and which is why you can act today, because we are *not* special. Everybody must be able to say, "I recognize her." Gielgud is no good for Chekhov. Gielgud is a mask, like England itself.

You don't play your personality, you play the character. Reinhardt was a very great man who created the greatest European theater outside of the Moscow Art Theater in his own style. But when he sat in the audience at a Moscow Art Theater performance in Berlin, he said, "We can do everything in our theater, but we can't do that kind of realism." That came from the technique Stanislavsky worked out for inner action and justification, truly understanding and acting from the inside.

Chekhov's technique is to use indirect action when the main action takes place offstage. When Arkadina comes in, we already know all about her. Chekhov explains her to you before she comes on. The character, then, has to do very little to introduce herself, thanks to the indirect action: somebody says something, whether or not anybody else listens. That is very prevalent, because he doesn't want a *play*—he wants what happens in life. He finds that in life—people talk. That is the truth, and that is why he created the "truth of the scene" type of play. He is original in that. He does not write a whole act. He writes one scene that has nothing to do with the next scene, which has nothing to do with the next scene. Masha whistles. Chebutykin is always reading newspapers and writing things down, out of context with anything that is going on. That is indirect action.

This is very interesting to actors. If you are in a play by Miller and you sit down at a table, it is very interesting for you to see that a guy playing solitaire didn't cover the queen. To notice what is around you.

These are the inner compulsions, inner secrets which make you behave. Stanislavsky's technique works here.

I will never pick up a play which doesn't relate me to the other people. Do you see how boring you can be if you don't do this? It is the technique Stanislavsky created for Chekhov, for every realistic play. For Miller, for Odets. This is Stanislavsky's contribution.

Do you see why I was such an enemy to that Strasberg misinterpretation? To that idea that you have to gain sixty-two pounds in order to play a part and feel the character? It can't be done. At least, it shouldn't be. Do you see that Stanislavsky is bigger, better, healthier? It can be done.

The way the Stanislavsky system is used in America is very shabby, like what happened to Christianity. Somebody said, "I'm right, I'm Catholic," or "I'm right, I'm Lutheran." Everybody said they were right, and it was all misrepresented. Working with Stanislavsky made you realize that it is not easily done. I will give you how he works from his own notes—not Stella's, but Stanislavsky's. Maybe I'll give you Stanislavsky's stage plans for *The Seagull* and *The Cherry Orchard* if you beg me.

From this, you will see how banal most schools are in giving you what they say is the Stanislavsky method.

The author is not left out in realism; he is added to by seventy-five percent. That's why nobody can play Chekhov outside of Russia. The French don't know how, the English don't, and we certainly don't. We don't know how to do it because we don't understand what Stanislavsky wanted: he elaborated. Realism needs great elaboration from the director and the actor.

Stanislavsky adds what makes it actable. He adds the candy and the waltzing and the sunshine. Some people sweat in the sun. Somebody else sings. Masha says, "I can't take it, it's killing me." She is so tired from the sun. Stanislavsky added the fatigue and the flirtation and the sense of family togetherness. Stanislavsky said we can't do Chekhov unless we add by creating the details of place and an atmosphere for each character in the class and conditions of that period.

For instance, in Russia, the tea is very hot, and they make noise when they drink because they want it very, very hot. They hold the glass by the handle and they sip it . . . slowly and loudly. They don't put the sugar in the tea. They wet it and put it under their tongue and suck on it. It's Russian. Don't put the sugar in the tea, because that is English. It is also English to put the milk in first. If you don't put the milk in first, you are certainly not English.

Once Howard Koch, a very big producer, came over to the house to ask me something. He came with a director who was English. Howard and I talked. The director never said a word. When they left Howard said, "Goodbye, darling," and kissed me. I kissed him. I said, "Goodbye, sir," to the English director, who said nothing, gave nothing away. English. No emotion. Very different from Howard Koch, who came from Russian-Jewish parents.

Stanislavsky puts it all together—the scenery, the props, the habits—out of all the objects of that environment. He adds how it should be lit, how nature comes in, elaborating to such a degree that the audience gets interested in the details of each character and in the truth of their living. At that women's prison where I talked, where all of them were there for life, the psychologist said to me, "You know, you can't lie to them. Nobody can lie to them, because they have been through so much. They know if you are a liar."

If you are not faking and if you come to the stage knowing the truth, you can survive. Chekhov says we are all artists in our own way.

If you don't read Chekhov that way, kids, you're in trouble. If I can read him, it means you can too. It doesn't mean that I am the goddess of the theater world. It just means that I am the only goddess around town that does this with you. Nobody else seems to bother.

NINE

THE SEAGULL

I WANT YOU TO KNOW how Chekhov works. It is not how other playwrights work. Others have direct action—what is happening on stage is really what is happening. With Chekhov, even more than Ibsen and Strindberg, what is happening on stage is what is *not* happening. It happened before the characters came in. What matters is not the circumstances but the character's reactions to the circumstances. Chekhov could not have succeeded without Stanislavsky, because he puts so much into the past of the character before he walks on stage that unless the actor knows the past he can't possibly get the present. Each person comes in with his former life. It's the past of the character that relates to the present and to the partner. It is important for you not just to play what is happening on the stage now but also how it affects your character's *former* life. That is something Stanislavsky had to do because the actors couldn't do it for themselves.

I'm going to talk a lot about *The Seagull.* In *Seagull,* nobody has a cent. That is because of the moment in history. It is very important for you to understand that you are not in Tolstoyland with the upper aristocrats. You are with a kind of society that has had the best of everything but is now going through something different. The transition is very hard.

> [Synopsis of *The Seagull*: The legendary stage actress
> Arkadina returns to visit her estate with her young
> lover, Trigorin, a famous writer. They and her dod-
> dery brother Sorin and her old lover Dr. Dorn,

among others, are to be entertained there by the unveiling of her son Konstantin's new avant-garde play—and, in the subsequent acts, by all the volatile emotions and high comedy-tragedy that lie in the confusion of art and life, and the connection between art and passion. Konstantin's play-within-a-play serves to parody contemporary symbolist drama. His mother hates it. He hates his mother for that. Only a murder or a suicide can end their struggle.

—B.P.]

The Seagull is a play about theater people. There is nothing in it but the discussion of theater, the understanding of it, the people who are kept out of it, the people who want to stay in it. It is about the catastrophes you have to survive. It is a play which deals with the intellectuals and a better grade of people who aren't busy with money or selling anything, the landed aristocracy. If anybody tells them anything about money they say, "Don't talk about it—you're upsetting me!"

What is happening in *The Seagull?* All the grain, everything from the land, is sold to keep up the estate. A manager runs it. The man who owns it doesn't know a thing about it.

God, how I understand him. Nobody in the world can bother me about a bill or money, because I go crazy. You wouldn't believe it, but until last month I never signed a check. In my bringing up, there was no money talk. There was no talk except about theater, Schiller, Tolstoy. So I am a nut. In this play, they all know about art. They all talk about whether the play is good. It is a class of people that did not get waylaid by thinking about anything except art. They are all involved in "What is a good play?" "Who is the best writer? Dostoyevsky?"

Konstantin, the son, says the famous writer Trigorin is "cheap." He says that because of the new movement in Russia and France, the symbolist movement, led by the great French poet Mallarmé. Konstantin's play is written in this symbolist style. No wonder his mother says, "I don't understand it." You can't talk symbolism to an actress who is going on the road. Konstantin should know he'll be criticized, but he can't take it.

So this old aristocracy was busy with art. In this play, the whole emphasis is on which side of art you take. Everybody is part of the fight of "What is art? Who is an artist?" This is one of the great Chekhovian themes: "Who really is an artist?" You have this conflict of art all the way through, motivating the excitement and tension in the play. It is not "There's a storm here, let's close the windows, please help me." It's not that at all. The storm is coming, but nobody cares about it. They are so filled with the tension of their own lives. You have the calm and the tension—the calm of the uncle and the tension of Konstantin. When Strindberg has tension, the other person has tension. With Chekhov, you have the complete opposite.

Chekhov deals a lot with the weather that surrounds these people. In the opening scene Masha says a storm is coming. If Chekhov puts that in, it means to reflect on the action. If a storm is coming, it means the characters are stimulated, agitated. An upheaval in one Chekhov character affects all the others. Konstantin is trying to stage his play and Masha is hanging on to him until he finally says, "Go away. Leave me alone!" He is the temperament of the storm in that scene.

So Nature comes in. "A storm is brewing" gives the actors a sense of restlessness in the first act. It tells you somebody is going to be very disturbed in the situation. In the next act, the sun is shining, which has a very different effect on everybody. The effect of the sun on each character is different. It fatigues Masha. She says, "I feel as though I've been dragging myself around for one hundred years." She can't take the sun. Whereas Arkadina is dancing and laughing and eating candy. Laughter and sunshine go together. Storm and candy do not go together.

Each atmosphere in Chekhov has to be created on the stage. A storm brings movement and discomfort. How can they watch a play if it's about to storm? "My God, the lightning. Listen to the thunder!" When there's a storm outside the theater, it's discombobulating. He gives you that to close the play down. What Stanislavsky adds is really very funny. The crickets are cricketing and the frogs are frogging and lightning is lightning and the shadows and the trees are rustling—he added so much to "a stormy night" that it was difficult to hold your seat down.

There is a great deal of tension created in Chekhov out of the weather and out of character relationships that started before.

Unless you go back to find out what the relationships are, you will not understand Chekhov or any other good play. No realistic modern play starts with *you*. Remember, when Masha comes on, that she was brought up in the same house as Konstantin all her life. Her closeness to him has been from twenty-five years of knowing him and being rejected by him as if she didn't exist as a woman. Masha is destroyed by this.

What can Chekhov do about it? Chekhov was resigned to life. He didn't partake. He liked to be with artists but he was mostly an observer. He built this play around Arkadina, Konstantin, Trigorin, and Nina, plus Sorin—artists with conflicts.

Arkadina is a famous stage actress. She is not the greatest actress, although she has played Hedda Gabler. You can't always do Ibsen. Not all of the plays were masterpieces. You don't keep the curtain up thirty-five weeks a year by playing Gorky and Chekhov all the time, even in the Moscow Art Theater.

Arkadina knows how to survive. She doesn't need a twenty-five-year-old son around. She doesn't need anything that will take away from "I am a star and don't you forget it." She needs to look thirty-five. All her glamour, all her anger, comes from being at a moment in life where she has to protect herself from growing old. No actress needs a son of twenty-five when she is forty-three. A reporter once asked my mother how it happened that she had a son of thirty-eight when she was only forty-eight. Her answer was, "He lives his life and I live mine." Very witty and very applicable.

So Arkadina has to protect herself. What does she need young Nina around for? She has a need to protect herself and her lover from this. Konstantin, a playwright in love with his leading lady? Who needs it? This son is an embarrassment. He writes crazy plays. This new theater is decadent. "Yes, I get it—you think I don't get it? I *get* it, but I don't like it." You have to have her whole inner action of being threatened.

The theater fascinates the people around Arkadina. They love her because she's glamorous. Whenever she leaves, all the servants come and the cook cries because they are taken by her, in the same way people are by movie stars now. "Do you know who's here? Burt Lancaster!" The intense personality of the actor has a way of making everyone aware that he is in the room. The excitement President Carter had—the humility with which he talked to the artists that came to the White House. I went to Yale and brought four men from Moscow to lecture on the theater. I was Mr. Brustein's* dinner partner. He said, "We at Yale aim high, but we don't have the inspiration, the effect, the dynamism, the importance of these artists from the Moscow Art Theater."

Arkadina went to the big city, met a strong guy from the upper peasant class, got herself pregnant, and then finished with him— divorced. The son is a result of this. He is not an aristocrat. This bothers him. On his passport it says he is the son of a peasant. That bothers him very much, because people looked down on the peasant class. So he is torn.

Arkadina knows she has sinned against Konstantin. She knows that she has not given him love, that she has neglected the one thing she gave birth to. Her attitude to being a dozen or so years older than her lover is a sense of indecency. She has an inner turmoil. She loves her child but not as a mother. If he shoots himself, she nurses him and then says, "You are a peasant. Get away. You disgust me." She is a complicated woman and her relationships are complicated. She will nurse you when you are sick like an angel, but just try to praise another actress in front of her! Instead, you have to be enraptured over her marvelous acting in *Camille* and *The Fumes of Life!* Those are pretty miserable melodramas, but very successful. Camille dies of TB and a broken heart. It's pretty crummy. But it is not crummy to the actress who plays it.

Do you understand the stardom of Arkadina? Why Polina sees her husband, Shamrayev, eating in front of Arkadina and says, "I think I'll die, I'll just die"? You must understand the stardom. People throw roses and jewelry to her on the stage. You have never really seen a period in which there was a star.

I'll tell you a story about a very successful producer named Jed Harris. He was living at a house we had in the country with my brothers Luther and Jay. My father was at the table. Somebody said something and Jed, sitting at the table, screamed, "Ahhh, what the hell do you mean?" The two boys took him from his seat, to the car,

*Robert Brustein, head of the Yale Drama School.

to the station, and put him on the train. Nobody screamed in front of Jacob Adler.

People don't misbehave in front of Arkadina. Whenever she is on stage, everything revolves around her. Konstantin admires her talent and loves her as a mother, even though she isn't. She can still hold an audience and she has a big following, like an opera star. She has influence in the society. She is aristocratic even though she married into a business class.

In my family, in four generations, nobody was ever in business. My idea of a businessman is that he is vulgar. I don't care who he is, Rockefeller—he's in a money game. Some of my cousins decided to be the Lerner Brothers and became multibillionaires. We always said, "Well, there are the rich Adlers and the talented Adlers." They never mixed.

The difference between Konstantin and his mother is that she is very professional. She wants the curtain to go up on time and the play to have an audience, whether it's *Getting Gertie's Garter* or *Hedda Gabler.* He says, "You and your cheap theater," but he has no right to insult her like that. He says, "You are a cheap woman. You have a cheap lover. And he's a cheap writer." That's Trigorin, who is considered one of the best writers in Russia. That kind of snobbism is in Konstantin.

Chekhov and Stanislavsky understood this young playwright. They knew people worshiped the theater, worshiped the actor and remembered every gesture he made. Shamrayev says, "Do you remember forty years ago when Pavel Chadin . . . ?" Like people who heard Caruso. It stayed for a lifetime. People still remember gestures that my mother did. Chekhov and Stanislavsky have an understanding of these people who love the theater.

Konstantin and his play are a social embarrassment to Arkadina. She is irritated by the play, by his age, by his bringing in a young, pretty girl who in two years will want to take her place. Arkadina doesn't need the competition. She doesn't need her lover, Trigorin, to say "How beautiful you are!" to Nina. Actresses never get older, never get tired, never have rheumatism, never need glasses. An actress doesn't say, "I don't feel well, I have a headache." I learned this from my mother. "My feet don't hurt. I don't sweat in the summer. I'm not cold in the winter." That was very strong in my life. There was never a complaint from an actress. Never, never, never.

It is very important that the actress doesn't age. Actresses must remain the same, and this is very annoying to the boy. "What is the matter with you? Why can't you be like other women, like a real mother?" They are in eternal, psychological strife. The man-boy wants a mother, not an actress. I don't know any actress that does not have trouble with grown-up sons and daughters.

Arkadina has kept him in the country. Everything she has is threatened by him, by his play, by the young girl.

You create the past from what she says. Stanislavsky makes you understand the past in order to deal with the present. Unless your character has a past, forget it. You cannot have a Konstantin unless he is neglected as a child, kept in a corner. This hurt him terribly. Everybody around her was somebody. He was nobody. You have to build that up in him in order for him to be so embittered. You have to build up from when he was a kid and she said, "Don't be foolish, you are not a playwright. I love you and you are my baby, but now, shut up." She babies him but then says, "Don't talk about theater, because you are an amateur. Also, you are a peasant's son." She does something to him that makes him hysterical. She has what she wants and she wants to hold on. No great actress ever gave up a career for her daughter-in-law.

He doesn't have the courage to say, "I'll go away from you. I'm twenty-five. I'll write what I want." Where would he go? The situation with the mother is not new. Chekhov didn't invent the mother who wanted a lover and maybe helped kill her husband. Hamlet has the same relationship. How old is that?

Konstantin has developed that Hamlet/Gertrude situation. He loves his mother, doesn't want her touched by another man. That is a big psychological thing. Shakespeare knew it and Chekhov knew it and you see it in life all the time.

Konstantin is in the grips of that emotional relationship and can't get out. He loves her and hates her. That is the pattern of a neurotic, and that is what he is. Back before he came on stage, he went to his mother's room to say hello. He hadn't seen her in a whole year. He knocked and she said, "Not now." He sent her his manuscript because he wanted to share something with her, but she sent it back without any money. Does she love him or doesn't she? When she comes home to visit, she comes with a man. Her attention is towards her lover, not her son.

That lover, Trigorin, is fifteen years younger than Arkadina and just five years older than her son. He is a popular writer, very Americanish, like Norman Mailer a little, disillusioned with life—like writers in the movie industry who have to make money. If you have to make money, you write what appeals to people. People who write like Ibsen and Strindberg and Chekhov didn't make a lot of money, but one hundred years later we are still talking about them and not about the other ones.

Trigorin is a good writer but he is very dissatisfied with his writing. He has no other life. Stanislavsky didn't understand Trigorin when he first played him as an actor. In that first production, he wore a panama hat and a white suit as Trigorin. He didn't want to give up that wonderful white European silk suit. Chekhov said, "Stanislavsky, you don't understand—he wears yellow shoes! He smokes expensive cigars, his fishing rod is crooked, he is a man who doesn't know how to use life at all."

He's not a great lover. He doesn't love the young girl; he never had a girl. He's a writer and he's passive. He is quiet and he is with a family who screams all the time. To play Trigorin, you must know that he is a deeply unfulfilled and unhappy man. He needs Arkadina to cling to. Trigorin says, "I am charming and cultivated and people buy my books, but when I die people will say, 'He is certainly not Tolstoy.'" Tolstoy is the big literary truth. The point is that Tolstoy is known for the same thing Chekhov has—the truth.

This famous Trigorin has not got anything from his writing but the compulsion to write, much like a Hollywood writer who has to conform to success and change the ending and say they lived happily ever after. He has this same sickness. He is at the point of the Hollywood writer who says, "I'm building a new wing to the house, we're extending. We're at the beach this summer. We just made four billion dollars from *Star Wars*."

Two other special characters I want you to understand are the uncle and the doctor—Sorin and Dorn. Sorin is Arkadina's brother, over sixty, the one who brought up Konstantin while she was away. Konstantin doesn't understand what his uncle went through by doing that, by not accomplishing anything or getting where he wanted to be. He wanted to marry but he couldn't be calm, nobody would marry him, and he learned to laugh about it. The laughter of hurt is different from other laughter. Konstantin says, "Uncle, look at your beard, your hair. For God's sake, comb yourself!" People always told him that, but he couldn't. That's why he was not attractive to women. He says, "I never married or had children"—with a nervous laugh—in the middle of anything. If I were the actor, I would build it up by thinking he got used to people laughing every time he said anything. His mind tells him, "I'm never going to stop being funny because I see that I *am* funny." So he has learned to laugh about it. You have to introduce into every character the essence you find in him from the external things.

This uncle isn't an old American midwestern uncle. Sorin is an aristocrat, and he'll keep this aristocratic thing forever. He'll ask for his sherry until he dies. He has form. His land is already three-quarters gone, but he keeps his form. He knows theater and philosophy and is a very articulate, educated man. His sister blows in for a week or two once a year. He has no luxury, but he still wears proper upper-class suits and owns an estate and he is generous. He doesn't take the money himself; he wants it to be there for his sister. He has a certain reticence. He is a man who never accomplished anything and compensates for it by cracking jokes, by noticing other people, by helping them. He is a giggler. Stanislavsky gives him a special laugh because he has found a way to counter his impotence by being the fool.

Stanislavsky builds him. As he comes in and things happen, Sorin talks. He is very busy. He always carries his blanket, smokes, sings and hums, makes designs with his cane—he has a lot to do. Four people fuss around to put him in his wheelchair. The circumstances are used tremendously and his dialogue comes out of it all. There is a very good scene when Masha describes the beauty and sadness of Konstantin's play, how it affects everybody—and Sorin is snoring. They wake him up and she goes on talking. Sorin takes out a handkerchief, laughs, wipes his head. The audience has to see how impeccably aristocratic his manners are from that one gesture of taking out his handkerchief after he snored and disturbed people. The doing in Chekhov is subtle; it must explain the caste he is in.

Sorin is very unhappy. He covers it up by laughing and joking and combing himself and saying cute little things from another era.

You have to play with a self and not expect the self to be created on the stage. You need this Stanislavsky technique to create a self that exists before you come on.

Sorin's best and oldest friend is Dr. Dorn.

If I want to understand Dorn, I have to know something about doctors. There is a Chekhov short story in which a doctor's own child is dying in his house. Suddenly, he's called out on an emergency. So he goes and drives all night and finds out when he gets there that it's not important. When he comes back home, his own child is dead. His duty as a doctor is never to think of himself or his own before the others.

A doctor's duty is to other people, not himself. That goes on forty years and wears you out. You're interested in what the chart says, "Show me your tongue," "Let me feel your pulse." You don't notice the flowers in the room, the book that patient is reading. You're not really with life in its whole. The rest of life fades.

You have to get to "worn out." When you see a horse, it has only one thing to do: pull that carriage. Every horse looks worn out. When you see a man lying on the street, he's worn out. He used up his body years ago. You have to really understand what a worn-out person is if you're going to play the part. When a tree hasn't got the strength to hold itself up anymore, it dies. So does a body. When the doctor says he is worn out, it means he can't go on, he's sliding down. Stanislavsky wants you to *do* the worn-out things, not *say* them.

To be a doctor in Russia in this particular class means a lot of sacrifice; you can't live too long. There is no money. You are overburdened. This culture was so worn down, nothing to work with, that the mere ability to be gracious is a tremendous thing, the graciousness coming out of that difficulty. In every play, there is a doctor who really explains himself very well. He says, "I've ruined my life. I've only been with old people, sick people, the most desperate kind of people. I've never had anything for myself." In each case there are differences, but it's the same doctor, taking the blows of society. The doctor here has no aim, but he works, he wears himself out in work.

Arkadina has an aim. She says, "I'm not going to die, I'm not going to get old, I'm going to kill Nina. Nobody is going to get in my way." The doctor respects that because so many people give up. He is a little bit in love with that. He tolerates it because she has, from an intellectual point of view, an exquisite vulgarity. The doctor expresses the author's thoughts. That is the purpose of the doctor in these plays, to give you what Chekhov is—the *raisonneur*, the man who explains to the audience what goes on, the person who uses reason to interpret.

The doctors in the plays are not up to their weaknesses when they come in contact with the emotional difficulties of the characters. In that moment, there was nowhere to go if you had troubles. For that matter, I don't think there's much of a place to go even *now*. "Doctor, help me!" Men and women say that to the doctor. But he is not a psychiatrist. He is a medical doctor. He cannot help much. He is small.

Most of the men in Chekhov are small, not heroic. Most of the men of his society have given in. The doctors give in. The people on the estates give in. Some of them give in because they are children. In each play I will show you who the child is. In *The Seagull*, Sorin is the absolute child. There is no fight left in him at all. He and his class are fading out.

Trigorin says to Arkadina, "Take care of me, for Christ's sake, I can't take it anymore." There is no steady thought of "I'm strong, I am going to rebuild the world. I am going to remake the theater."

Artists cave in a lot in Chekhov, and this play is about artists. They are not without compromise. When they meet uncompromising people, they get angry. You do a commercial and then you do Chekhov. You make a buck where you can. But keep that inner fire going so you can restore this thing he says gets worn out by doing commercials and junk. You see what happens to the actors out in Hollywood: their souls get worn out. This is what Chekhov is afraid of. He says if you don't keep working on what your soul needs, you are going to be wiped out.

Key Scene Analysis: Stanislavsky Applied

Every text is bare.

I'm going to show you what Stanislavsky did to the text. There are two plays he staged that are translated with the staging—*Othello* and *The Seagull.* It is Stanislavsky's staging. I have it. I'm going to give it to you. I will show you that you cannot play Chekhov without Stanislavsky because you will just go to the lines. I will take you in detail through certain scenes in *The Seagull,* which are some of the most important scenes in all of Chekhov and also some of the most important scenes in all of modern theater.

In all of them, something is always happening offstage that feeds the inner action. When you open a Chekhov play, nothing seems to be happening. "I am in mourning for my life." But the inner actions always make a modern play come alive in a sense of quiet poetry, even when nothing is happening. The characters involve you in their inner action.

ACT I, SCENE I: MASHA AND MEDVEDENKO

Okay, darlings, let's get up and read—and don't wait ten thousand years. At the first reading, see what is spoken about, what the action is, and when it shifts.

{A student reads.}

Don't mumble, dear. I don't understand you. What is all that mumbling? *Talk,* for God's sake. Talk and discover it while you're reading. It's human right away. Who are you talking to? A girl who's wearing black. So tell her, darling! "I have a hard life. You have a better life than me." Right away!

Certain characters are not capable of surviving—the apathetic ones, like Masha.

They don't have "iron in the blood." That is good for you to remember when you start hanging out at bars. That Masha drinks is the beginning of going down. "Love" is the most important thing to her. Chekhov says, "If that is the most important thing, you are going to go down, because it is *not* the most important thing, and every love affair ends."

Men know that, but women don't. Women die because they don't know that; men survive. If you start looking dirty and smoking and cracking nuts and taking snuff—it is the end. Whenever you see a woman drinking in public, she is losing her hold on life. A woman at a bar drinking is a woman that is sinking.

In this play, the reticent characters are reticent for good reasons—like Semyon Medvedenko, the schoolmaster. Understand what the teacher represents: a teacher knows facts. If you study botany, your teacher is going to teach you the same botany class he has taught everybody else. There is no creative aspect to him. When Masha says, "I am in mourning for my life," that is not his idea of a "fact." He can't hang on to that. He comes from another class. He is poor.

He says, "My life is harder than yours." He is speaking to a girl whose soul has died. When the soul dies, *you* die. You don't need anything except whiskey.

"Why do you wear black?" is an open question. The teacher doesn't understand anything that isn't solvable. He is talking to somebody who talks back to him in terms that are not solvable. She is part of a wealthy household with carriages.

She doesn't have to be dirty; she could be clean. He doesn't understand her failure in love, hasn't experienced her desperate inner sense of failure. They are talking to each other about experiences that they do not understand.

They will never connect. He says, "I love you, I walk four miles to see you." His soul is alive, but hers is dead to him. He is talking to somebody who hasn't experienced "I have to feed a family, I can't borrow a horse, it takes six hours to walk, I am not paid anything. . . ." She doesn't get it: "I think your poverty is a pleasure compared to my life. My suffering is so much greater than yours." He does not understand. Why should her suffering be so great?

This is indirect action. She is dressed in black; her hair is not combed. She is an aristocrat, but she drinks, she has lost control, doesn't believe in her life anymore. She sees it is going down. She is not interested in herself or in other people. Today we would say she needs an analyst. Maybe if she were lucky an analyst could pull her out. I know a lot of people today who are going down because the social situation is going down.

Would you say that she and Medvedenko are fit to be together? What good is his love to Masha? She is deeply alcoholic. She does not react to anything but her feelings for Konstantin. She can't get out from that love, which drags her down. Chekhov says, "If that's the only direction, sweetheart, forget it, you are going to die. You cannot base your life on love. It is too fragile to put such a high value on it."

My sister was like Masha, and an actor I knew named Ben Ami was very much like Sorin. Ben would come in when my sister served fish. He'd look at the fish and say, "Ah, little fish, swimming in the stream, how beautiful, how beautiful!" My sister would say, "You know, this needs a little lemon. . . ." She smashed the mood. You have to know the tone if you say an extremely extinguishing thing. I'm trying to get you to activate the character in the circumstances. Chekhov establishes the mood. Activate it.

You don't reveal except to somebody who catches it. These are the colors he wants you to show. Complete revelation. "Look at my soul. Look at how I'm dying." She's in trouble.

ACT I, SCENE 2: SORIN AND KONSTANTIN

Masha is in love with Konstantin. But Konstantin is in love with Nina, the young actress, and he has written a play for her. Very rarely do two people ever connect in Chekhov.

When Konstantin comes in, you immediately get his enthusiasm about the theater, which is frantic and wonderful.

He has talent and he has a vision, but he doesn't have what Chekhov calls "iron in the blood"—the thing you must have in order to get past what is defeating you. Chekhov had it to his deathbed. He had people come to his room when he was dying. He sent for his friends, and they came just to watch him be sick and die. Jesus, what a man!

Konstantin is excited. It's his opening night. He has preperformance anxiety. Chekhov says that's good—don't get to be peaceful, it's not good for the artist. So Konstantin is in this anxious, hysterical condition when he comes in. It's his first play and he's there in front of judgment—his mother, the great actress, and her lover, the great writer from Moscow. His girl, Nina, is coming, and she is the star. But the first person he sees is Masha, and his first words are, "You shouldn't be here—please go away." Doesn't he know Masha is dying inside, dying to be close to him? He doesn't know or care. He says, "Get out. I don't want you here. Yes, you're my sister, but leave it alone, already—go away. I'm nervous." Konstantin dismisses her. He doesn't want to be bothered or mothered by her.

Now Sorin says, "Masha, dear, I wish you'd tell your father to take the dog off the chain so it won't bark." Masha turns and looks at him with poison and says, "Tell him yourself," and stomps off. She takes out her rage on poor Sorin. He wonders, "Why is she so angry?" He doesn't have the sense to say, "Hey, I still own this estate and your father is my servant!"

Now Konstantin opens up to his uncle and says, "I'm fighting with my mother. . . ." Sorin can't understand: "But she loves you, Konstantin—your mother adores you." He is thinking, "Why, when we were kids, we always played together and I made her laugh and she loved me and she loves everybody. She loves you, too." But Konstantin's experience is a year without a letter, a year of her knowing that he had pneumonia and not bothering to find out if he got over it. Sorin doesn't understand what is going on inside Konstantin, doesn't comprehend what he brings from the past in relation to his mother or his art. Sorin says he thinks it would be nice to be even a second-class writer, not realizing how offensive that is to Konstantin, who feels, "That son-of-a-bitch *Trigorin* is the second-class writer—a liar in every line!"

Sorin says, "By the way, what kind of a chap is this novelist? I can't make him out." It means that when Trigorin arrived, Sorin ran to the library and got out a book and when the novelist was presented to him he said, "I know your work," and he showed him the book and Trigorin looked at it and said, "Yes, thank you," and walked away. It is like later, when Trigorin says to Konstantin, "You're a great success, I read your article and everybody's talking about it." But when Konstantin looks at the magazine he sees that Trigorin didn't even cut open that page. He just mouthed the words, which is what he does in his fiction. So Sorin asks about him, and Konstantin has a few minutes while he's waiting for Nina and the play to start, so he answers in a page-and-a-half monologue:

"He's an intelligent man, a bit on the melancholy side, already very famous. As for his writing, well, he's no Tolstoy. . . ." From this you get that Konstantin belongs to another school—Zola, maybe—avant-garde.

Stanislavsky says Konstantin delivers the whole speech while smoking, taking cigarettes in and out of his mouth, inhaling. The smoking is a big thing in between the words which gives it an agitation. It's a speech with a rhythm that is not written.

Now if you can do that, you can be greater than Pacino. Just be a big smoker in order to get rid of the big monologue. You mustn't say a monologue unless you divide it in three parts—pacing, talking, and explaining. This is what Chekhov and Stanislavsky taught us. It is not "To be or not to be." You must do it with its own rhythm, because over a page and a half it's going to vary.

Then there's a pause. Sorin says, "Well, my boy, I can't help liking literary chaps. Long ago I wanted to be two things passionately: I wanted to marry and I wanted to be a writer, and I'm afraid I failed in both my aspirations. It must be nice even to be a second-rate writer. I mean, after all, if you write . . ."

Stanislavsky says that while he's talking, Konstantin lies down, which means he doesn't listen to him. The moment the uncle starts talking, he thinks, "Here he goes, I might as well lie down." Just lying down, being with his own nerves. Stanislavsky has made a scene that is actable. He has created for the actor what Chekhov didn't give him. Sorin talks, pauses, whistles, hums, then another pause, then, "You know, my boy, I can't help liking literary chaps. A long time ago . . ." . . . then hums, absurdly, *da dum da da*—. . . . No wonder Konstantin takes a rest. It's taking Sorin ages to say these six lines, whistling, reminiscing, singing. . . .

The key to Sorin is that he fills in his life and he doesn't really speak to anybody. This is typical of Chekhov. Don't go to the words. Go to the character of the words. Sorin is not contemporary, not to be rushed. He lives in the country. He is slow. He thinks about the past, doesn't listen much. "I hear but I don't listen because most of it is questions I've answered a thousand times." If somebody says,

"Where is the bathroom?" Sorin would say, "The bathroom? Oh, my boy, in the old opera house, when Caruso . . ." He's interested in that particular bathroom. "It was on the third floor, so beautiful . . ."

Finally at the end of it, Konstantin jumps up and says, "I think I hear footsteps." He embraces his uncle. "I can't live without her. Even the sound of her footsteps is beautiful. I'm so deliriously happy." He goes to meet Nina. That is what is written, but this is what Stanislavsky adds: "Konstantin hurls himself upon the uncle"— jumps up and jolts him. The difference between "embraces" and "hurls himself" on his uncle.

Sorin's hat falls off, and not knowing what to do about it, he gets up from the bench, smooths his hair—he always does that—and then hooks his hat with his cane, which takes quite a long time. He's too old to just bend down and get his hat. So he's not listening to Konstantin at all. He's always busy doing, doing, doing.

ACT I, SCENE 3: KONSTANTIN AND NINA

So you finish with the son and the uncle, and then a new character, Nina, bursts in—terrified—with a completely new scene. "Oh, I shouldn't be here!" She runs in with her life that you don't know. To be an actor then was the lowest thing you could be. No one wanted his son or daughter to go out with an actor—the morality of actors was considered so low.

In America, when Gloria Vanderbilt started in with the Bohemians, her family put a stop to it. Vanderbilts didn't go out with actors. That kind of money doesn't. A Rockefeller with fifty billion dollars would never marry an actress, because what he owns really belongs to the firm. He can own it up to a point. They'll give him just so much to fool around with for a year or two, but the big money is never, never touched. It stays in the family. So this thing in Chekhov is taken from the real world. "Please don't make me stay!" she says. "I'm not allowed to be here. They say this is an immoral place!" She's frightened out of her wits and she's saying this to Sorin, who has no idea why she is afraid, because he doesn't experience her fear.

Again, one character doesn't understand what the other is going through. Sorin has no clue why Nina is attracted to Bohemia, why she's frightened—but she is drawn there, to this artistic life, and that is the beginning of her escape.

Konstantin has brought her in and now kisses her hand ardently. Russians declare themselves. Konstantin tells Nina, "I feel close to you, my darling, I love you, I want to kiss you." His heart is open. The Russians kiss you and die for you by really *doing* it, not by talking. They are not like American men. He says, "I'm deliriously happy!" He kisses her hand ardently and then helps her off with her cloak and shakes it and folds it and puts it on the table, which is much more actable than just kissing her hand and waiting for a cue. Somebody coming in from stormy weather has a cloak. You help her off with it. You don't just kiss her hand and wait for your cue.

Nina says excitedly, "I hope I'm not late. I'm not late, am I?" Chekhov writes "excitedly." Stanislavsky agitates it even more and says: "She can't catch her breath. She takes off her hat, which is pinned. She was running from across the lake. She fixes her hair, the hairpins fall down. She puts them back in."

Being late means she has to do something in front of people which should not be done. She drops her pins, has to pick them up. . . . Use that! She can go and look at Sorin's watch. "Oh my God, am I terribly late?" She can do something with the watch. She can rush out and put something in the hall and run back in again as she's saying, "I'm not really that late, am I?"

You have to *do* something when you talk. It's about what *happens,* not what is said. Take ten different situations of being in a terrible hurry. I'm in a hurry to get out of a restaurant. What do I do? I can pick up the check, look for the waiter, get the money out. . . . This is your work in acting. This is what you can contribute. Don't just wait for the director. You will be lost if he does your creative work for you. Do it yourself.

Do the words instead of say them. A play about art is boring unless you fill it with the inner thing of the artist.

Then Nina says to Sorin, "All day long I've been terrified that my father wouldn't let me come. But he's just gone out with my stepmother. . . . The sky is so red. The moon is shining. Oh, I am so thrilled. . . ." This is what Chekhov has written.

This is what Stanislavsky adds: "Nina goes up to Sorin. As she does the monologue, Sorin lights a match when she says, 'I'm so frightened.'" He can't see her. It's dark. So he lights a match in the middle of her monologue and says, "I do believe I see tears in those pretty eyes of yours," and then laughs. Stanislavsky has a note that Sorin laughs very unexpectedly, jarring everyone around him. This old man sees this girl crying. He is charmed, he laughs. She blows out the match and moves away because she doesn't want him to see her and says, "I'm afraid I did cry a little, I was in such a hurry. . . ." She does five things because she is late, and if you do two it would be considered genius. If you did none you would probably get the prize. They give the prize to the worst people. They'd say, "Oh, that must be Jewish what she is doing, or Italian."

During this whole thing Konstantin goes toward Nina, but she waves him off and moves away because she's sweating, she's not together, she's afraid he's going to scold her. So she's running away from him and he's running after her to bring her back, urging her—"Please, it's time to get started!" So you see it's a riot, with Nina and Konstantin running back and forth. Sorin says, "I'll go." He doesn't want to interfere with the young people. He heads out, bursts into laughter. He will play the fool to the end, what else can he do? Sorin puts his cane over his shoulder and marches off singing—maybe he has a coughing fit—while Konstantin and Nina are left alone on stage. Chekhov puts it all together and makes a scene in which each character does what he has to do so you have, as in music, a counterpoint.

Nina is very shy when she is alone with a man. Now there is "a Stanislavsky pause" where nothing is said, they just look at each other. Finally, Nina says, "My father and his wife have forbidden me to come, but I feel so drawn here to the lake, like a seagull. . . ." She is drawn to her fate, which is to be like the seagull and maybe get killed. Chekhov says you risk that in the theater; your life is going to be brutalized. You'll have an affair with a man who says he will love you forever, but he'll leave you pregnant and desert you. Or you will have a breakdown and won't be able to go on. That is the fate of the actress.

Nina has now sat down near the hothouse in the back. Konstantin sits down beside her and kisses her hand. She pulls her hand away and says, "I thought I heard someone." Konstantin gets up, goes and looks behind the hothouse, and says there is no one. He comes back, sits on the bench next to her, and kisses her. As he kisses her she says, "What kind of tree is that?" Konstantin gets the message. You see that the proximity of Konstantin is not interesting to her. She keeps avoiding him.

Now, if he just kisses her hand, it's over. But if while they're sitting there, you hear the uncle singing, and he lifts her hand and she withdraws it and jumps up and says, "There's someone there," and he takes the same hand, puts it down again, and we still hear the singing—this is what Stanislavsky added to give them a scene.

I'm so overwhelmed by his nobility of understanding: Konstantin is with the person he loves. Love is not quick or noisy. Love is quiet. It is love, not sex. He is not touching her bosom. An aristocrat doesn't do that.

Only in America do you say "I love you" and reach for the bosom. When you say you love me, please don't touch me. You have to teach American men this. That's why they can't do Chekhov.

Read the play; deepen yourself. I played these plays at your age. You have intuition and you're getting firsthand knowledge. You're not getting it from me. Surely you didn't get it from Strasberg. You're getting it straight from Stanislavsky, who couldn't stage Chekhov without it. He had to create a new method of using the stage, gestures, props, everything. He had to find a new way.

After the kiss Konstantin says, "Don't go back." She says, "I must," and he says, "What if I went to your place? I'd like to spend the whole night in the garden looking up at your window."

We don't think like that. Once there was a guy who was very jealous of me. He spent the whole night waiting to see if another man came from my apartment so he could shoot him. He was a shooter. It was more interesting than not doing anything.

So the moon is rising, and it's time to begin Konstantin's play. Konstantin is now a different man. He's authoritative. You never hear him authoritative again.

He raises his voice, gives orders. He is pinning her costume on her and he says, "Are you nervous? It isn't my mother, is it?" She says, "No, I don't mind her a bit." It's Trigorin, the famous writer. She says, "Is he young?" That's the payoff. You know she's not in love with Konstantin because she's asking if another man is young.

Understand that the actor must not depend on the director. I'm saying this to directors, too. This comes from Stanislavsky to Stella to you: modern acting means the literary side and the histrionic side. The literary side gives you the characters, the themes, the keys, gives you some words. But you have to add ten thousand more pages to the background. You can change it a hundred times, but you must see that it feeds you. You cannot do the present unless you have ten thousand more pages about the past.

When Konstantin walks onto that scene, he knows he is going to do something that is bigger than his mother. He is going to create a new theater. He is going to bring on a young actress. He is going to make that place work for him because he knows what he wants from that place.

The uncle doesn't want that from that place. Each person comes in with the knowledge of what the circumstances mean for them. Does that change acting a hundred percent for you? One hundred percent.

ACT I, SCENE 5: KONSTANTIN'S PLAY

Arkadina is terribly irritated. Why? Here are these old fogies around her. The mosquitoes are coming out. She smells kerosene and it's going to burn down her estate. You'd think they could start before everything is burnt. It's late—when is it going to begin? He says, "In a minute, in a minute." That reminds her of *Hamlet.* Suddenly, she's free. She's the freest woman in the world. He says, "I beg you, be patient." Where does she go? To *Hamlet.* "Ah, Hamlet, speak no more . . ." She's an actress. It's marvelous what she does. It's kidding, you know? That big speech you recite in class. She has all the commas. "All living things, in the cycle of sorrow . . ."

Don't miss the whole ensemble scene of everybody coming in and sitting down for the play.

Trigorin is there, with his ugly yellow shoes and shabby clothes. Sorin is talking antediluvian stuff and Arkadina sits behind him and gives him a blanket and Yakov runs around with the sulphur while she and her brother are bantering and joking and singing. Konstantin is fussing around and maybe says, "Mother, stop fixing my hair!" It's not the lines. It's an attitude that we've got to get. Do you see how it's mixed with comedy?

Arkadina is a diva of the stage. She has toured all over Europe.

She upsets people. *She's* not upset. The whole point is that she upsets *him*. She interrupts his play. She's saying, "Is this a joke? I don't know what I'm supposed to look at. Oh, he wants a new thea—he wants a—this is art? What kind of play do you want me to listen to? You mean you smothered us with sulphur as an *artistic* venture?" It's like when people bring me one of those underground literary magazines where the print's upside down, I say, "Ha, another one of *those.*" She's saying, "Oh my God, here he goes again!" I want that fight between them. That real naked fight. Nothing polite. One of the funniest lines in the world is when he says, "Draw the curtain, my play has been ruined!" The curtain is a *sheet.* It's so sad, it's funny. When they draw it, she goes, "Wha—what . . .? What are you so excited about? You haven't got a play to start with. Write like that if you want to, but leave me out of it!" She's thinking, "He is a pest, that boy. I'm not angry at him, but I'll destroy him . . . Oh, here's my shawl. . . ." And then you go on to the next thing. You can't miss that with Chekhov, or you have entirely missed the method.

What you have is the typical build of an ensemble scene, for which Chekhov needed the Moscow Art Theater—to get in the being there, the lousy stage, the curtain going down. Konstantin goes off and cries. Arkadina says, "Hamlet, weep no more. Mine eyes turn away. . . ." This is the understanding that Gertrude neglected Hamlet. Chekhov has Arkadina reveal she is deeply aware that she has hurt her son. He quotes Shakespeare to do it. You never have Arkadina without some inner excitement. Did Trigorin sit next to her? She's aware of where everybody is; she's nervous about everything—the party, the play, her son Hamlet. It's a farce and then it becomes a tragedy.

Curtain down. "What did I do? I've hurt my child." Suddenly everybody is in tragedy.

Now what happens after he runs off? Suddenly she says, "Oh, don't let's talk about plays." She says, "It's a lovely evening, people are singing across the lake." In the distance there's music. Everybody settles in for "the Russian evening." The mood must affect you. This is what Stanislavsky worked on. The lights go down; Arkadina walks around. The doctor is flirting with her. Everybody finds himself in this atmosphere. You can't in Chekhov go logically from one thing to the next. This whole scene has nothing to do with the last one. "Years ago, there was so much singing on the lake every night. . . ." A whole different scene, having to do with poetry and magic. "I remember there was so much music, so many love affairs, and of course the favorite of the ladies in those days was our dear doctor here." And she motions with her head to Dorn, who has moved close to be near her.

Do you see that she's related to Dorn from the past? He was the big lover of that day, when she was young. Did she let him go or did he let her go? He had Polina and other girls, too—a few years of whoring around. She says, "He was the idol of the ladies. He's a very handsome man still, but *then*—" she goes back to her affair—"he was simply irresistible." She does not just *say* it. She *experienced* his irresistibility. Do you see the difference? If you think the words sound the same without the experience, you're a lousy actor.

It's no good just for me to know this. I would like you to take it away from me. If you don't take it away, it will die because I won't be here and nobody else will give it to you.

ACT I, SCENE 6: SHAMRAYEV REMINISCING

Masha's father, Shamrayev, the steward, comes out and sings . . . "La donna è mobile" . . . You can sing any song that's not in your own American tradition. Have you ever heard a really beautiful singer? Imitate John McCormack, or somebody wonderful from the past. The memory is beautiful. I once heard Caruso. People are still saying, "Remember when Caruso sang 'Ridi, Pagliaccio'? . . . Ah, you don't know what you missed!" He is not in you or your American culture. He's with some miracle of the past. Shamrayev says, "Do you remember so-and-so, thirty years ago?"

Arkadina says, "You're driving me nuts. Don't talk to me about dead people. I'm not interested." It is so typical for an actress to say that. "I'm not interested in your recollection of Bernhardt, so shut up." Isn't that marvelous?

A woman came up to me recently and I said something about an agent and she said, "Miss Adler, you must act." I said, "Why?" She said, "Because you're going to die soon." Marvelous . . . real Chekhov. I'm talking about a contract and she's talking about something on a high plane. Fantastic, isn't it?

It's beautiful to act. If these Chekhovian people didn't live and philosophize this way, they'd have to commit suicide. Don't start with the words. "Oh, yeah, 1873 . . . ha ha ha." It's "Oh, 1873! What a night that was! What a night!" I don't start with the words. I start with the sense. Give me what it was really like in 1873, sitting at the opera or, a few years later, like watching Duse. Don't make it sad. It's their chorus. Reminiscence is their only happiness. "I remember the cherry orchard . . . how they made all kinds of jam." People who have no future live in the past. They go on and on. "Do you remember that opening of *Waiting for Lefty* in 1932? I'll never forget it. The people stood up on the chairs when he walked out and . . ." You must take it as something that is alive, not something that is dead.

You need a technique for this. I once played in a Gorky play in Philadelphia, *The Lower Depths.* They had two rehearsals. And because we didn't know how to do this, the audience started to boo us. You can't let that happen to you. You will kill your audience.

So what happened in 1873? It has to be, "Oh, remember when Caruso went on in *Samson and Delilah* with his hair cut off and he sang. . . ?" That's what their life is. Do you get it? They're full of life. He says, "Marvelous, exquisite." You can not pull down things that are marvelous and exquisite just because it was in 1873. It was *exquisite* 1873. Shamrayev is so much in it. "I wonder, madame, what happened to that actor who was—"

"What the hell do you want with me with 1873?" she says. "What are you asking me antediluvian questions for?" If you ask her about 1873, you're killing her. Do you remember that song written in 1850? "No! I wasn't around!" That's why it's funny. "What the hell's the matter with you, 1850?" He's fifteen years older than she is and he's trying to carry her back into his past. Be in it yourself. You respond as if you're talking to somebody else. Get that difference between overhearing and conversing.

ACT I, SCENE 7: DORN AND THE FAMILY

One of the things you must understand in all Chekhov plays is the closeness of family life, including all the neighbors. Sorin and Dr.

Dorn were brought up in the same town together, played pool together, went drinking together, and now they have their sherry and cigars together. The doctor says, "You're going to die." The uncle says, "What do you care?" It's two old buddies talking and kidding each other. He doesn't mean, "Go and die." He means, "What do you want? You've done what you've needed to do. Come on." One's fifty-five, one's sixty. They kid each other about these things because they've been together all their lives. Life ran down and the estates ran down, but they are still together.

What is the doctor doing all through the play so far? He's only said a dozen words. But he is there, he observes, he hums, he makes a link. He is a part of this Chekhovian family. If there is music across the lake, he picks it up. When he does say something, don't give it too much salesmanship. You have to take your time, make some link. How do you get from discussing the moon to green cheese? From green cheese to "I think I'll waltz"? You have to do it inside, think inside. You have to say, "Hmmm, spirit . . . matter. How do I get from one to the other?" The doctor is concerned with matter, philosophically. He likes to know about such things. Konstantin says, "Doctor, I've got something to tell you about spirit and matter—it may take five minutes." Why is he telling this to the doctor?

He has chosen exactly the one who doesn't understand. Do you understand what a poker game this is? Take your time. Don't lose the humanity of Chekhov, what it means. The way they visit is to be overheard. They come to be overheard. They are not restless the way we are. It is the Chekhovian thing. The actor thinks inside. Before Chekhov, before the Method, that miserable word, it was impossible to get the actor to take the time to think on the stage. Stanislavsky gives you time to think. He gives you music. He gives you an atmosphere and the mood to reflect on. The mood catches on and helps you relate to your opposite—even if he can't answer you logically.

A C T   I I ,   S C E N E   I :
A R K A D I N A ' S   " F I N E   F I G U R E "   D I S P L A Y

Now, the second act. What is the Chekhovian situation, the mood? This act is wholly different, very gay. When the curtain goes up, the sun is shining, there's a table with tea and cake. Arkadina is drinking tea, eating cake, waltzing around showing off her figure to everybody.

What are the relationships? What is she doing? She's taking center stage, but what else? Trying to say you'll go down unless you do something. You mustn't get fat. She's exhibiting herself, yes, but she's also teaching you how to survive. "I'm not a youngster. Look at me. I'm holding myself up, I do it all the time." An actress has to preserve herself. It's her life. Joan Crawford is a monster, but she preserves herself. "Look at me—men like me!"

Who is she saying this to? To Masha, who has just said, "I'm going to destroy myself." There's a total lack of emotional identity between them. There was a wonderful *New Yorker* cartoon with a tiny shrunken Jew, bald, glasses, and the psychiatrist says, "Go out into the world and circulate." That's Arkadina talking. "I stay up all night working on a part. I have no wrinkles. I can stand on my head. I do that. Why don't you? Who's got a better figure, huh?" And she waltzes and hums. . . . Chekhov says Arkadina often walks with her hands behind her back because that's how she bows on the stage. He says two gestures are beauty, but six gestures are vulgarity. This social class doesn't use so many gestures. We do because we are classless.

Unless you use the stage, you are obsolete. Give it up, throw it away. There isn't a moment when each person doesn't use the stage according to his character. One whistles, one hums, one laughs, one is passive, one is excitable. Each brings his inner character to the scene which the other doesn't understand.

Get the Chekhovian situation. What is Dorn doing there? It's so funny when you get it. Arkadina is talking to two people who couldn't be less interested. Dorn says, my bodily pleasures have been over a long time. Masha has just said, "I'm going to commit suicide." He's looking at these two women, what can he do? The play doesn't move on. These Chekhovian things you will never get more brilliantly. Chekhov joins Sophocles, Shakespeare, Ibsen, certain epochal dramatists who created forms which never existed before— not to "advance the action" but to reveal psychological truth, the deep humanity. This is your heritage. It's divine.

My sister says, "The fish needs a little lemon." Masha says, "It's all over for me." Her position isn't so romantic in the revelation. Revelation isn't God, you know. It's just talk. "I'm busy with my crappy soul," she's saying. "My life is boring. Gee, you should see my wardrobe, Madame Arkadina. You know what my nightgown looks like?" Stop going to sadness. Through character and contrast, it's a very funny scene. She's saying, "You see what I am, I'm a god-damn bore, Madame Arkadina." Masha always does that, and afterwards she cries.

Hard work, isn't it? This is breakdown. This is what you need the technique for. You have to know Masha through characterization, you've got to laugh it off. Play with it. They play with the sadness. Don't be so sentimental.

That's what's funny. Arkadina says, "I want to live all the time." Masha says, "I don't want to live at all." To make it worse, Arkadina says, "Look at how beautiful I am." Masha is not concerned with beauty. Her soul is dying, and Arkadina is talking about her figure. Masha is saying, "I can't even schlep this little soul of mine along." At twenty-two, her future is behind her, because she'll never get Konstantin. Arkadina says, "I can do it all!" A real star. She takes over. "Oh, I'm so involved and fretting about everybody. My boy is such a difficulty, if he would only be a banker. . . ." Very Chekhovian.

Arkadina says of Nina, "Her mother left an immense fortune." If you say it as if you read it in the newspaper, the lie rings out from you. In these plays, you do not lie. Understand everything to the last kopeck. She says, this girl has nothing because her father willed everything to the stepmother. Arkadina is a neighbor and knows that. What a terrible thing to do. To leave his daughter penniless and give the whole fortune to his new wife—how awful, how vulgar. Arkadina knows a lot about these people. And it's not in the text.

Masha says, "I don't like my father, I can't talk to him." Her father is a businessman. Her mother was in love with Dr. Dorn, had an affair with him when she was young. Masha says to the doctor, "I can't talk to my father but I can talk to you." He says, "Be quiet, people are coming." It means maybe Masha is really the doctor's daughter. I picked that up. It is more interesting to build Masha that way than to build her as the daughter of this boring, tiresome businessman.

Masha is becoming a drunk. They all see it happening. In the second act, she says something to Trigorin and keeps pouring the vodka. He says, "You drink a lot." She says, "I'll tell you something—most women drink alone, I don't, I drink wherever I want to."

Masha is going to pieces. No one pays attention to her. The superfluous person is always one of the characters in a Chekhov play. The one nobody needs. In the next act when she says goodbye, she says, "Don't write 'To my dear Masha,' write 'To Masha, who wasn't needed and doesn't need to live.'"

Give me something Masha does that's an inner action. When Konstantin is alone by the lake, who can help him? Nina. But Nina says, "Where's Trigorin? I want to be with him." Who wants to help Konstantin? Masha. Does she know how? You flatter a man, tell him wonderful things. But Masha says, "Your mother's looking for you." She does just the opposite.

In Konstantin and Masha, you have two types that are not meant to be mated. There is no way. They've known each other since kids. They both are impotent. They've had fun together. She looks at him and says, "God, you're getting old." Family teasing. It's like Luther and myself. Dramatize it. Otherwise, you'll make the play go down the toilet. Do something. Play with it. The whole scene is play. Her foot's gone to sleep, so she must kick it. So she kicks him, and he says, "Ouch." They laugh. It isn't in the line. Look for things that make the characters clear. It's funny when your foot is asleep. You kick it to get it back. Give me a situation. When I work on a text, I see what the action is and from my part take my action. I do not see what the words are.

STUDENT: But you have this genius.

ADLER: It's no genius.

STUDENT: Yes it is. I just want to know that there's hope for us. I mean, will we be able one day to pick up something you haven't worked with us on and be able to do what you're doing? I follow you when you do it with us. But each time you say, "Now what's he doing here?" it's not what I thought, so how can we get it if we don't have you and the director doesn't give us these things?

ADLER: Darling, I'm telling you, I never got it in my life. But I knew that I had to. I stayed up all night for years and years, digging and digging. A director won't do it for you. He'll do it for himself and use you. You don't want to be used, because it's not creative. Of course, there's hope. You're catching on. It's a lifetime's work to read Tennessee Williams, any of these plays, and find out what's going on. This is the job. From now on, when you're finished with me and start working in the theater for a public, you will never again come on thinking, "I'll do the words." You'll know you can't live on the stage without understanding the situation and looking for the different keys.

ACT II, SCENE 2:
DORN AND POLINA AND ARKADINA

Let's get to Dr. Dorn and his old love affairs. You have to build it up from the doctor's past—twenty hours a day, no money, going to poor homes and birthing babies. It was only two or three of those houses where he's really with them, drinks with them, where they love him and take him in. He grew up with Sorin's family. His own life is worn out, but he saved one thing in himself: he really admires Arkadina. He admires her as an artist, the fact that she has this boldness, that she functions. He sees very few other people functioning.

Remember this is Chekhov, who said, "I never loved anything. I understood everything, but I think electricity did more for people than praying. I have a soul. But I respect my medical side more." When the patient he operated on died right in front of him, how did Dorn feel? The scientist is hit by the downfall of society differently from the artist. He knows he isn't a great lover. But Polina is. She is a beautiful, aristocratic woman. They had an affair. He says, "For God's sake, don't make so much of it." This is very Chekhovian.

Polina is angry. She says, "You're carried away by Arkadina.

Don't do that in front of me. It makes me sick. Be with *me,* you know I love you. You don't even notice me."

He says, "Darling, I'm fifty-five, I don't have it anymore. I can't give it to you." He says, "I did a lot of good for women. They liked me because I was a goddamned good doctor. And furthermore, I've always been an honest man." But how does that reach her if he sits next to Arkadina instead of her? Polina is jealous and anguished, and when her husband comes in she has to pretend not to be.

You see that they are all mismatched, misunderstood. Jesus, this is interesting! Do you see the difference between a man's attitude toward being a lover and a woman's? Polina is also Masha's mother, so you see where Masha gets her obsession. Nina loves Trigorin but not "that" way. Trigorin loves Nina that way. Konstantin and Masha don't love each other that way. He loves Nina. Masha loves Konstantin. It's all mismanagement of the souls. In Chekhov, if you talk about your problem to someone who hasn't experienced that problem, they don't know what you are talking about. It is very important to see that not-meshing with the mind of the other person.

To Polina, the doctor meant more than a love affair; it meant her whole life. She had to marry into a lower class. She is dying because of the vulgarity of a husband who chomps into sandwiches when he talks. Stanislavsky gives you his vulgarity. Polina says to Dorn, "If you don't take me away, I will die." To him, it was a just an affair. "Don't take it so seriously." He doesn't understand that she is dying of pain.

For that matter, he feels pretty much the same toward Arkadina, even though he is more enchanted by her. Once when Harold Clurman wanted to write about Ethel Barrymore, he said, "I don't know if she's a good actress or not." He went to see her performance and said, "It was so full of the melody of her beauty and her voice—but I still don't know." So he went again and came back and said, "She's so fascinating, so hypnotizing—but I still don't know."

That is Arkadina. Dorn is hypnotized by her.

She is a big star. She has slept with Dorn. Practically openly she says it. But she was strong and Polina is not. You get Dorn's fascination with having two wonderful women always in love with him. But he was so busy all his life with everybody's babies and sickness.

He has no money, no life, he's old, he sings a lot. People who sing songs of the past are thinking about who they were at twenty-two. If you sang "Bicycle Built for Two" then, and you sing it now at fifty-five, something in this song betrays in you a lost romance.

If you understand that as a technique in Chekhov, you can use it in modern plays all the way up through Tennessee Williams, where it's the same class only in the American South. I want you to see how a writer builds through memory.

All Tennessee is memory. A great deal of *Death of a Salesman* is memory, and such memory! Miller is a genius. But Miller goes with Ibsen, not with Chekhov. Tennessee goes with Chekhov because it is a class society, and Tennessee writes about Southern aristocracy. In Tennessee's plays, there is always one character resembling the teacher who likes Blanche DuBois in *Streetcar*—the guy who has a fascination with her artistic temperament. The pedestrian soul is often drawn to the artistic—to the thing he doesn't understand. In all these plays with characters who are dreamers, there is always some plain guy like Dr. Dorn who likes that.

Memory has a way of making the event beautiful. You don't often remember and talk about ugly things. "At that parade, all of a sudden the horse let loose with . . ." You don't say that. You say, "Did you see the comet?" "Did you see the sunset?" It lifts you. It is not just ordinary prose. It is the prose of memory.

Arkadina says, "You know, fifteen years ago we had music on the lake every night. There was lovemaking and laughter and noise. I remember, there was this doctor. . . ." She lifts it. Then in the next moment she says, "I've hurt my son, I know." Memory on a deeper level. "Where is he? . . ."

Understand where the mood affects you. All this is reminiscent of a life that you like to go to. It's songs your grandmother sang. It's a swing you had as a child. Somebody picks up a daisy and says, "She loves me, she loves me not." Somebody's looking for a four-leaf clover. Don't promote the play. Choose what you want to do within the character, within the mood, within the action. For God's sake, stop selling dialogue. After Chekhov, don't sell *anything*.

If I were Arkadina, I would go over to the swing. "Oh, how nice. . . ." Her brother joins her, singing. See the family. It's slow. It's the melody of the brother and sister. The singing connects them and they connect it. You can connect with anything that's disconnected in Chekhov.

The harmony they can't make in life, they make indirectly. Otherwise, it's direct and very boring on the stage. Good writers create "mood actions." Walk around in this mood. Have an action here where nobody does anything. Take five minutes before she says "Oh, how nice it is," so you can show where the "nice" comes from—the swinging and all. That is acting. Everything else is baloney. Have one person not talk directly, and you'll have the biggest success in the world. Do it on a symbolic rather than logical plane. Try it. Get five minutes of Chekhov, kids, you're over the hurdle.

Throw all that sadness out. The Russian thing isn't sad and it isn't phony. What life they have is in the past. That's what people live by. We say, "Remember eight years ago when Marlon was in the class and there was some tootsie who . . . Remember that?" Everybody shares the past, that's what unites them. Think of the inside action of a wonderful past. Be *in* that. Be with the crickets and birds and night noises. That makes Arkadina talk in a certain way. If you think of that night music, you will act and react differently.

[A STUDENT *reads.*]

You've got a big mask on, honey. You're playing a character who talks a lot. People listen to Arkadina. She doesn't have to have a mask. She's free. She's open. People want to hear her. Everything comes to life when she speaks.

[STUDENT *tries again, reads.*]

Goddamn you! Now you've read this play a few times, and the least you owe it is the pronunciation of difficult names. At the first rehearsal you should say, "How do you pronounce this, Miss Adler?" and not go on mispronouncing like morons. "Alexeyevich." Say it! Read them off—"Nikolayevna, Arkadina". . . . Now do it easy, second nature. "Konstantin Gavril'ich." . . . You can't even imitate. Come on, for chrissake! Say "Nina Mikhailovna." Say it one at a time. Everybody. "Boris Alexeyevich"! Make it your own. If not, you'll always be ignorant. The moment you get a name that isn't familiar to you, that you can't pronounce—German, French, Turkish—find out!

ACT II, SCENES 3 AND 4:
NINA AND KONSTANTIN;
NINA AND TRIGORIN

In the second-act scene between Nina and Konstantin, what is the
mood? What is the Chekhovian thing when Konstantin comes in?
She's with the discovery that life is not what she thought it was for
these people. She's with her own ideas. Somebody comes in and falls
at my feet and says, "I can't pay you, Miss Adler, I have such troubles." I say, "I know, you have a new car, you're in a jam." But I am
looking past their soul. I will not fall for their soul's problem. What
is it I'm doing? I'm looking through their soul. Give me the
Chekhovian situation here.

> STUDENT: I went up to an agency to see an actress friend
> of mine who was becoming an agent and I said, "What am I
> going to do? There's no theater in America—I have to do
> solid work as an actress." She said, "You've got to stop play-
> ing old women, get an agency. You're afraid of agents, aren't
> you?" And I said, "Oh . . . don't you remember the old days
> when we sat together and we had repertory theater?" And
> she said, "I'm telling you, you've got to make a few phone
> calls and get an agent."
>
> ADLER: You were both in a moment of your own reality.
> Very good. Now let's see what Konstantin does.
>
> STUDENT [Konstantin]: "I was so mean as to kill this bird
> today. I lay it at your feet. Soon I shall kill myself in the same
> way."
>
> ADLER: No! You're promoting the action. You're asking
> her to understand something illogical. This isn't Chekhov.
> He seldom gives you something to convey logically. You
> convey it illogically and she answers when you're done. "I lay
> something at your feet which means something to me and
> may mean something to you." But you're giving it to her
> and saying, "Here's five dollars, give me two dollars change."
> What is his inner action? In what Chekhovian manner?

"Nina, I'm bringing you the symbol of life." It's not a mask; it's poetic realism. Don't bring the logic down. There are certain mystical elements of life Chekhov deals with. The seagull is the symbol of something that has wandered from home and is lost and will be killed because it's out of place. "You and I are out of place." Don't act the character, act the situation.

STUDENT [Konstantin]: "I was so mean as to kill this bird today. I lay it at your feet. Soon I shall kill myself in the same way."

STUDENT [Nina]: "You have changed, I hardly know you. . . . You have become so irritable of late. You express yourself so incomprehensibly."

ADLER: There it is! The whole thing, isn't it? The barrier is too great. They can't reach each other.

STUDENT [Nina]: ". . . I am too simple to understand you."

STUDENT [Konstantin]: "What is there to understand? My play was not liked . . . you consider me commonplace. I feel as though I had a nail in my brain."

ADLER: Here comes the real genius: that passing-by, like two strangers. Konstantin says, "You are disgusted by me now." He is not revealing *his* soul, he is revealing *hers*. Her inner action is not really "I'm too simple," it's "You're too dramatic." He says, "I disgust you, I've failed you." She has to find that patronizing way you talk to a failure. Ethel Merman talked to me like that—"Oh, you poor thing, you're in *that* kind of theater?" She didn't mean to hurt me, but it was "Oh, you come from *that*—with the symbols and seagulls and all." It's talking to somebody who is not really a part of your life anymore. Try it again.

STUDENT [Konstantin]: "I was so mean as to kill this bird today—"

ADLER: Yes, but it isn't alive. "Nina, you're a bird, you're out of place. I killed this bird because it's better dead than to see what you're doing when you smile at that faker Trigorin or fall for my mother. Do you know the symbol of this bird? The seagull is what has to *die*. . . ."

STUDENT [Nina]: "You have become irritable of late—"
ADLER: Don't play irritable. If you just play irritable, you're finished. You have to get from her something that merits his laying the seagull at her feet. Get the counter-point action. Her values are false to him. He wants her to see that. Chekhov said to Stanislavsky, "If they're both serious, we're going to cry." But we also have something here that is a little funny. A man comes in when a girl is primping and puts a dead seagull at her feet. She says, "Oh, what's that?" Get some counterpoint. In the first act he said, "Art should change, we need new forms," and in the last act he says, "We need no forms at all." Nina goes from idealizing him to not knowing him. These are the reversals, the growth in the characters.

It is very Chekhovian when you are reaching out to somebody but they can't understand you and you don't understand them.

In the next scene, Nina says to Trigorin, "You're so successful, if you only knew how I envy you, your life is so splendid." What he brings in from the past—his rejection slips, all that waiting in publishers' offices—she doesn't see. She doesn't see that his shoes are torn. It is how I described seeing Stravinsky in Venice. She just sees Trigorin and says, "You have such a great life." He says, "Me, a great life? I'm the most miserable person in the world. Day and night, writing. I finish one novel and then start another, a third, a fourth. What's so splendid about that?" In that sense, he is modeled very much on Chekhov, who just wrote, wrote, wrote. . . .

They are on two different planes. He's a peeker-in at life, never wholeheartedly in it. She is just the opposite. He has a way of taking everything and conventionalizing it. She takes everything and raises it. Make some fiction out of it: he's a bum, and she's the only one who finds out he's a bum. Use it.

Nina thought Trigorin and Arkadina were very glamorous. But in the end she says, "There is no glamour. There is only death. I am not a seagull. My child died in my arms. The man I loved deserted me, it was an insult from beginning to end. But I have to survive. I know that I am surviving."

She becomes the true Chekhovian method actress. She understands that you cannot be on the stage unless you understand pain. Understand that when you look at autumn, it is dying.

Look at the poverty, indecency, the lies in human life, and take it in. Look at most people and know that their minds have died. She understands and brings in that deep understanding of having loved, lost, suffered.

Nina is saying, "I almost got killed by that." It is indirect.

In the beginning when she says, "There are no living characters in your play," Konstantin doesn't take her seriously, because she's not a "real" artist, she doesn't know. His mother *knows*. When his mother says something, whack! Down comes the curtain. In the last act, he finally has to accept that Nina, who knew nothing, became the real artist.

In the last act Konstantin is a well-known writer, but he is defeated because he can't deal with emotional difficulties. If his girl doesn't love him, he wants to shoot himself. He does, eventually. If his mother makes fun of his writing, he doesn't defend himself. He doesn't feel, "I'll fight this through, I'll try to accept the fact that my mother is fonder of her lover than she is of me." All this disturbs him. Chekhov says, "I am sorry it disturbs you, but you are going to die. You haven't the will to fight through."

Konstantin, the most ambitious, in the end is a suicide. He gives up. That's the reversal in Chekhov.

When Arkadina is bandaging him, she's absolutely maternal. A second later, she's an enemy, because he challenges her. "I won't take it from you! You're an amateur. Don't talk about Trigorin or me or my plays!" When he shoots himself, my God, she's all mother again. Chekhov does not write a plot where one scene follows another. He says life is not lived like a play. You do one scene and then you do another. Don't look for plot. Look for the change of mood. Where is the plot? It's in indirect fragments. Chekhov is a mood playwright, not a plot playwright, because the mood of what people do changes so frequently.

The reversal makes for drama, for building a part from "I'm a seagull" to "No, I'm an actress." Chekhov shows you what a real artist is in the end: Nina, not Arkadina. The forces against Nina were so great, but she pulled through. Because Konstantin didn't know how to shield himself, he had to commit suicide.

*　　*　　*

The Seagull is about no place to go. Trigorin had to write cheap novels. He had no place to go in literature. Konstantin demanded art but had to compromise. Even the Moscow Art Theater was a compromise. When I was there, they played *Beyond the Train*—all about the glories of communism—and melodramas. Here, you have to do commercials. You get stuck along the road. Nina plays cheap plays in vulgar cities for vulgar audiences. But that is a way to survive, and Chekhov admires her more than anyone else in the play. The play is about being stuck.

In Chekhov, something in each character makes him relate to the other characters in an unexpected way. It's very human and very much what we do in our own lives. You cannot say those lines unless you understand the nature and the aliveness of every word—unless you universalize it, make it epic, make it large. Your society is on too low a plane. But your profession needs words. Prose poetry needs to be spoken not just with conviction but with total understanding. It has to be translated into truth.

This is called acting. This is the job of the actor. This is your art. Most artists feel like Trigorin—a failure—no matter what they do or what claim they have. "Who, me? I am without a life, I have never lived, I never loved, I just wrote and wrote . . ." or "I just acted and acted and acted. . . ."

Chekhov says creative artists are not happy. They are deeply hit by the blows of nature, life, history—everything knocks them down. You cannot have a Tolstoy from just what he lived through personally. He is endless history. You cannot have a Chekhov unless he knows every human being, the sickness of every peasant. He says every man and every feeling is different. Part of him is on fire because he writes. But the other part of him is Dr. Dorn, the scientist—watching, listening, taking in. The artist in him felt he was a failure. "I hate writing this play. I don't care if it's successful. It's a bad play."

When I read the prologue to my father's autobiography, it was terribly upsetting. At sixty-two, he was so full of doubt and anxiety and pain. The only thing creative people can try to do is *to learn.* It's not easy to act and get up in front of everybody and take the blows of the critics and try to understand Chekhov and take him on the road.

TEN

UNCLE VANYA AND
THE CHERRY ORCHARD

Uncle Vanya

W E S A W I N *The Seagull* what we see throughout Chekhov: that when the weather is unsettled or thick with storm, things are disturbed and accelerated. This affects the acting. If a storm is brewing, there is a certain inner anger brewing, too—a dissatisfaction awakened by the climate. There is much talk about stormy weather and its disturbance. People sleep late, one doesn't want a draft, one wants air, another feels dislocated. It stimulates these country people, whose energy level is low.

Chekhov speaks a great deal about this lack of energy, the lack of will in his people. From this lack of will you get a certain poetry, a certain sense of beauty in them. But when their "will-lessness" is stimulated from the outside, these people can become hysterical.

Uncle Vanya exhibits those signs quite early. He is passive before the curtain goes up and when the curtain goes down. His passivity is his ruin, but what can he do? Chekhov doesn't believe that experience changes you. You are born a certain way and the external circumstances happen to you, but what the people were originally they go back to at the end of the play. Nothing changes. They live through the storm and then return to their lives. They remain passive. The poetry in the characters comes from their passivity, or from their revolt against it.

Follow the revolt of Chekhov's characters—the key to Konstantin's failure and suicide in *Seagull,* for example. Here, Uncle Vanya is in revolt against his passivity; the others are not. Yelena doesn't revolt. Her passivity is central to the play's development. She does nothing, she seems to want nothing, and when she does want something, she doesn't take it. In both *The Seagull* and *Uncle Vanya,* city people intrude and upset the calm will-lessness and lack of energy of the country people.

Uncle Vanya and his family live a quiet life on their estate. But when the old professor comes with his young wife, Yelena, everything changes. The play is about the devastating effect of beauty. Not only the woman's beauty but the beauty of the land-scape—the beauty of Russia fading out in the same way Yelena's beauty makes the people fade out. When Yelena comes to the house, Vanya suddenly becomes aware that he has passions, ambitions. He had not experienced this energy before. It is awakened in him. At forty-seven, he is suddenly filled with the desire to accomplish something. It's a little late. He is shattered by the sudden emer-gence of these needs he never felt earlier.

This is Chekhov, and it isn't easy: beauty makes you aware of your own insignificance, of the wastefulness in your life. When the doctor asks if he looks the same, the nurse says, "No, you have lost your looks." Sonya says that she is plain. When Uncle Vanya enters, he looks drunk and unkempt, but he puts on a special tie for Yelena. The effect of her beauty on people is to make them feel their own lack of accomplishment. I have a quote for you from a Chekhov short story about a railroad guard:[*]

> The guard was standing with his elbows on the railing, look-ing in the direction of a beautiful girl. His battered, wrin-kled and unpleasantly beefy face, exhausted by sleepless nights and the jolting of the train, suddenly took on a look of tenderness and of the deepest sadness as though in this girl he saw his lost happiness, his youth, his purity, his wife and children, as though he were regretting in his whole sub-stance that this girl was not his and that for him, with his premature old age, his clumsiness and his beefy face, the ordinary happiness of a man was as far away as heaven.

[*]"Krasavitsy" [Beauties], written in 1888.

The feeling when suddenly seeing something so beautiful is that you have lost something along the line. Chekhov takes it up not in terms of action—"She did this to me, so I'll do that"—but as an aesthetic or symbolic thing. When you kill the seagull, you kill the beauty of life. Beauty gratifies you but also awakens a sense of your own defeat. You didn't do what you could have done. This is what *Uncle Vanya* is about.

> [Synopsis of *Uncle Vanya:* Vanya and his niece Sonya have for many years managed the estate of his late sister and her husband, Professor Serebryakov. Their self-sacrificing labors have permitted the selfish Serebryakov to live a carefree urban life with his young and beautiful second wife, Yelena. Now retired, he descends on the estate, thinking at first to settle there, then suddenly deciding to sell it, heedless of the consequences for Vanya and Sonya. Vanya is startled to realize he has spent his life supporting a man he now despises. In his rage, he attempts to shoot Serebryakov but fails in that as in all else. Yelena's beauty awakens not only Vanya but also his dear friend Dr. Astrov, who ignores Sonya's true love for a superficial flirtation with Yelena. Any recognition of their wasted lives comes too late for change.
> —B.P.]

Vanya's name is Uncle. That is symbolic. He is not Mister or Daddy. He is Uncle. It was his destiny that he did not have the will to become father or husband or grandfather. He lost that. For everybody he was Uncle. The same was true of Sorin in *Seagull.* They can blame it on outside forces, but they lacked the will to do anything bigger with their lives. There are a lot of parallels. This is a play about the critical periods in life. It is critical in Uncle Vanya's life and in the Doctor's life. They are no longer young. They have both failed; they will not marry. No matter what they accomplish, they feel it is wasted.

Uncle Vanya says he doesn't believe in anything. The old nurse says she believes in God. If you believe in God, everything is all right. If not, you blame other people for your problems. Konstantin blames his mother and Trigorin for putting out false values in art. Uncle Vanya blames the professor. The Doctor is also taken by Yelena's beauty, but he is tougher than Vanya. The Doctor is not capable of accepting pain to the extent Uncle Vanya does, because he is a doctor and has other pursuits in life. Love is of secondary importance to doctors; their souls are less apt to be disturbed by beauty. Vanya is disturbed to the very core; he is absolutely destroyed inside.

It is the most fantastically beautiful play.

Remember that in Russia there has not yet been a revolution in 1897, when *Uncle Vanya* was written. They are anticipating a change. They have a tsar, Nicholas II, who will be extremely reactionary to the bitter end. In France they have already had their revolution and their disillusions, but in Russia they still look forward to something different. What the difference will be, they don't know and Chekhov doesn't say. He doesn't think any all-encompassing change can take place. He says he hopes things will change, but he doesn't know how.

In the play, Yelena has a problem of her own. She experiences her own deadness, her own boredom, her own inability to change or risk even for a moment a relationship with Dr. Astrov. She has a terrific lack of energy. At one point the professor says, "For God's sake, jump into the lake, even if you drown! Get yourself some vital human experience." But she can't—not because she doesn't want to, but because her "morality" is stronger than her will. Chekhov says the deepest immorality is to be untrue to your inner desire to fulfill yourself. That is a deeper duty than the social morality Yelena clings to.

When Vanya insults the professor, Yelena reacts by saying it is a lovely day. She wants peace. She can't stand all this upheaval. The weather affects the psychological actions of everyone. It provokes and enhances their emotions. Yelena's presence shakes everyone into a desperate realization of their own hopelessness. Their quiet little atmosphere is turned into a furious storm. There are moments when the excitement is so great in Uncle Vanya that he explodes with it. That is what makes him try to shoot the professor. Once the storm starts in him, it takes a form and grows to the end.

In the opening of the second act, the storm is coming and Yelena's husband says do this, don't do that, until she says, "Leave me alone!" It is all provoked in dramatic terms by the weather, so to speak—by the impermanence. Vanya wants to live and is going to die, and once this energy provoked in him explodes, it recedes. After the explosion, the situation gets an equilibrium and life again is calm and the tensions settle down.

Yelena, too, is in tension. She is a conservative and virtuous person, in a social sense. Her beauty excites people and eventually their excitement comes to her. She would like to express her feeling for Dr. Astrov, but her nature has an inner conflict that nothing can resolve. Yelena has a choice between jumping into the fire of passion or going back to a life where you get up in the morning, you have lunch at one o'clock, then you rest, and you have a secure income—that sturdy rhythm of life. She goes back to the husband she despises.

Before Yelena showed up, these people had their own rhythm of life. They weren't really happy, but they were quiet. Chekhov says he can't explain why beauty makes people sad, but it does. If you see something very beautiful—a sunset, a garden in spring—it touches your heart. It is possible in the theater to convey this and make others experience it. It may seem to have no meaning for you at first. When you first read it you say, "This doesn't mean anything." But then you see that Uncle Vanya—in all his comic clumsiness and articulateness—has the deepest meaning. He is about failure. He tries to shoot the professor twice but fails both times. Through his failure, you get a deep understanding of people who have this inadequacy, this aimlessness. Chekhov has great compassion for them.

Sometimes their passivity is overtaken by anger. Yelena tells Uncle Vanya to please go away, but he persists in his masochistic love, in being rejected. Rejection has a tremendous effect on people who insist on being defeated. They become terribly aggressive. When it reaches a point at which they can't function, they become violent. That is why Konstantin kills the seagull and tries to kill himself, and that is why Uncle Vanya attacks Yelena, attacks the professor, attacks life, attacks Russia. The professor is inflated with his own importance. He has a painful illness—gout, arthritis—and when he spills out his frustration, Uncle Vanya attacks him unmercifully. Vanya blames everything on the professor.

Yelena's beauty has a lesser effect on the Doctor, who is tougher and younger than Vanya. His soul is less perturbed, less available to pain. He has made love of secondary importance to more useful pursuits. Yelena, through the Doctor, is aroused to get out of the situation of two men she wants to leave.

Yelena herself does nothing to produce the situation. She is, however, activated by it and saves herself from its consequences by suppressing her deepest desires. Yelena is put into a tense predicament between her beauty and her unyielding virtue. Nothing can rescue her. She is like another Helen—Helen of Troy—who also returns to the husband she despises. But this Helen has no adventure. It is not funny, but a little comic. Her misfortune is her beauty, which entangles other people in a terrible way. Maybe nobody was happy before, but they were quiet and maybe even content. Until she showed up, Uncle Vanya did not realize he was no longer young and the doctor was occupied with his work. They were not tortured by desire.

Yelena unbalances the scale. Chekhov says beauty is a burden. If you glimpse it, it takes away one's illusions that make life bearable. She brings to everyone a sense of loss—the hint of happiness too far removed from possibility. Chekhov says it's not easy to define this unhappiness. He felt no obligation to explain it, but to put it down truly. Chekhov says it is not possible to say why beauty makes one sad or why life should give us a sense of waste. He is as incapable of leaving his own cage as is Yelena. He constantly complains of his own passivity and the lack of vitality from which he himself always suffered. Chekhov's characters suddenly feel a sweeping desire to *do*—but they are thwarted by their tragic lack of energy. An intense experience is frightening to them and the humdrum existence to which they cling. Yelena flies from the possibility of escaping the horror of her despotic husband. She rejects the opportunity to live as she desires, which reveals that she has given up her humanity. It reveals her lack of vitality and her weakness and fear. She rejects freedom for the security of a soft couch.

Chekhov's understanding brings out his compassion. The characters in *Uncle Vanya* are sympathetic, even the professor. Sonya—a plain girl, very open and sensible—would make an ideal wife, but Dr. Astrov doesn't want her. He's a fine man but incapable of a love that is not physical attraction. He is bitter, contemptuous, even cruel. He is harder on himself than on others. Astrov is vital and has a brain. Uncle Vanya is more sympathetic. There is not much left of him.

In a sense, all the characters are ill. In their own way, all of them are secure against the upheaval of the outside world. They can't face the world. They do not want to escape. "Life passes, that is all." The worn-out tensions of aging souls—the slings and arrows of misfortune—is the mood of *Uncle Vanya*. The characters have been refined by nature—by their languor, weariness, resignation—not to experience their circumstances. Konstantin and Vanya are both idealists, country adolescents supplanted by decayed, glamorous men from the city. Uncle Vanya feels contemptible in Yelena's eyes. He is coming to the end of his life and has never lived. He suffers from loving and being humiliated. Love in *Uncle Vanya* is sad.

Chekhov says the discord in people puts them at odds with themselves and others. There is no cure for the soul sickness which infects the world. Chekhov sees the world as a dying man. He writes about futility. It is different from any other writer. It saves them in some way. Tuzenbakh in *Three Sisters* and Sorin, the uncle in *Seagull,* have no life—their speeches are about the futility of living. But Uncle Vanya is an idealist, and he has done something with his life in a very Russian way—sacrificed it for something he believed in. He is not, in his defeat and futility, like Tuzenbakh and Sorin. He is the neurotic, the man who is so angry, with that explosion in him. He shoots the professor but can't kill him. It's terrible. Chekhov makes you smile at Uncle Vanya and cry at the same time. He is defeated differently from anybody else, but he is still defeated.

The end is like the beginning: everyone is shaken, yet nothing changes, and the only purpose this summer storm serves is to reveal each character in his nakedness. They are terribly beautiful people. Their souls are elegant. No other playwright gets to that the way Chekhov does. These people are not ashamed of revealing their souls. They have the perfume of losing.

When the English National Theatre came here and opened with *Uncle Vanya,* the big critic on *The New York Times* said, "*Uncle Vanya* is not Chekhov's strongest play." In order for him to be a step ahead of Chekhov, he felt he had to say that. The theater at one time didn't need such critics—didn't bother with them. You don't need *The New York Times.* You need Chekhov.

The Cherry Orchard

Chekhov's people live with a great sense of space. They are not crowded in. When I did a British TV interview about Chekhov and Stanislavsky, the BBC man said he'd been to Moscow and had never seen anything so beautiful as the opening of *Seagull* with the trees and bushes and Konstantin's little makeshift outdoor stage plat-form—that sense of the Chekhovian landscape. Chekhov was famous for framing every story he wrote with the beauty of the countryside. So when you go onto a set, for Christ's sake don't say, "Oh, so it's a garden." Say, "It's like a Monet garden!" or "The colors are like a Cézanne landscape!"

The point is, know and notice the difference. A decaying Russian estate still has great beauty. There is nothing in the world more beautiful than those white cherry trees in the orchard when she opens the window, thousands and thousands of blossoms. Don't say, "Yeah, it's a cherry orchard." For God's sake, use paintings, begin to understand where you are. If you don't do that and make it yours, it is going to be a fake.

> [Synopsis of *The Cherry Orchard:* The old way of life is drawing to a close. The magnificent cherry trees on Madame Ranevskaya's estate no longer produce income. When she returns from Paris, she is over-whelmed by nostalgia and the orchard's beauty. But it's going on the block. Everyone has an unrealistic fantasy of how to save it. Lopakhin, the son of a for-mer serf on the estate, suggests selling parcels of land for summer cottages. But that would mean destroy-ing the orchard. His idea and warnings are ignored. Finally, he purchases the estate himself: in a total reversal, the landowners must move out, the entre-preneur takes over, and the sound of axes cutting down trees closes the play.
>
> —B.P.]

Each character in *The Cherry Orchard* has his own attitude toward the orchard. The old valet, Firs, says, "In the old days, forty or fifty years ago, the cherries were dried and preserved, made into jam. . . ." Everybody says, "Shut up, Firs," but he goes on: "Whole cartloads of cherries were sent to Moscow and Kharkov, and oh, the money they fetched! The cherries in those days were soft, juicy, sweet—they really knew how to do it then, they had a recipe. . . ." Is that very tragic? No. But it reveals his attitude. It is what the cherry orchard means for him.

Lopakhin says, "Up to recently there were only gentry and peasants living in the country, but now we have all these summer residents and all the towns, even small ones, are surrounded with villas. In the next twenty years, they will multiply tremendously. At present they only drink tea on the veranda, but they might start cultivating their land, and then your cherry orchard would be gay with life and wealth and luxury. . . ." What is his attitude toward the cherry orchard? To commercialize it. To make it into something else. Firs's is to wax nostalgic about the old days.

Now go to the attitude of Madame Ranevskaya: "Oh, my childhood, my innocence, I used to sleep in this nursery, used to look onto the orchard from here. Happiness woke with me every morning. Oh, my orchard! After the dark, stormy autumn and the cold winter, you are young and joyous again. If only this burden could be taken from me, if only I could forget the past. . . ."

So you get the three different attitudes. Hers is an aesthetic, poetic understanding of the orchard. She does not focus on the orchard being sold or how sad that this beauty will be taken from the world. That social aspect is non-Chekhovian. "Sold" and "bought" are not Chekhovian. What is Chekhovian is their utter inability to save the orchard. That is what makes it not about the defeat of the upper class and success of the middle class, but about this dream quality and Chekhovian sense of beauty.

You and I understand it differently from Chekhov. Chekhov understood, in every play, that the old way of life had to go. He was the prophet of that. He said it's going to go, there is no hope for it. Stanislavsky at first, in his interpretation of it, said, "It's such a tragedy that it's going." But Chekhov said, "No tragedy." No matter how deeply offending, it is nostalgically sad rather than tragic— it is poetically sad.

Gayev is not a tragic character. He is a patrician. I saw Stanislavsky play Gayev, and he was absolutely perfect—an elegant aristocrat, his gloves are put on for him, he never touches himself. When the young footman Yasha is insolent to him, annoys him and treats him as if he weren't the boss, he whines and complains to his sister and says, "I want you to choose between him and me."

It's a big moment, but it's ridiculous. Chekhov points out that Ranevskaya's character can never be subdued by suffering. Nothing but death could subdue her. Nothing can put her down. She is unrelated to anything. She has thrown away her life on trifles, which forms her comic essence. She is full of all kinds of trifles and sentiments. If you do not do this, you will just be playing the old outdated romantic concepts.

Comedy is not big laughs; it is something ludicrous in the character. Everyone here except the young daughter has something ludicrous in them. The real theme is not so tragic. Chekhov is telling you something not tragic but, rather, dismal. He is saying the Lopakhin types are taking over every cherry orchard they can get hold of, speculating on it, not only in Russia but everywhere. To Lopakhin, it's just business; to Ranevskaya, it's an aesthetic thing; to Firs, it's a cartload of something you sell. None of these three attitudes in the play are tragic.

Chekhov says Lopakhin is dressed in a white waistcoat and brown shoes, "walks along a straight line" and waves his hands, always deep in thought. He is not a merchant in the vulgar sense. He is full of his success, which is why he waves around. He is a self-made man who wants to do the right thing, but success has killed the artist in him and he walks around with a great sense of frustration. One character says of him that he has fine, sensitive hands. He is aware that these people have this "thing" about the cherry orchard and he says, "*Don't* keep it, because you can't afford it in life." By the end of the play he is absolutely wild, because he sees success facing him and that the orchard has to go. He's got the cherry orchard, but he feels in front of them that he has failed. He has this dual thing.

Get the social situation. In *Cherry Orchard*, the man who comes in and knocks down the trees is the same as the hired hand in *The Seagull* who says, "You can't have the carriage." It is the same vulgarity. Lopakhin is sensitive to this family and to the beauty and quality of their land, but he has killed this sense in himself. If he were tragic, the conflict would be active. But in the play, he really has no conflict and he goes ahead. That is what makes him funny— the absence of inner conflict. In the beginning, he genuinely tries to save the orchard, and in the end you have the Chekhovian reversal: he buys it. He is a rich businessman, yet in front of these people he always feels awkward. He says, "Why do I feel that? I could buy and sell them." Because he cannot get rid of the fact that he is a servant. This is funny, not tragic.

Lopakhin says, "Oh, Ohmelia, get thee to a nunnery." He can't say Ophelia, but he has enough of it to quote it. That is funny. He says, "I was reading a book, I don't even know what it was, but I fell asleep and missed the train because of the goddamn book." It's funny. When Varya says, "Don't joke about my engagement," he misinterprets what she says, like when two people are waltzing to different rhythms. He says another rich merchant is trying to buy the estate. So who is he competing with for the estate? With the family? With another merchant? He's not in competition with them, he's in competition with commerce. This is very twisted, reversed, Chekhovian.

When Ranevskaya comes in and sees the student, she says, "My God, how ugly you are." He says, "Yes, people say I look moth-eaten." Terribly amusing. Chekhov says whatever Dunyasha, the chambermaid, does, she does because she is a crybaby. Lopakhin in the opening scene says, "We haven't met for five years." She has been away that long. It is dawn, the cherry trees are in flower with the frost of the early morning, and there is something expectant. But this man doesn't relate to that. He says, "I'm a pig." A girl in a cold sweat is trembling and says, "I'm going to faint," and he says, "What's the matter with you? Sit down, behave like a servant. What are you sick about? It's not your business to be sick. It's your business to wait." He is very peasantlike with this servant.

Nothing belongs. That is Chekhov. Chekhov says the cherries and the frost don't go together. It is winter even in the summer here, and out of this Lopakhin makes no contact. He says, "I am full of rheumatism, there is frost, the cherries are blooming, and the goddamn birds are whistling." He is absolutely on edge. Yepikhodov has fallen asleep, and Lopakhin doesn't know why—he is mad. When Yepikhodov wakes up and comes over and says, "My shoes squeak," Lopakhin says, "Will you shut up! Who cares about that?"

The madness of coming over to him with a detail as repulsive as that is a great shock to Lopakhin.

Yepikhodov has fallen asleep over two chairs, but Dunyasha looks at him and says, "You know, he has proposed to me." You must understand this is very funny. She is in a sweat, her hands are trembling—what is she doing? A Chekhovian thing: she is explaining the character of the ridiculous man. "We call him Twenty-two Misfortunes," she says. "He's a schlemiel—oh, he's not bad, just ridiculous. Maybe I'll have to marry him." She is fainting, Lopakhin is bored to death, it's a wonderful situation.

The family's entrance is very funny. You cannot build a family that isn't funny with that entrance—especially with Ranevskaya's maid, Charlotta. Chekhov once visited a family with an English nurse and said, "I didn't know whether she was a boy or a girl." He based this asexual creature on her. When Ouspenskaya played Charlotta, she somersaulted in for her entrance with the dog and kept on going. Ranevskaya, who is like a child, travels with this meshuggah nurse who somersaults with a dog. Her brother plays billiards and is always thinking of what shot he could make. Her friend Pishchik's name means a bird's chirp-chirp. Nothing makes sense. The lunacy of this environment makes it impossible to call *The Cherry Orchard* a tragedy.

These people all talk at cross-purposes. As an actor, you must find out what these cross-purposes are. Charlotta is absolutely fatigued, she is with the dog, and she says to Ranevskaya, "I have something terrible to tell you: boy, am I tired." It's like talking to a drunk. This is exposition of the background, which no one sees. The foreground is about nothing. It is diverse and not direct. Lopakhin says, "Moooo . . ." That is the dramatic clincher to "The estate will be sold." He sticks his head in and moos, and he buys the estate. That is funny. The devil is presented as not being a serious menace.

The Russian character who hasn't a cent and spends for a banquet is easy for me to understand. My mother had nothing and went out and bought the most expensive rug in America. "It costs $4,800? So I'll buy two." The intellectual aristocrats used money to cultivate themselves. But in a materialistic society, you don't use money for culture, you use it for more *things,* more money. We are bankrupt in America because it is not used for culture. That is the last thing we use money for.

Ranevskaya stayed five years in Paris; she lost her child, her husband. Now she comes in with this crazy entourage and acts like a little girl, but she is the only grown-up person here. She is the mother, the one in the end who says, "I am going out after a new life, I don't care about the cherry orchard." In Chekhov, what is nostalgic is what they live off. They don't have movies, telephones, pressure cookers. It's "The sun is going up, the birds are whistling, the cherry blossoms are blooming, twenty years ago we were children. . . ." Don't pretend. Read simply. Ranevskaya needs her coffee, her flowers, her little delights. On her small level, she is a life force. She is very Russian. She puts cream in her coffee and cries into it and wipes her eyes. Don't make it too sad. Chekhov and Stanislavsky make you invent a technique in which the actress has no mask. Gayev tells her the nurse died while she was away; he talks about death while he eats his caramels. It's part of the nostalgia. "Our nurse is dead, but we're alive and the cherry orchard is here and I'm so happy I could die." They are two children happy to be back in their nursery.

She picks up an old doll, he is eating caramels, the birds are singing, the wind is blowing, Lopakhin is saying, "You cut up the land into fourteen—" They're tired, they've been up all night, but Lopakhin is very clear-headed, talking about cutting the property up, and it is very comic. It's like someone talking to me about stocks and bonds. I have been told about money for forty years and I could never listen to the end, it's too confusing. Ranevskaya can't follow that business thing, but she gets that the orchard is going to be cut down and asks, "Why?"

She is giving him the aesthetic thing. This kills him. He sees the light in her eyes and he could cry, but what can he do? She brings you the aesthetic picture; he brings you the encyclopedia. Between the encyclopedia and the aesthetic thing, he is a goner. Don't play the direct action. Lopakhin's thing is "I have got to make clear to them what is happening." He wants to get out of it, but they just think he is crazy. He is stuck there with the perfume of her being there. This man is trapped.

The brother can't work, can't do anything. The uncle in *The Seagull* wasn't allowed to work. They are paralyzed. Baron Tuzenbakh in *Three Sisters* tells you how he was dressed, his socks were put on for him. He is exhausted by his background, by being taken care of. All his life he has been made to feel, "I can't take my own shoes off; somebody has to do it for me." In *Cherry Orchard,* the brother's servant runs to him with his overcoat and says to this man of sixty-five "You forgot your coat" and treats him like a child. He is impotent. It's like the South in Tennessee Williams—the downfall of the aristocracy. In *Three Sisters,* Tuzenbakh loves Irina, but not like a man. He loves her like a spirit. Where does his impotence come from? He never was allowed to grow from boyhood to manhood. In the aristocracy you get a great deal of this overdelicate refinement. "I can philosophize, but somebody has to put my coat on." In *Cherry Orchard,* Gayev is like that. The porter says, "You haven't put on your coat, bad boy!" That is not very good for a man of sixty-five.

There was a tremendous upheaval in the privileged classes. The estates ran down. They couldn't work it out. There was nowhere to go, no trains or cars. You were stuck. Chekhov writes not about these big things but about people who sit and say, "Have them change the water. . . . By the way, I wanted to tell you about a picture. Where is it? Here it is. . . ." He goes into a million trivialities. I once tried to live like this for an hour. I walked out and noticed the thing you wipe your feet on was so muddy. And who put those stones there? I never noticed them before. I don't know about the stones. They must have come from that boy next door. . . . I have to do something about him. Now, what did I come out for? Oh, yes, I wanted to sunbathe. Is the sun out? That is life. And Chekhov is able from this trivial life to become the poet of all time.

If you don't pray and you don't have a sense that you are being uplifted in your work, if the work becomes monotonous and you have to do it every day, it wears down your spirit. If there is nothing in the society to build you up, people get run-down. When you wait on tables, you get worn out. He recognizes this and says it is sad, but it can't be helped. He understands that and goes to something else. He says that you must find a way.

In one of his short stories, Chekhov has a man who rows people from one bank of a river to the other.* People get in the little boat, pay him a penny, and he rows them across, which takes about four minutes. When he gets there, they get out and other people get in, give him a penny, and he rows back. He does this for forty-five

*"V sylke" [In Exile], written in 1892.

years—back and forth in his little boat. It's always the same thing, crosses from here to there. Chekhov says, what can you do for this man? Up and down for forty-five years. What is going to replenish him? What is going to save his humanity from dying out? What is going to lift him up?

He says that is a bad situation, but that in the middle class we do something worse. We make more money and then we eat more and buy more clothes. Your appetites five years later are more filled. You eat a little more and drink a little more and play cards a little more and watch television more. This is our life—more appetite, more clothes, more drink. He says the man proportionately dies. So when we meet men of sixty and seventy, they are not really men anymore, because they gave up long ago on fighting through to some real evaluation of themselves.

Almost everybody I know, man or woman, by the time they reach fifty they are completely worn out. It's gone. I see it. I see it in my friends. A kind of nothing has happened to them. Nothing has reached out to them. They didn't know where to go, so they eat more and they have more money and buy more clothes and go to Saks more. "Let's watch some more television—why not?" You do it at thirty, you do it at sixty.

This kind of life is what Chekhov sees. His dialogue is not the way we speak. It is not vernacular. The seeming naturalness of the dialogue is spoken by people of a high intellectual class, landowners. Watch yourself when you read it—don't go to *your* fatigue. Go to the fatigue of the spirit. Peasants are closer to you when they are tired. People who are trained never to bend their backs, always to walk straight with a certain deportment—they don't get the way we get. When they become old and can't walk, they don't get like the peasant.

Listen to this:

RANEVSKAYA: Why on earth did I go out to lunch? That disgusting restaurant of yours with its stupid band, and those tablecloths smelling of soap. Why did you have to drink so much, Leonide? Or talk so much? You kept talking in the restaurant today about the seventies and the deca-dents—and to whom? Talking about the decadents to the waiters!

YEPIKHODOV: Apart from everything else, what I ought to say about myself is that Fate treats me without mercy, like a storm on a small boat. . . . Why should I wake up this morning and suddenly find a spider of enormous dimensions on my chest? Or pick up a jug of kvass and find something quite outrageously indecent in it, like a cockroach.

These two speeches will give you more Chekhov than any explanation. People have to talk and so, intellectually, who are they going to talk to? Each one is so isolated. They live so far from everything. There are only the peasants and one or two servants who wait on them in the house.

Yepikhodov is complaining about his fate as a servant. He has a lot of character business, the way he speaks and sings and plays the guitar. His complaint about fate is not pedestrian. There is something charming about his complaint. There is something about Ranevskaya not liking it. There is also something charming about the way she complains about her brother: He talks too much, eats too much, drinks too much. When you have no work, you do that. It is downhill for them.

Chekhov says they have great elegance, childishness, and simplicity, they are the most beautiful people in the world, but they will never come again. Ranevskaya is charming, gorgeous, and silly. She has had a silly life. Things got difficult and she did what she had to do, adjusted to the difficulty. This is very Russian. They are not like us—they are demonstrative. They kiss and hold each other, reach out. They are very physical in their expressions. It is not Russian to say, "Oh, God, I'm poor now, what'll I do?"—not in that class. It is very Russian to say, "Here's my jewelry, take it!"

It is the ability not to solve a problem. It is a kind of fragility.

In her last scene and farewell to the orchard, Ranevskaya's daughter Anya says, "A new life is beginning." Gayev says, "Before the orchard was sold we were worried, we were wretched, but now that the question is settled irrevocably, we feel calm and even cheerful." Ranevskaya says, "You know, it's true, my nerves are better, I'm sleeping well, I'm going to Paris to live on the money Auntie sent to buy the estate." Is she devastated? She says, "Get me my galoshes and let's go to Paris and spend the money, I'm going back to my lover. . . ." She might cry a little, but she's hardly annihilated. Anya is looking forward to a new life. Gayev is looking forward to being a bank clerk, which is ridiculous. So, actually, the cherry orchard is not a fatal loss, only an aesthetic loss. It is not really so dramatic. This new way of life doesn't kill them. They are all fine.

The theme of Chekhov is the destruction of beauty in the world, which is always sad. We go past a lovely old building being torn down and we say, "Oh, I remember when I was a little girl, that lovely old Vanderbilt house—it can't be, my whole life is in that, my father and I used to see it every day on the way to the park. . . ." But it is not really tragic. It is nostalgic. It is a memory.

Cherry Orchard is the funniest Chekhov play of them all.

ELEVEN

THREE SISTERS

WITH *Three Sisters,* you will see another side of Chekhov and Stanislavsky. In breaking down and understanding Chekhov, don't be dumbheads. There are two sides to an art form called the drama. There is the literary side. Chekhov, Tolstoy, Ibsen, Shakespeare—that is literature. That side is not the actor who gives a show. The actor's part of the art form is called the histrionic side. That's when you put the playwright away and shut the book, and you have an audience, a stage, a director, lights, scenery, costumes. What do you call all that? You call that the interpretation.

Chekhov lived down south on the Black Sea. He didn't live in Moscow with the Moscow Art Theater and the circle of actors. There was an awful lot that he didn't know about that. That is why Stanislavsky said, "I have to *do* something with him," and created the most important theatrical movement of the century. The realistic form was the biggest thing that happened to the theater in two thousand years. It was desperately needed, because the society had changed, the audience changed, the way you got to the theater changed—everything changed.

In Chekhov, somebody always comes in and gives you the news of someone else who's coming in, and what he is like. From what one person thinks of the other person, you can gather a lot. In Chekhov, you don't come in to find out what you do. You come in *knowing* where you are going and how it is going to affect you. Don't come with *your* situation into a different situation which you must anticipate. That is the extreme need. Your acting is kindergarten unless you do this. It is naive, boring, ignorant, vulgar. It is like playing the "Moonlight" Sonata with someone singing along and telling you what it is—*da-da-dum-da-da*. . . .

You must bring something in. How do you do that? Each character has a past. Know it and build up the difficulty. If you don't, you are a dope. Get out of the acting business. There are easier ways to make a living. The Greeks chose the drama as their main art and communication form because it was better. Why? Because it is easier to convey an idea to people who listen than to people who read. Reading is a more difficult way to awaken. Acting, theater, is the most extreme form to awaken an audience into understanding itself through the problems in the play. It has been a very popular form.

But if you don't find and take that thing that excites you, the maximum choice of what makes you experience, you are just adding fiction to fiction. The adding of the imagination is the adding of the maximum choice to excite. We say, "Oh, it's such a sunny day," but we lie. In life, we lie. You can't do that on stage. If you take somebody that's never seen the ocean and show it to them, they say, "Oh, my God!" But the hundredth time they see it, they say, "Oh, yeah, an ocean."

Life runs you down. Which is why art must not. Do not take the dead experience. Take the imaginative thing of the sun shining in on a house that is not *your* house, on sisters who aren't *your* sisters. Then your whole imagination will start working and grow. It is very hard to give up life for art.

There's a Chekhov story in which a man is offered two million rubles if for fifteen years he never opens his mouth.* He's put into a cell, never speaks to anybody. In the fifteenth year when they let him out—he refuses the money. He says, "I don't need it. I have learned all about music, literature, poetry, art. I am so full." It is Chekhov speaking of the ability not to be pedestrian in the pedestrian life.

If I say to you as actor, "Here's $100,000 and your own gasoline station—but don't ever open your mouth about the theater," you'd have to think about it. You'd say, "Hmmm . . . $100,000 is a lot of money"—especially if you lived outside of Milwaukee, where there are cars and supermarkets but not a really stimulating environment. People who live in New York have a feeling that it's better here than it is outside of Milwaukee.

*"Pari" [The Wager], written in 1889.

The sense of what we have in New York is what the three sisters have about Moscow. It's the opposite of a small, drab town six miles from the station in 1901. In three hundred years, not one artist or philosopher has come out of it. It's a place without intellectual stimulation. If you play the piano beautifully, who are you going to play for? It's a trap. You've seen rats caught in a trap. There's no way to escape, but they still run around, against all of their animal logic, and try to get out.

Once I rented a house in Antibes for the summer, but when I realized I'd have to be there for three whole months, it became a trap for me. I'd go to bed thinking, "I've put all this money in for the summer, and now I'm trapped in this house with the French servant girl and . . ." There was no way I could leave the bloody place. I just felt I couldn't leave.

That's how the three sisters feel: trapped. They were born in Moscow, but their father took them to live in a provincial town three hundred miles away. The seagull got killed because it wandered away from its base, where it could survive. It belonged to the sea, not a lake. Here the symbol is Moscow. It is not a city. It is an idea to which you can attach hope.

Our country is made up of immigrants. The idealism of getting to America is not to be believed. America's streets were paved with gold. People idealized the coming to America. I wouldn't want to come to America now. I think it's vulgar and ugly and brutal and you can't walk safely in the streets. But it used to be like Moscow— a symbol—like New York is for people who live in Idaho. The emptiness there must be awful. You hear the drunkards, see the lack of education. It's not like New York. It's rough.

There is a thing in many people that makes them say, "If I don't go, I'll die." Emigrés have this. So the thing about Moscow has nothing to do with the reality. It is not dancing that they want. It's that something in their souls will be happy, will be restored. "I have to go—I just have to."

Moscow is a dream. In a dream you will be loved, you'll be happy, you'll meet the man. The dream is an ideal. An idealist does not see the truth, only his illusion of the truth. He fixates on it. The sisters think it's only "here" where there is such boredom and claustrophobia. Against the magnificence of Moscow, everything seems trivial and diminished. The quest grows more and more until it's an outcry: "We've *got* to get there to save ourselves. We will do *anything* to get there!"

So the Moscow thing is big. It is much bigger than "I'll marry and be happy"—that pedestrian stuff. Not just, "I want my guy. I want a husband." I never wanted to be with husbands and wives because it's so boring. They're so together, you can tie a string around them. There is no expansion. Young Mrs. Rockefeller—she married a second cousin of mine—once said to me, "We just read a book." I said, "What do you mean, 'we?' People don't read a book *together.*"

So don't make it that lousy little twosome when you say, "I want to go to Moscow." It's, "I want my soul to expand. I want to be a human being again through love. I want to meet my own love and my own soul and be a human being again, through loving a man, through being in the streets where my mother is buried."

[Synopsis of *Three Sisters:* The Three Sisters are really the Four Siblings—Olga, Masha, Irina, and brother Andrei Prozorov. Their provincial estate is a salon for the aristocratic officers of a military brigade stationed there, a remnant of their late father's glory days as a general in Moscow, where they grew up. No sisters could be closer or more dissimilar than Olga, the teacher and surrogate mother; Masha, the married, disillusioned pianist; and Irina, the young innocent. They long for Moscow, and for love. Major Vershinin and Baron Tuzenbakh provide it briefly. Old Dr. Chebutykin provides comic relief and perspective. Andrei's slutty wife, Natasha, provides the vulgarity that wrecks their domestic peace. Life itself provides the frustration of their illusory dream—Moscow!

—B.P.]

Chekhov wanted to give you how life goes. He's the only one who wanted that. He didn't want to do what he did with the earlier plays—melodrama and all. In *Three Sisters,* which is his masterpiece, what is emphasized is not what happens. Nothing really happens. It is the tension. Underneath the tension of "I want to do this or that," and "I love her but she doesn't love me," there are no resolutions.

Stanislavsky's notes on *Three Sisters* make you understand, first of all, the importance of the seasons. The play opens with a joyous Spring—all the mice and the human hearts are jumping around— and ends in a melancholy Autumn. Chekhov builds from joy into deep thinking. Spring means happiness. You walk in the park, boys and girls get together, you go rowing. The feelings come out of the doing, and the doing comes out of the experience you take. If I'm rowing with the ducks in the pond and the other people rowing there are throwing us the new cherries they've just picked—I'm all right as an actor. Then I have a place. Mine.

In the Prozorovs' house is what used to be a large ballroom with columns, which is now divided into a drawing room in front and a dining room. It is not like *your* dining room. It is a big room where people dine and play cards and discuss things. There is a piano in the corner. In front there's a table and chairs and settees and commodes where they keep china and beautiful things. You can sit at the piano or lean on it when you talk. You can play the piano and then get up and talk. You're very frontal. You have areas, space.

What kind of people occupy this space? The most important aristocratic group in Russia then: military people. They were the most educated, most brilliant, and most lawful element of that society. My parents were Russian, and my mother fell in love with the old man because he was wearing a uniform. My mother sat like Arkadina. Nobody could touch her. She once told me, "You'll never find a man in America. Go to Russia and find a man in a uniform. You don't marry a man without a uniform." Years later, I was on a train from Moscow to Leningrad and for Christ's sake, a general walked in. Such bearing! The Russians still have that—even Brezhnev. When he puts on the uniform, he doesn't carry jelly beans. The uniform is such an emblem. The army has the larger sense of Russia. It has size.

So understand that if the sisters marry a pedantic schoolteacher or a baron who is milky white and sleepy and elegant but not really masculine—they aren't good enough for these girls. When an actor gets that and gets information about a character's past, he can do things. If someone calls Vershinin "the lovesick major," you know he's a kind of romantic idealist. If you get that and you're playing Vershinin, you will not come in without paying attention to women. He sees Masha and Irina and says, "There were three sisters. . . ." He wants to know, "Where's the other girl?" Men know about girls—whether there are two or four, whether they're nice. If not, they're businessmen.

What I am trying to tell you is that when you get a clue about your character, eat it, swallow it, develop it. Every Chekhov play depends on the actors. That is why he needed Stanislavsky to bring these three sisters and their brother to life. Their mother has been dead for ten years. Their lives are built on the deepest pain—the loss of their father, the general. Each one is in tremendous pain about something.

Find out what.

Olga, the eldest, is twenty-eight but looks forty-eight. She became a teacher, lost her youth, works day and night, comes home, takes care of the house. She is without a romance or a moment of relief. Her mother and father died and she became the maternal figure. The maternal figure can love somebody else's child just as strongly as the real mother. You can love somebody else's dog, too. I wish you'd cure me of that habit. I stop everybody with a dog and nobody likes it. Anyway, someone had to look after the two younger ones, so Olga brought them up and ran the household. How does she feel about Masha and Irina? How do they feel about her? These sisters are so entwined—a symbol of family life and togetherness. But they have secrets, secrets! You can only find out how they feel by what they do.

Irina is the youngest, just twenty, hardly knew her mother. Olga's attitude towards her littlest sister is "I brought you up, I dressed you, I know you totally, you're an angel, you're so beautiful." It is full of love but full of pain because there is no hope, and Olga knows that. How can she get Irina away to Moscow? There's tremendous pain when you love somebody and you see they are failing.

Masha feels Olga is lost, too. "I am sick when I see Olga, and I'm whistling with pain because Olga is still so brave even though she knows there is no escape for any of us."

Masha sits there in black whistling, because she has died already. She's revived by love for a few hours and then she dies again. Where can Masha go? She's married. You didn't divorce in those days. She is married to a very educated boy. Who isn't? He is middle-class, boring, intellectual. A man who gives you a lot of information is a bore. It doesn't matter what information he gives you. If that is his tendency, he's finished. He is not a match for Masha.

Masha grew up in Moscow, she is educated, she knows three or four languages. She's a concert pianist, but she doesn't play anymore. She gave it up. You start to wear black when you give up your art. There's nobody to play for in this town. At eighteen, she married a teacher in his middle thirties. There was bound to be friction. You mustn't mix the classes. Should Blanche DuBois's sister have married Stanley Kowalski?

Masha is the sister who is the mystery. You cannot reach her. You can't reach the artist. There is no logical way. Keep her in a special pocket of feelings that are complex and different. She smokes. She is very direct. She says, "Shut up!" The others never heard such a thing. She says, "Give me a drink!" Her husband says, "Two marks for bad conduct." Either she will become a drunk or kill herself or, as you will see in the last act, she will have understood love for the first time, which will give her at least something that very few people get. Irina will never have it. Olga will never have it. But Masha has some one thing that reaches her and might make her survive.

Vershinin is a romantic idealist. Masha likes and needs that. He is a cultured army man of good habits, and she has never been made love to by someone like that. See how good men relate to women, how free they are. Vershinin says, "Darling, my soul is so full of love—I love you." Love loves love. That's Chekhov and that's the society. American men don't dare be that free, and it's pretty boring to be with them. Not *pretty* boring; it's *killing*. Something happened in America that messes you up and makes you want to get into bed right away.

This is not the bedroom. The love in *Three Sisters* is not on the level of sex. It is not "I want to feel between your legs and touch you immediately." It is not in that society to touch. You don't do that right away. For God's sake, learn this.

When Vershinin speaks to Masha, he's so crazy in love. When he speaks to Olga, he understands her sweetness. He loves the house because Olga keeps it like that. The difference between Vershinin and the other men is that he is the only one who is a father, who notices children and girls and falls in love. "I love my daughter— and this daughter, too." He has the aliveness of being involved with family life.

Baron Tuzenbakh is a romantic, too, but more like Byron. Byron needed to be heroic. He was the aristocratic Lord Byron, and England bored the hell out of him. So he slept with his sister, with Italian girls, Spanish—anything but a proper Englishwoman. He loathed their coldness. His inner fire led him away from England and into some crazy war between the Turks and the Greeks. This great man went and got himself killed in Greece for nothing. It was a truly aristocratic gesture. Byron truly loved. "When we two parted in silence, tears half broken-hearted to sever, cold brood I kiss. . . ." What are you going to do with a poet? Put some of that great elegance into Tuzenbakh. The Baron has that. "I will work in the brick works, I will really love." When he says "I love you" to Irina, it is different from the way anybody else in the world says it. It's like a poem.

The real aristocracy doesn't care about much, but it cares about being first-class in manners, mind, and taste. The Baron says, "When the singers come, I'll play all that rotten stuff people like." He's a classical musician. He'll play the junk if they want him to, but it's a first-class mind.

Yet he has been exhausted by his background, by being made a child, taken care of. All his life he has been made to feel "I can't take my shoes off; somebody has to do it for me." He is now thirty-five and still in his baronial house with four servants. He feels that impotence. He loves Irina. But he doesn't love her like a woman. He loves her like a spirit. He never was allowed to go from childhood to adolescence to manhood. He loves her with such purity. He's so above it all. That's why you have Solyony—all physical, as if he wanted to eat her. Irina is revolted by him. But she can't respond to the Baron, either. The Baron, knowing that, doesn't mind dying, doesn't even try to prevent it, because he feels "I can't really give her what she wants." Your clarity of the Baron has to be "I am what I am. I can philosophize very well, but somebody has to put my coat on."

Vershinin, too, has the habit of philosophizing—of saying, "Well, if there's no tea, then let's talk about the future." A Russian upper-class army officer has a sense of moral justice and order. He can't run away with a married girl and leave his wife and children. He is the symbol of his army. When his army has to go, he says goodbye and goes. He and Tuzenbakh each have their own way of saying, "It might not be better for us but someday it will be better for someone." At any rate, they discuss life, which is one of the things a man of culture does.

That is very interesting. When the Kennedy boys sat down to lunch, their mother, Rose, wrote down on a blackboard what the topic was going to be at the table. They were not brought up to say "Gimme some more." They were brought up to discuss a theme or analyze something to do with government or culture. It came from the cultural makeup of that mother. The old man was a lech, but he was going to have sons who would be senators and Presidents. He knew it and he built it and he paid for it and he did it. So don't knock it. His boys were pretty good men in history.

Chekhov says a man of that class and quality is not static. They have a social sense of living in a world they want to be better. The Baron has the social sense to say, "I was brought up to be useless, but I'm going to work in a brick factory because I feel every man should work. It may take three hundred years, but something will rub off to improve this corner of the world."

Vershinin feels that when the lower classes start moving up, everybody will be happier. That was a mistake. It was Shaw's mistake, too. In *Man and Superman* Shaw says man, if given the chance to rise and enough money, will use his free hours not to go to the ball game but to educate himself. Mr. Shaw lost. It was a mistake of socialism to think money would raise the masses. It doesn't. When the working class gets a car, it wants two cars. It just wants more money and more comfort. You must accept their vulgarity because they don't want to change.

The greatest example is Natasha—Andrei's wife.

Understand that the sisters can associate with a soldier who comes in, fences brilliantly, is impeccable in his behavior, because he's a military officer like their father, which means learning and discipline. But brother Andrei got fatigued. He wasn't of his father's or his sisters' mettle. In Chekhov, you either survive by the iron in your blood or you don't. Not everybody has the guts to pull through.

Andrei is the Oblomov type. Ask any Russian if he knows Oblomov, and he'll say, "Certainly—the Russian guy who's always tired and immediately gives up." He is not driven like an American man. No one is as driven as that. The Oblomovs are exhausted by the situation, drained of their vitality, and surrender without a fight.

That's Andrei. The few women in this small town are mostly middle-class girls looking to better themselves. A general's son does not usually mingle with that class. In *Anna Christie,* a Catholic sailor falls in love with a syphilitic whore and says, "I'm going to marry you," but you know he can't. He can't give up the Catholic thing and marry a whore. It is the height of foolishness to think that will work. Andrei, because of his lack of energy, is sexually attracted to the most common girl, marries her, has kids, and becomes a zero as a human being.

Natasha is utterly vulgar. Olga says to her, "You mustn't wear that green sash, dear, it's not right." Like me in Paris, when the dressmaker was so appalled by the shades I wanted. The French are brought up with a sense of color. Natasha is like me. She comes in with a loud green sash and it throws off the whole party. Natasha has no values. She's a provincial who comes into the house of a general's son. She's frightened. But she's a climber. Once he marries her, she becomes a despot because she knows how to climb. I want you to know the climber because you're very close to her. Aren't we all?

Chekhov's point on marriage is that it's no use producing children if the mother is so vulgar, because the next generation will have this same vulgarity. She's shrewd, loud, selfish. All through the play, Natasha's vulgarity grows. She has no feeling for anything but her body and her children. All she can talk about are those dreadful kids.

The cultivated class doesn't know how to combat this.

The Prozorov sisters take care of their servants, for example. When old Anfisa walks slowly, Olga understands and pets her because she's been there fifty years. What else is she going to do with her? But Natasha says, "Don't you dare sit down in my presence!" She takes on what she thinks are aristocratic ways. "I have money now, I pay the servants, and that gives me power. Don't you sit in front of my power! This crazy old crippled peasant woman—take her away!" When Olga hears this in the third act, she is absolutely undone by it.

Natasha is stupid but she's strong. She gets what she wants. The sisters are too well bred to defend themselves against her vulgarity. She becomes head of the household much like Lopakhin buys the cherry orchard, and for much the same reason: in the last act, Natasha announces that when the sisters leave, she's going to knock down all the trees.

Tennessee Williams uses his genius to deal with similar people in the aristocratic collapse of the South. He is very much with what he considers the best people, who are going down. He goes to the mixture of people until he gets to Kowalski and Blanche. Kowalski is the lowest form, very much like Natasha.

Chekhov mixes Natasha with the one who could have been a great professor in Moscow. In the last act, when Andrei finally sees that the nice middle-class girl he married is a dreadful, opportunistic liar, he too picks up the hopeless refrain: "If only I could break away, go to Moscow. . . ."

The one happy person who has no desire to go to Moscow is Masha's husband, Kuligin. Masha, an artist, was trapped in this small town by the intellect of a teacher. We know what Chekhov thinks about them: a teacher is a person who learned but who has no life. Kuligin is a nice man, but when he hears her play he says, "Jesus, that's different from making money." He's very puzzled by Masha. When he speaks, bring in that puzzlement. He says, "I love her, she's so lovely, but what was she doing out all night?" He sees Masha play a score without studying it, then throw the score out the window. He wonders, "What is this work of art doing with my stupidity?" You see Chekhov's attitude towards academic life in Kuligin, who has the habit of illogic. If you talked about art, he would talk about the state of the union. His interruptions never express anything important.

Masha married a stupid man who can't match her feelings. She is very destructive toward almost everybody. An artist often is. She'd destroy a home, throw out the baby with the water. She's working from a source nobody understands. Freud said we can touch everything but the artist. We don't know where it comes from or how to deal with it, so leave it alone. Don't monkey with the artist. Don't say, "You know, it would be nice if you led a normal life" to Van Gogh. He has one ear. I'd like you to see me when I'm myself, acting, not all dressed up for you like now. When I act, nobody can be near me, talk to me, even say hello. People hated me. I hated people. The moment I work, I'm not nice at all, because what I work with is the demon in me.

The real demon in *Three Sisters* is Solyony. I want very much for you to get the important types Chekhov gives you. Andrei as Oblomov is one. Solyony is another—the neurotic, serpentine, satanic type that runs through Russian life and literature, in Dostoyevsky especially. He has a desperate quality. He duels brilliantly and is very disagreeable and dangerous, always quarreling and saying something rude, nasty, and against the atmosphere. He is Moscow—he has that Asiatic, Byzantine quality even the churches have there. He is constantly at Tuzenbakh. He has that Brezhnev quality to fight, to kill.

Baron Tuzenbakh is St. Petersburg. European. They spoke French there—very different from Moscow. People like the Baron don't fight with people of lesser caliber and intelligence.

When Marlon Brando first did Stanley Kowalski, he broke the body and broke everything—he was the first to do it that way. Everybody imitated him. Solyony is the Russian equivalent of a Kowalski. Solyony is a problem for an actor, but Chekhov gives every character his particular habits that help. In Solyony's case, it's a thing with washing his hands. Solyony carries around a bottle of perfume and talks and then wipes his hands.

That habit of washing with cologne is interesting to develop. It's funny. Neil Simon is madly in love with Russian literature, and he wrote a kind of old Yiddish play from another era [*The Good Doctor,* 1973]. He took it from Chekhov. And in *Last of the Red Hot Lovers,* he has a character constantly smelling his hands. He knows where to steal.

Solyony and Tuzenbakh are both in love with Irina. They make up one of the important trios. The play is about trios. The sisters themselves, of course, are the main one. Kuligin, Vershinin, and Masha are another. Andrei, Natasha, and her offstage lover Protopopov are another. When one triangle goes off, another one comes in and develops. Each of these triangles is complex and unsolvable. They make for a very complex play.

Scene Analysis

In the first act, we get a certain breadth from the indirect action. Somebody says something and nobody listens. That is prevalent in life. Chekhov doesn't want a play, he wants what happens in life. In life, people don't usually kill each other. They talk. So he has created what is called the truth-of-the-scene type of play. He is original in that. He writes a scene which has nothing to do with the next scene, which has nothing to do with the next one. You will have six characters and five of them will not really care or hear or understand what you are saying. But don't choke your partner. Don't come in without a definite relationship to those other characters. What is indirect in the scene? What is your relation to the others? What is the particular difference between you and them?

Get used to understanding how this particular author is applied. Get the ability through Chekhov to open up a monologue. The big monologue is no longer a soliloquy. It has another modern function. The old soliloquy is only done by the giants of royalty. If you are the king's stepson, you do a soliloquy: "Thy suffering is not unique in the world. Suffering has been here since mankind was born. . . ." You don't say that to a real person. Regular people don't chat like that.

The modern large monologue is a way in which you unashamedly talk about your inner self. It is the inner revelation of the actor. It is self-revelation. But it can also be discursive, as when Konstantin says, "I believe a new literature is coming which will not be filled with cheap morality." That is no longer revelation. That is thematic material about ideas.

You have to have some brains. When you get to this epic thing that the playwright says through you in a modern play, let it rise. Chekhov understood that you are unrelated in what you say and nobody really knows what you are talking about. I, for instance, when somebody comes in and says, "The Yankees really just . . ." I don't know whether they won or they lost. I don't deal with sports. It passes through me. Or somebody says, "Did you catch the news on TV?" Four people are there, one is talking about mathematics, one is eating, the other one is . . . This goes on all the time in Chekhov. He builds a play as a series of small scenes, which is how we live in life. He didn't construe one thing to fit the next. On the contrary, he said, "This thing does *not* fit the next thing." You never really catch up to the first thing. In life, you pass a morning in small scenes.

ACT I, SCENE I:
OLGA'S OPENING MONOLOGUE

This is an upper-aristocratic house with a ballroom. On the piano are pictures of Mother and Father, and sheet music. The sisters all play the piano. The brother plays violin. Music is in the family. There is a great big clock. In the corner are billiard sticks—you might pick up a billiard stick and do something very charming with it. There's a samovar, books, flowers. The flowers are mentioned often, which gives you a key to the lyrical quality of these three girls. There's a big portrait of the father in uniform and his sword is underneath.

The props are right for the class. You have cigarettes. Masha smokes. You have a chess table where Solyony and Tuzenbakh play.

On the dining-room table there is lots of shining silverware, set for lunch. Lunchtime is no time to weep very much. You can weep a little, but it's not the hour for hysteria. Right away you get lunch, birthday cake, guests, presents, celebration. But you also get Olga's opening monologue:

"Father died a year ago on the fifth of May, your name day, Irina. It was very cold and it was snowing. I thought I would never live through it. But now a year has passed and we can talk of it freely and your face is beaming. . . ."

A Moscow Art Theater director told me he couldn't make the actress playing Olga do the speech right. He could not get her to say it without tears. Even the Moscow Art Theater man could not get an actress to understand she couldn't cry, because a year has passed. The play is built on pain, but for now it is over.

The first act is in sunshine. If it's sunshine, you don't play tears or "I'm so tired." Irina looks out and for the first time she *sees:* "The weather is beautiful today. My heart is so light. I saw the bubbles in my bath, the colors in them. I heard the birds. I remembered it was my birthday and suddenly I felt happy. I'm twenty, I have life, my heart doesn't hurt so much now. I remember when I was a child and Mother was alive."

See the mother picking her up and running in the garden with her. She had curls. Running together. This is all in the background: see it and experience it. "Such wonderful thoughts kept coming to me. Thoughts that I want to work. I won't be lazy. I will do something with my life." The background must be expanded. You must get to where you remember your mother in a *place* you remember. The place you choose must give you joy. If it doesn't give you joy, choose something else. "Mother was trying to catch me running up the stairs and I fell and she fell down with me. . . ." Choose something that gives it to you. There is no fun choosing something that doesn't have radiance.

Moscow is brilliant and big and beautiful in their minds in a thousand ways. At the opera, the whole audience got up when the general walked in, because he was the safeguard of Moscow.

You must embroider. These girls know what their Moscow was like in spring. Moscow was flowers and birds and visitors and music. This is what they had and this is what they want.

Olga says, "We almost died, but now it's spring." Irina says, "It's my birthday and I feel happy." The only person who doesn't feel happy is Masha. Masha is in black. She's not mourning her father. She's mourning the death of her soul. When you mourn, you see nothing. You look at a person or a tree or a summer day, but it doesn't register, because your soul has been so deeply wounded. Death does this, takes the life away from you. That is mourning. When the widow greets you at a funeral parlor, see how much life there is in her. She says, "Hello, nice of you to come." But she doesn't really see you. When you lose what you really love, whether it is a husband or a child or an animal, there is a time element during which life disappears.

But now it's "My God, I'm free! I see that it's spring. Isn't it wonderful?" You hold your heart and rejoice. You're not hurting so much anymore. That is how Olga says, "Father died a year ago—in spring, just like now. . . ." She remembers how cold it was, how downcast all the soldiers were, her agony when she bent over that earth that was thrown on him and thought she would never live through it. But *now* . . . You felt it, but now you are free from it. It is like having a severed finger put back on: "When I saw that finger lying there—oh, my God, no, no! I saw it there and it was so horrible, but now it's back. . . ."

Olga is alive again, seeing life in addition to memory, and trying to re-create it with all her tiredness. Why is she doing this? *Because she wants Masha to see, too.* Masha is dead. She is trying to awaken Masha. She is getting Irina to feel it, but she cannot get to Masha. Nobody can. But Olga is trying. *Masha must stop wearing black.* Olga's point is not "I Remember Papa," but that it would be a good thing for Masha to face it. "Masha, remember how happy we were?" Not how happy *Olga* was. I'm now reading in: "Father would come home with his whole staff, and so much was always going on. The light from our house lit up half of Moscow. He had such joy in life, and he wanted us to know that life would bloom for us, too. When Mother died, he took the three of us and said, 'You will live and be as beautiful and happy as your mother was when I married her.' Papa didn't want you to wear black all your life. He wanted you to go on."

Olga is saying, "I am tied to you. My life depends on your getting well. Don't do this, Masha. Don't discard your life. Don't hurt yourself. Don't hurt us. I'm in trouble, too, but I am trying to fight it. I'm at school every day, headaches all the time—I look like an old woman but I'm trying to keep up." She is trying to uplift and hold everyone together.

Get some fun out of Chekhov. When Olga says, "Look at me, not the beauty I was!" have her go over and pose next to Irina for comparison. "I feel my youth going out drop by drop but, Masha, listen—" have her pull Irina over to Masha—"we have our dream left. We'll wind up everything here and go to Moscow! Yes, Masha, Moscow! Andrei will be a professor there!" And they all three laugh with the joy of that wonderful thought.

That is the sense of it. You must build it. You don't play it for what it *says*. You play it for the reasons you bring in. If not, you're just bums. I am giving you the real Stanislavsky technique. It works. How he influenced me—I will never again play a part without relating to the other people. How boring you are if you don't do this. He created the technique for Chekhov and every realistic playwright thereafter—Miller, Odets, all of them. Use it. See why I was such an enemy to that Strasberg misinterpretation. This is bigger, better, healthier. It can be done. Strasberg can't be done—the stupid idea that you have to gain sixty-two pounds in order to feel the character.

Use Olga's clothes for a start: She's in a school uniform—very constricting. But when she thinks of Moscow, she sees herself at eighteen, in white and pale yellow dresses with her hair up. When Masha sees herself in Moscow, she is in lace petticoats and starched aprons on the way to the academy with little Irina. It is not in the play. But unless you see them in clothes that fit their lives, you will not know them. Olga was a debutante, the one the men came to dance with at the balls. All the young men were there for her. See her in the gowns she wore then.

But now she is in her teacher's uniform, surrounded with papers to be corrected, books for her classes, curriculums she has to look through. She's very conscientious, picks up one load, puts it down, picks up another and another. No wonder she has a headache. It comes from an overwhelming amount of work. It's not just "Oh, I have a headache." It's *why* your head aches, or *why* you are dressed in black. Why, why, why? Unless you justify every line from the moment, you are out of business. Unless it's justified, Chekhov is just [*in heavy Russian accent*], "Acchhh, how zis foooot hurts!" Don't play her as just a tired old teacher. You have to play her as the woman who understood her mother and father better than anybody else and who loves her sisters as if the three of them were a single person.

What a shmuck you will be if you only play the lines. You will never get to Moscow! You will never get to what the play means. *Three Sisters* is the name and the symbol. They are symbols of family life. They are one person. There is nothing about them that is disconnected.

You better tie them together in every act.

ACT I, SCENE 2:
THE SOLDIERS AND THE SAMOVAR

Olga speaks a big monologue and then Irina speaks and then Olga speaks. Olga is interested in Irina; both of them are interested in Masha. There are three other people on stage: Tuzenbakh, Solyony, and Dr. Chebutykin. They are not deeply involved in Olga's and Irina's scene. There are interruptions, but it is basically between the three sisters. Now comes a transition. The scene between the sisters stops. Tuzenbakh says, "The new battery commander, Vershinin, is coming," then sits down to play the piano. Solyony and Chebutykin start to bicker.

The two scenes are not connected. The sisters are not involved with this, so they do something else. Masha whistles; Irina is feeding the birds; Olga goes over to make sure the table is set with the proper silver. Solyony is talking but not relating to anyone. Chebutykin is reading a newspaper and talking about his life, but nobody really cares or listens except the audience. The sisters are not interested until there's a knock and Chebutykin says, "Hear that?— they're calling me downstairs," and hobbles off stage as fast as he can.

That constant breaking away is characteristic. That is how Chekhov writes. See who each scene belongs to. Nobody listens until they get a cue. But it is good for you to know who owns each scene, not just that they are cued for different monologues.

So here's another threesome—Chebutykin, Solyony, and Tuzenbakh. Chebutykin is always writing down items from a newspaper in his book—"Ah, Balzac was married in Berdichev!"—because he thinks something will accumulate from it. He reads newspapers out of context with anything that is going on. He is a busy, crazy man. He is never without doing something. That is indirect action. Tuzenbakh's indirect action is to be alone with the chess set or to go to another table, maybe with a deck of cards. Let him do things he can do alone—move the chess pieces, with or without a partner. He could play solitaire.

That would be very interesting to an actor. If you are in an Arthur Miller play and you sit down at a card table during another guy's speech, it is useful to notice that some solitaire player forgot to cover the queen. Notice what is around you and use it for yourself. These are the inner secrets which make you behave. They will give you a framework for Chekhov.

Tuzenbakh, out of nowhere, says to Solyony, "I'm tired of listening to you." If you are tired, you do something about it. Walk away. Lie down. Go out. The only thing you mustn't do is talk. Close your ears and go out and say, "I'm sick of listening to you." Learn to use the place and you will save yourself. In this style, you are a liar if you just *say* it. It's the only style in which you shouldn't lie. "I don't care about weights or how much you can lift. I'm sick of this talk." If you're sick of something and walk away, you must know *why* you are walking away. You must not just talk. Tuzenbakh and Solyony have been playing chess. Tuzenbakh bangs down the piece and says, "I don't want to talk to you anymore. I want to get away from you. You're crazy." Like when someone gets out a Ouija board and says, "Put your hand on the table and I'll put you in touch with your grandmother." You say, "I don't want to get in touch with my grandmother." The other person says, "Just do it." You say, "Will you go away, please? I'm an intellectual, I graduated from the university. Stop it with my dead grandmother!"

So he goes over to the piano, and as he sits down and starts playing, he says, "Oh, I forgot to tell you, we are expecting a new guest, Major Vershinin. . . ." Irina is leaning over the piano and asks, "Is he old?" There's laughter. "No, about forty . . . nice chap. He's got a crazy wife or something." It is not important for him to make a big speech about it. It is only important that he gives everyone the information—interrupted information—as he plays: "A major is coming; he has two kids and a crazy wife." Everyone listens except Solyony. Solyony is always with himself. We learn a lot about Vershinin through the person who tells you about him. Tuzenbakh is the messenger. Chekhov is a poet. He is going to explain it under a waltz and establish a new mood. There is an entirely different mood when the Baron talks about the Major with the playing of the piano.

Tuzenbakh is very gentle. He doesn't talk as much as anyone else. He corners himself away from the action. There was a good production by the Moscow Art Theater and in the middle of a scene Tuzenbakh, being bored, fell asleep. Irina said, "Baron!" And the way he woke up was marvelous. "Huh? Wha . . . ? Oh, I'm so sorry. . . ." That awakening of a baron who shouldn't have been asleep in a drawing room but was just so tired of all the talk. Tuzenbakh doesn't need the chatter. He's the only baron in the house, and his walk, speech, and behavior are different—much more formal than Solyony's or the doctor's. Don't be intimate in Chekhov. It's about a certain class. If you play old Anfisa, don't go to *your* servant sense. Anfisa mumbles and grumbles, "Where's the samovar?" She's one hundred years old. They let her talk because she talks to herself the way all good Russian servants do. They talk to the plants, they scold the pots. There is a constant conversation that comes in and goes out with them.

By this time, Irina is no longer dreaming about her birthday but about "how great my life will be when I work," in a fantasy all by herself. Everybody is doing something else. The doctor is reading. Solyony is fuming about what Tuzenbakh is doing with Irina and says, "If you open your mouth again, I'll shoot you." It sounds like a joke, but pick up on it for the next act.

Stanislavsky was anxious that there be uninterrupted movement during the performance. The movement should not be broken at all. The talking should come out of doing. If Irina says "I'm happy," she is embracing the doctor, messing up his papers, one falls down, she picks it up and, as she does, says, "No, I won't give it back until you tell me why I'm so happy! Why? All right, now you can have it. . . ." Constant doing.

None of this business is in the play. This is the Stanislavsky breakdown. Does Solyony have things to do? Does Tuzenbakh have a way to behave with the laughter? Does Irina lean against the piano? My biggest advice is to figure out how they move around the stage. If Tuzenbakh speaks to Vershinin, remember that they are together and the girls are not in the middle when two men speak. They are a few steps behind. I do that automatically because I am so willing for the men to be men. See how the stage works, how each character walks within it, where the indirect action is, how one reaches the other.

You have a great opportunity to do that at the end of this scene, when Chebutykin returns and brings in the samovar. Nobody gives a samovar to a girl of eighteen. A samovar is given after twenty-five years of marriage. But he presents one to Irina. It's totally inappropriate. If you don't know that, you won't understand why she says, "Oh, how could you do that! It's simply shameless!"

It is always better to walk and then talk. Remember that. Never start with words, start with moving. In realism, don't come in with the words. The doing makes you talk. If you start talking before you start doing, you are an idiot in the modern theater. Invent the doing and make the words come out of it. Reach over to the samovar first and then say, "I wanted to celebrate your birthday. . . ." If you say, "I wanted to celebrate your birthday," and then reach—do you see how foolish it is?

ACT II INTRODUCTION:
FAMILY BONDING AND IDENTIFICATION
(IRINA'S DECLINE)

The family of man is in every play. You don't have to say, "Ah, this is the Scandinavian family!" or "This is the family of the American South." The family with its infinitely complex problems is in all of us everywhere. The three sisters are so compatible they have complete identification with each other.

When Irina comes on in act two, it's a shock to the audience. In the first act, she's alive and it's spring and she speaks of love. Now, just a few years later, she's pale, her hair is cut, she looks like a boy and sounds worn out. She says it's not love, it's work. Everybody must work. "But I can't work like this, without poetry," she says. "It's killing me." Masha starts whistling—a sure sign she sees Irina is going down. It is very Russian, and very Chekhov, that they *feel* so strongly and are so aware of their own and of each other's emotions. Irina looks fifteen years older. How do you feel about that if you are Olga and Masha? "For God's sake, she mustn't fail, she mustn't!" She is your blood—she's *you*—and you see this happening to her.

My brother and sister appeared in a play my father did. It was their opening night and they were so nervous. I was in a little room in the Albert Hotel with them, and I experienced that. So I can go to this experience of togetherness when Masha starts whistling and Olga says, "Masha, stop it! I know what you're going through."

You go to a situation that gives you the feeling. Don't go for the feeling, go to the place: "They're opening in five minutes. My God, don't let them fail! They're trying so hard. They can't go down." That's good enough for me to take and say, "God, Irina looks like Olga now. She's going to have no life. This must not happen to her." I go from my own situation to Chekhov's. The truth of art is the truth of the situation you are in, not your own situation. That's Stanislavsky.

I have a bowl of fish and the mother has just given birth to all these babies, but now she's dying and I look and say, "You can't die now—you mustn't! They have to have you just for a few hours. Don't desert them now." I can go to the fish—or to fifty other situations. I can't teach you how to act. I can only tell you that you can open up the situation from yourself.

In act two, Olga says to Masha, "Don't do this, don't have a love affair. No, no! Don't you know he'll leave you? He is married. You will go down." I'm a sister, so I have in me the seed of being able to play one of these sisters. I am tied to them by not wanting them to go down—which they are, act by act.

Have a little talent and use the action and truth of the *play's* situation, not the situation in your own bedroom. That's what I fought with Strasberg about. He was afraid of me and he didn't tell me much, but I saw what he did. He said, "Stay in the pink bedroom while you're on stage with the three sisters." I said that would drive me and the audience insane.

I'm all right in *Three Sisters* with the fish if I'm fed by the circumstances. Stay with the play—let it feed you. If you don't understand the family closeness, shop for it in your own way. When you separate two animals, they get melancholy; when husbands die, wives often die soon after. The one can't survive if the other goes down. The sisters feel this way not only about each other but about their brother, too. In the second act, the big withdrawal from the family is by Andrei.

ACT II, SCENE I: ANDREI'S WITHDRAWAL

The theme of the play is the power of banality. Think of what you experience every day on television, the banality of the programs and the advertisements. You can't get away from it. These people can't get away from the banal life around them, but it's worse because they are so isolated.

Act one, full of hope and confidence, is followed in act two by the banal reality that everyday life envelops people. It is not about art, it is about living. A lot happens in act two. There is a party, but it's with drunken people and the state of mind of what goes on is banal, prosaic. You aren't uplifted by it. In act one, spring uplifts them. In act two, it is evening, winter, an accordion is playing way off, and there are no lights in the house. In the first act, it's a birthday party, Andrei is playing a waltz on the violin and he's in love. In the second act, he is not playing a waltz. He knows he has made a fatal mistake of marrying beneath him and that he's not going to Moscow. He's stuck with children. The banality is an aggressive force that eats into the most intimate aspects of life. His dreams are smothered. The Moscow dream has become a stupidity; an inaccessible thing. He will never be a professor. His sisters depended on him for that.

His father made him into an overstrained intellectual. Once the General died, Andrei relaxed and got fat. He says, "You want me to be the General? I can't." He withdraws, feels a failure in their eyes. These three girls adore him. He plays the violin like an angel. "Listen, that's our brother playing! He can do anything with wood." A stranger like Vershinin walks in and they say, "Look what our brother did," and he says, yes, uh-huh. . . . They worship this boy, and he feels he doesn't deserve it. He's not just "shy." That isn't deep enough acting. Get deeper: he can't live up to the love poured out on him.

In my own life, they offered me the repertoire of a great actress when I was twenty-one. I said, "I don't understand this thing that is coming to me." When Einstein died, they asked me to read a funeral address at the Psychoanalytic Society in New York—me. Stefan

Zweig wrote it. But I, Stella Adler—nice Jewish girl from Russian parents—never breathed the air of Germany, didn't speak the language. Einstein deserved someone of German earth to read that. They said, "You do it." I burst into tears. I said, "How could you ask me? I have no sense of what it is to be German. You have to grow up where Einstein did to feel that. Ask a German actress. I don't deserve your honor."

The action is to retreat from love and honor and admiration you feel you don't deserve. That action is very strong in Chekhov and in Andrei. Stanislavsky in act two conveys that feeling of retreat in a house which until now was warmed by the hope of Moscow. How does he diminish the hope? I'm going to give you what nobody in America knows because they think the Method is hysterical insanity to squeeze something out of you. That doesn't make you act. This will make you act:

In the dark living room, the fire in the stove is dying out. There is only a streak of light from an offstage lamp. A shadow flickers in that light. We hear Andrei walking up and down his room, going over the lectures he was preparing for his Moscow doctorate. Otherwise, silence; just the shadows and steps and mumbling of Andrei. Now, this is Stanislavsky: "Hear the monotony in the footsteps, the coughing, the blowing of a nose, the shifting of the chair, the tears—you jump up at that sound! It's the first time you hear that a man is crying."

Andrei is going over what he could and should have been, and because he is Russian, not American, he is not ashamed to cry. The past is so overwhelming. Andrei's past, Moscow—you must understand how he feels about being caught in this trap. The oil lamp is low, it flares up and down. The windows are frozen over. It's winter. If you only have one thing, it's that the windows are frozen. You say as you look out, "Ooh, it's so cold, the snow is falling. . . . Life must be so much better in Moscow. . . ."

Stanislavsky points out that the room is now in Natasha's taste. He gives you that to work with. She has filled it with herself and the baby. On the couch are blankets and diapers and toys. On the table by the sofa is a barrel organ that plays a squeaky harlequin air. On the floor next to the piano are pillows with more toys. She has made the whole room into a nursery, with her bad-taste materials and

scissors on the piano, which she moved against the window. If somebody touched a piano of mine, I would kill them. Natasha moved it
away. She has no sense of where she is, only of what she wants. We
can understand that because we Americans are from the same opportunistic class that climbed up from being a butcher to owning the
store, then a whole string of stores, and filled them up with our vulgar idea of good taste.

You have to know that there's something in a man that likes a
whore. Andrei knows Natasha is a whore. His attraction to her is
because she is common. She's got nothing that the sisters have. They
have haloes. She has available flesh. Going to her relieves him of the
retreat. When in the end he says, "She's vulgar, indecent, and dishonest, but I love her," it means, "I don't have to retreat from her."
My father was very handsome, liked women. But he didn't like
ladies. When he was on the prowl, he didn't like perfume or fancy
dress. He didn't like to have to live up to anything. When he fooled
around on the side, it was with women who were no challenge.

Understand that if Natasha whores around—and she does—it
doesn't offend Andrei, because he doesn't expect anything better
from her. He knows she's sleeping with other men. It doesn't affect
him. She's flesh. That kind of vulgarity is not so hard for an intellectual man of his caste to accept. It is not seen as particularly immoral.
The immorality comes from marrying into another class. If I married a rock singer you would say, "Jesus, that's not quite right for
Stella." From Ibsen on, especially in Strindberg, you see that the
mixture of the classes destroys. If an aristocratic woman sleeps with
a coachman for some reason, she kills herself. She has to. It's a lousy
mix.

When you study acting you study life—how to live life—and
one thing you learn is not to get carried away by somebody who
hasn't the mind you have. You can't substitute a good body for a
good mind. It won't work. Minds go to minds. Bodies go to bodies.
There used to be a better understanding of that. If a man wanted a
body, he went out and bought it. Now, he marries it. That's the mistake. If he wanted a mistress, okay. But marriage was on the level of
mental and sociological rightness. You can't have a whore bring up
your child. You just can't.

ACT II, SCENES 2–7:
PHILOSOPHY AND FESTIVITY

Actually, Russian men love much more passionately than Russian women. The women hold back. Tuzenbakh worships Irina. Vershinin adores Masha, even though he has two children. He is a man of tremendous moral force and integrity. He has a right to say to Masha, "I love you. My wife is insane." He is *able* to love. This is not Stanislavsky. This is Chekhov, in the play.

I saw a production once where Vershinin and Masha never moved in this scene. One was on one side of the stage, one was on the other, and they talked. Carroll O'Connor thought it was well done. I said, "You know, if you use a chair, sometimes you can lean over it or sit on the edge of it. You don't always have to take a position and do nothing—one here, one there, talking at each other like stand-up comics." I noticed it and I made Mr. O'Connor notice it, and he said, "You're right, Stella."

Now Irina comes on, looking so tired and so much older, with Tuzenbakh. Vershinin has been begging for a glass of tea since his entrance, but nobody in the Prozorov household seems to be able to produce one. He finally gives up and says, "Well, what the hell, if we can't get any tea, let's at least philosophize." And Tuzenbakh replies, "All right, let's. What about?" They both like to think. They both have imagination. They are both good for loving. So Tuzenbakh says, "What should we philosophize about?" Vershinin says, "Let's dream about what life will be like in three hundred years." There's a pause. Tuzenbakh has found a little music box and he turns it on and it emits some sounds and the conversation stops for a bit. It is better than just sitting and talking. The music makes it pleasant. It lifts it. It gives it a kind of humor, and at the same time it becomes poetic.

Vershinin says, "After two or three hundred years of working and suffering, our happiness will come, I know it will, I feel it. . . ." In the script, opposite those words, Stanislavsky wrote: "It is important to stir up the audience, speak with spirit, raise the voice." Two minor soldier-characters are playing a guitar and harmonica in the background, and Stanislavsky adds that "their music and drunken voices seem deliberately to bring to mind that everything about which Vershinin speaks is a long way off." So Vershinin is speaking against that distant music. He doesn't have to punch it. The Russians don't do that. You don't punch the monologue, you can say it quietly.

In the middle of the men's discussion, Masha laughs softly. That is all we get from Chekhov. She seems happy—she laughs. But Stanislavsky says, "Masha's laughter is nervous, she could as well burst into tears; she quickly puts out both candles." The scene is winter, dreary. Winter is all right for men. For Masha, it is not all right. She knows the whole thing is going down. It's the men who philosophize. Women don't do big monologues about three hundred years. They do not express these ideas. What do they do? They wait until these conversations are over. But instead of just waiting, he has Masha do something to show she is nervous, something very good: she blows out the candles.

So the rest of the scene is done in near-darkness, with only moonlight and cigarettes. Stanislavsky says, "How expressive it is. The lonely glow of cigarettes in the gloom as people dispute 'passionately' about happiness, work, the future." He says that in this scene, to philosophize, it is better to have darkness, nothing to help it. So in this very dim light, the men continue to talk and she is nervous. There is nothing to do when men decide to discuss life on a grand scale. If a man says, "People are going to fly and wear spacesuits," I think a woman would normally shut up, even today—unless you are vice-president.* It's not good to talk to a man when he's talking philosophically. Women are not so philosophical by nature. They may be in a couple hundred years, but they're not yet and they weren't then.

Stanislavsky measures it. He says the talk dies down and ends with the quiet singing of a song about "wasted youth." Masha is a woman who has wasted her life, so he puts in a song like this—a bit out of tune, but it makes people react. When the philosophy stops, so does the singing, and then you get something we don't have anymore in the theater—the pause. In Chekhov, there must be pauses. The lights are low. Even if there is no music, listen. Hear a dog

---

*Adler's reference is to Geraldine Ferraro, Walter Mondale's running mate on the losing Democratic ticket in 1984.

barking far away. Hear something. Be quiet. Don't always talk, for God's sake. What you need is a pause once in a while.

It's silent. It's dark. She moves to another chair. But he follows her and he says in the darkness, "I love you, I love you, I love you. . . ." When a man of that stature says it three times, it isn't the same as when we say "I love you." It is not what you think of as a love scene. It means, "I want to give you my soul, my soul belongs to you." It means giving yourself away completely. It means you don't own anything anymore, you have given it all to another human being whom you love.

But then a letter arrives for Vershinin: his wife has taken poison. It is very annoying for an important man to have a woman constantly threaten him with suicide. It is a way of sabotaging. A woman who does that is trying to frighten him into submission. It happened to that friend of mine who was head of the Psychoanalytic Society. His wife took poison and he went to the hospital and said, "Now, you've done it—I'm leaving you. You wanted to enslave me by the threat and fear. I will not succumb to it." So he left her, and he was right. But the letter about his wife succeeds, for the moment, in tearing Vershinin away from Masha.

There is a constant emphasis in Chekhov on the contrast between the characters' inner state and what they *say*. The whole second act is worked out this way. Vershinin's inner state is "I am in love with a woman who is married. I have two children who are in danger because my wife is insane." That is his inner state, but he talks about happiness. It is a contradiction. Masha's inner feelings are "I will never have any happiness, but I will have a few hours, maybe, with this man. I am desperate." They are in a different state from what they are saying. You don't just say the words; you say the words against what you feel and what you are striving for in the face of defeat.

A lot of people are hungry, even now in America. Five percent of the population—eleven million people—have no money, no jobs, no Thanksgiving dinner. A lot of men are sitting in dark apartments where they haven't paid the rent, telling their wives, "It's going to be better." It is part of man to work against it. "Don't worry, life will be good again." How does a man feel on Thanksgiving with an empty table and two children in bed and one on his wife's lap? Does he say, "Look what has happened—we are destroyed!" No. Something in mankind fights that. "I will go to war, but I will come back." That is how man built the world. He will not give in to the defeat.

Chekhov felt it was important to show that people don't give up; that their thirst for life does not die but on the contrary revives them, as in the encounter between Natasha and the guests who have gathered at the Prozorovs' house for a party that Natasha wants to cancel so she can duck out for a rendezvous with her lover. So Stanislavsky introduces a whole "laughing scene" with Natasha, who now enters with all her vulgarity and crassness and her attitude that "it's the sisters' house but I'll grab it—I'll get what they've got."

She is the new middle class. She is a tourist there. So these cultured aristocrats watch her take on the tone of their class—speaking bad French and reprimanding Masha for swearing: "Dear Masha, why use such expressions?" It sends them into hysterics. They all spoke perfect French. Tuzenbakh is choking with laughter. He says, "Give me some cognac!" He just dies at her daring to say this to Masha.

It's an ensemble scene, and it's all about fun. Natasha speaks French with a dreadful accent. It's so funny because she is so vulgar. She is talking about her child to people who could not care less. The first rule of exchange is that you don't talk about things other people know or care nothing about. These people are well bred and they don't want to laugh, but she is just so absurdly out of place. That makes them hysterical.

It's very funny but also serious: you have Strindberg's warning that when vulgarity comes in and the lower classes start mounting, you're finished. They are so ruthless and their energy is so strong and what they want is so available.

ACT III: THE FIRE AND THE CLOCK

Act III begins with the great fire scene. The alarms are sounding. The sisters and soldiers are rushing in and out. Everybody is exhausted from fighting the fire—everybody except Andrei, who sits in his room and doesn't pay any attention. What does he do? He plays his violin. He fiddles while Russia burns.

What does Vershinin do? He philosophizes optimistically, even now. Chebutykin, Solyony—everyone else looks at him like he's crazy. He is alone in his optimism. He chooses a time like this to speak, in the middle of misery and disaster. The town is burning; everybody is grabbing clothes for the poor people; his own children are out in the rain in their nightclothes. But he is saying, "In the future, things will be great. . . ." It is absolutely in the Russian mood and the Russian way.

Masha never opens her mouth. People are yelling, "Oh, my God, the fire!" But while everybody is in turmoil and the town is burning, she is lying in black on the sofa, watching. Then Natasha crosses. Masha says, "She looks as if she's the one that set fire to the whole town." That is very funny to me. Natasha is the one Chekhov is after.

The other important moment in the third act is when Irina says, "I guess I will be leaving too," to marry the Baron, and Dr. Chebutykin suddenly drops and breaks her mother's clock. This is a great key for you to understand the great anger in him. You must build this complex character carefully. In the last act when they ask him what's happening in town, he says nothing. Two minutes later, the Baron is shot. The Doctor could intervene, but he doesn't stop the duel between Tuzenbakh and Solyony. He allows Irina's fiancé to die. Why? I shouldn't tell you—I should make you figure it out for yourself—but I will: Irina is the only thing he has. He wants her there in his old age.

ACT IV: FINALE

The Doctor and the other characters are defeated, but they all strive against it—except for Andrei. Andrei is a member of the district board. The head of the district board is sleeping with his wife. Andrei's new child in the fourth act is probably not his own. He has been cuckolded. Everybody knows it.

In act four, Chekhov wrote a tremendous monologue for Andrei on what he thought a wife was. At the first rehearsal he cut it down, and later he cut it more, and then a little more, and more, until, in the final script, all Andrei says is "A wife is a wife." It's a good sentence. That says it all.

"Where has my past gone," Andrei moans, "when I was young, gay, clever, when my dreams and thoughts were so exquisite and the future so bright with hope? Why is it that before we begin to live, we become dull, drab, lazy, useless, unhappy . . . ?"

Can you identify with Andrei? Would you say you've lived up to your own potential? He is young, not much older than you. But he did everything Strindberg said not to do: he married into a lower class, and that disastrous relationship pulled him down. It is a monologue of outright defeat.

But his sisters will not give in to defeat, even though they experience it. The youngest is a romantic, the middle one is a cynic, and the oldest is a stand-in mother. The women in Chekhov are still very protected by men. They know it is time to stop being so protected, but the culture still keeps them that way. The three sisters are girls in relation to men. They are not butch. They don't run factories yet. They have the education but not the freedom to untie themselves from men. "Somebody will come and marry me, I must be married." That idea is strong. It is still strong in 1984. I don't know any woman, I don't care what age she is, who doesn't say, "Well, there's always a chance. Somebody may come along—happened to a friend of mine." A few women now can say, "I don't need a man, for Christ's sake, I can have a baby by insemination." But they couldn't then.

The three sisters are weak—until the end. Masha in the last act sees that the answer is, you are going to die and you have to accept what is here. There is no other place for you to go. The cranes are flying and you can envy or rejoice with them and say, "Fly, fly to your freedom." But you can't. What happens when most people face their lives is, they accept it. Chekhov has found another way out from killing them. He used to say, "I don't know how to solve this character's problem, so I'll have him shoot himself." But he says to the sisters, "Stay with it, you can't help it, it's there. Love is transient, it has to go. Accept what is around you, even if it's not very creative."

Chekhov says whether you are in provincial Russia or Idaho, there is no life, only fragments of life. Things are accidental. What's missing in this town is energy. Keep that in mind when Masha comes in with no music. Equate it with your own boredom when you're far away in some dreary little miserable town. The result is a continual running down of the present in favor of a dream that will never be realized. The longing of the general's daughters for the brilliant life is justifiable. "There used to be forty or fifty officers in the ballroom when we were girls," Masha says. When you're young, you look for someone to rescue you. A girl thinks she'll meet a man who will solve the problem. But that is finished. Now Olga tells Irina, "Marry the Baron . . . I would marry anybody who asked me, even if he was old. I don't think you have to have love, you just have to have kindness."

Another kind of dream is Vershinin's: "If we aren't happy now, people will be in the future." His idealism appeals to a certain kind of person. It wouldn't appeal to me if a man said, "In fifty years there will be thirty sisters and in one hundred years there will be three hundred sisters like you, and they'll all be happy." I'd leave the room, because I'm a realist. But it appeals to Masha.

Chekhov is sorry that these girls are living in a provincial wilderness away from culture. He himself was isolated and wanted to live in Moscow, which is why he wrote about this. But he says people don't live in a connected way. They just live. They get up for a cup of coffee, they talk to each other, and nothing much happens. He re-created life out of the passing of time, not the building to an end. You never get to Moscow. That's written in the stars. But maybe someday someone will.

Chekhov is not too optimistic, but his characters are. Chekhov is a poet. Don't bring him down. Raise it. In *Three Sisters,* every character except Solyony wants to rise. They say it can't go on being this lousy. Irina in the last act says, "I won't ever go to Moscow, but I'll go and teach and maybe help a few people with what I know." She becomes someone who wants to contribute. That's what Mr. Chekhov believes in. He doesn't believe in the dream.

TWELVE

CRAFT AND CREATION

Exercises In and Out of the Void

A N   A U T H O R   L I K E   C H E K H O V   can only do one thing—kill you. That is what he wants to do. "There are a couple of actors out there? I'll give them *Uncle Vanya* and really kill them." When an author died, we used to say, "Thank God." From now on, he wouldn't be sitting out there listening to the play and making suggestions. "Is he still alive? Is he coming? Oh, God. . . ."

The artist is a revolutionist in society. An actor wants to go into the theater because life is too limited. I am here to equip you to take your place in society as a theatrical artist—not to teach you to be an "actor." What can solve the problem of repertory theater in America? What is a better way of artistic life than typecasting, the movie-star way? The answer is craft.

Only craft releases talent. If you learn the *craft* of acting completely, it can become the *art* of acting—a healthy system that will equip you to play a full range of parts. It requires only a normal body with normal talent. The instrument has only to be normal for the music written. But the size of the actor must be the size of the profession—two thousand years old.

The first thing an actor of size and craft understands is that the play is in the present but deals one million percent with the past. That is the actor's work to create. It is not in the play. Shaw said, "I'll do it—I'll put the whole past into the present so the actors will know what I'm thinking." He tried. He said, "Candida is not really real. She comes down because Zeus and the gods have lent her to mortal people for a while so she can live like them and teach them." The curtain goes up and Candida is sitting there knitting and you see she is somebody's wife. But you don't know that she is also a mystical figure with deeper meanings. Hard as he tried, Shaw couldn't really put that in. All that has to be in the actor.

I want to be clear. I think I am known for clarity. I don't like a mixed-up director who says, "Well, there's mysticism in this play, and . . . oh, it's just so very mystical." I say, "But what should I do next?" I am the kind of a person who likes to know what I do next. Mysticism I don't know. I want to give you some keys to how you approach a play.

Chekhov chose to write about the people he admired. He admired them because they were brave and he liked their minds and he was drawn to that society. He said it would never come again— that kind of elegance in the Russian aristocratic intellectual moment when you had the fading out of an entire upper class. It was not at all the same as the English upper class.

If you need somebody to play Henry IV, you send to England. An Englishman knows the speech before the first rehearsal. "Once more into the breach, dear friends. . . ." He is already finished with it. He doesn't have to learn it. The English can do that. But the English can't do Chekhov because they don't *feel*.

Chekhov is all feeling. Everything Russian is feeling—every bit of music, every poem. Everything in the Russian landscape is full of the melody of the inside. That is Russia. It is not America. We are agitated, but we are not emotionally free people. We don't cry when the snow falls. The English are not like that either, and neither are the French. There is only Russia left, with that extreme sensibility of reacting, caring, feeling, laughing with a tear, failing with a smile.

You don't have that kind of feeling, and you can only get it by the most intense concentration of studying and listening. My advice is to be alone when you read the play. Always throw out punctuation when studying a script. Periods and commas are meant for reading. Go over the script one character at a time. Get the things that talk to you. Masha in *Seagull* cracks nuts. She knows a woman of her class should not crack nuts, but she is a rebel. She is really delicious. She has a grievance. Always go through the complaints of the characters.

In *Cherry Orchard*, in *Seagull*, in *Three Sisters*—people complain about their lot. There is always a sense of "Something is crying in my soul!" It is crying for a love that is not coming. It is a soul cry, a love cry. Keep that sense going, which Chekhov gives them.

To learn is better than to know. Whether it's a rehearsal or this class, don't meander in. Don't be late. Don't gossip. Don't discuss your technique. Don't talk about your teacher or your fellow actors. Never say anything anywhere unless you need to. Convey ideas, not words. An idea is presented in a sequence. Learn to listen for the sequence. Don't listen for words. Listen for thoughts. Don't ever talk about what you don't understand. The most important thing to understand is Chekhov's idea that life goes on.

Stanislavksy was very interested in that. He told me that when Chekhov died and his widow was on her way to the funeral, she suddenly stopped and picked up a pin. She noticed a pin on the ground, and she picked it up. In doing that, you break the cliché of going to a funeral: life goes on and you notice things, instead of just getting into a trance of "I'm sad."

That pin is a perfect example of how you can use the stage. There is a lot of food on the stage—tea, samovars, glasses, everybody drinking. By the way Masha pours the vodka, you know how she drinks. This is what Stanislavsky did with Chekhov, how Stanislavsky made one aware. It was a great discovery for acting. Until then, acting was the way the English act. It is impossible to make an Englishman sound like a person. It is not their fault. The language is filled with a certain rhythm which makes it difficult to get the reality. England goes for this kind of acting. The Moscow Art Theater does not.

I saw a lot of the Moscow Art Theater. Stanislavsky said to me, "If you want something, *go*—don't wait." So I went a lot. Once when I was sitting in the Moscow Art Theater, I noticed that the actors on stage noticed *me* in the audience. They hadn't seen anything like me in a thousand years. Gloves and makeup. That was not their audience. It was not like our crazy theater here at all. Their greatest actor, [Vasiliy Ivanovich] Kochalov, in *Resurrection* had some steps leading down to the pit, and he came down to speak his speech and there I was, and he saw me. He was late with his cue. He didn't mind being late with his cue by taking the time to *notice* me. All the actors did it once in a while. Every actor in the Moscow Art Theater with their great Method did that. They looked at the audience to see who was there. So they are not dumb. When they don't want it, they throw it away.

What matters is you and your own creativity and your own choices at every level in every element of the equation, every step of the way. I cannot give it to you. I can only give you some keys and some exercises to help you out of the void.

In realism, big ideas come out of ordinary language. It is the actor's responsibility to live with ideas and know how to find them in the conflict of values and period of the play. The great realistic plays are not entertainments. They use middle-class elements to serve the exalted idea. Find what is universal in the common language.

In all great writing there will be an idea that pertains to all time—transcends the local and goes into eternity. "Man struggles for survival, with God, society, family, morality." It can't be solved, but man makes an effort. Theater means ideas that pertain to man. Take them as high as you can reach.

The ideas are the stretch for the actor. They must speak to him and he must fill them and make them his own. The realistic form demands it. Let the idea that has size affect you—let it give you the size it deserves—DO IT MAXIMUM. Your presentation must be as large as the idea.

E X E R C I S E :

Bring in some revelation—a miracle, perhaps—and do it without words. Make us see it. The birth of Christ or the resurrection, maybe. *Reveal* it, lift the veil off. Work on revelation. Then do it with as few words as you possibly can.

E X E R C I S E :

Find ten different circumstances where you cannot compromise. Take a big idea you will fight for—from life, from a play, from an essay. Is it Lincoln at Gettysburg? Kennedy at the Berlin Wall? Joan of Arc leading her troops? Whatever you choose, paraphrase it. Take it off the page. Be ready to present it. Find the thing that fascinates you. What arrests your attention? What is beautiful about it? What is horrible? Take it and, in two minutes, develop and complete it in your own words. Words mask us. Fancy words mask us more. We must use words to reveal, not mask, ourselves.

E X E R C I S E :

In your speech or your essay, pick out the words that are enormous—words with dramatic impact. Develop a sense of words. Be passionate of words. Develop your love of words and a real choice of words. Cultivate your ability to see something new in them a hundred times, not just the tiny physical things they indicate. It will help you to know the difference between "vile" and "evil," or "divine" and "fabulous." If your text says, "That woman is fierce," live up to the word "fierce." Give it its worth and inherent value. If you don't know exactly what it means, look it up. Look it up even if you *do* know. Then make the selection of meaning that is proper for you and the situation. Invest commonplace language with emotional truth.

E X E R C I S E :

Now combine those last two exercises above and use them for the Warren Report on JFK's assassination. Have you read it? If not, you're a fool. Get it and read it over a few times. Do you believe the single-killer or the conspiracy theory? I don't care what you think personally. Take both ideas and put them in your own words. An actor has to be able to present an idea, pro and con, on any subject in or out of a script. The truth of the idea must be second nature in your stage voice.

Make the difference in ideas big. Don't rush them—take the time to find and express them.

If you hear something terrible about somebody you love, your reaction must be on the basis of what you *know,* not what you *say* you know. Do not play personal conflicts. Always play the conflict of significant ideas. The discussion of opposing ideas opens up and goes beyond immediate reality. When a change is portended in that discussion, you have a large situation. Is it right? Is it good? Where will it lead? Depth in realism means what is under the lines *in you*— that part of the idea, the relationships and the issue that is beneath the prosaic lines and *in you.*

In realism, make the small action complicated and deep. Immediately put the literary idea into the theatrical size that the theme demands.

In *A Doll's House,* the last scene between Nora and Torvald is a fight to the death. Know what that fight is about. In the action of fighting, *all* of you goes outward. As you do the action, give birth to it. Let it happen as it goes on. If you work to get the maximum, then you can do any large or small action with the belief and experience in you. Then, if your partner attacks you from her deepest beliefs, you can fight back with *your* deepest beliefs. Justify your own sense of right deeply.

When you see the beautiful or the miraculous thing—speak it out. Go from one wondrous thing to another. When you see it, stretch to the sky. Such passages in Ibsen or Chekhov are above the reality—they go out to the world that is created by the actor. They are not just intimately delivered to a partner.

A modern play makes the actor dig for its meaning and find out why the playwright wrote it. You go first to the meaning, then to the circumstances. How does the play grow? You must know the important moments in the play, where the growth is, and conversely you must know what is *not* important. This first stage of approaching a part—finding the idea and plot as well as the style and form—is best done alone.

When the idea can be lifted from the page, you are in the second stage. That begins when you have the sequence in your mind. You start saying it aloud. In your room, on the street—anywhere. Then in a rehearsal space. Then you get used to the playing area and you get additional action from the partner.

You must communicate the real meaning of each word you speak and motion you make, but never by rote memory. You must always leave room for improvisation and spontaneity, which is the third stage of your art. The key to that is conflict.

Obstacles help the action. Put them in if they are not there. The element of an obstacle yields growth. Overcome the hurdle and go on to what exists *now*. Make it oblique—don't make it direct. Make things oppose your action. Put the urgency in the action. In realism, find the way to *do* it rather than say it. Start using creative surprises in the action. Bring in planned accidents that you need. There are no real accidents on stage, only planned accidents. Don't be afraid of your voice, body, or approach. If you are afraid to fail, you will never succeed.

When working on any scene in a script, it would help you to do some work with a pencil and paper first and put down the following headings:

> I. Action
> II. Physical Objects and Controls
> III. Mood and Soul

This is the breakdown of what you must know and use and take advantage of in the process of creating a character. Draw the set, too. If you know the place and your own and all the other characters' lives before they enter, you will be able to relate to them and to idea sequences instead of words. If you take the things you compile in the first three categories and arrange them into a series of clear steps, you will be able to come into each scene knowing how to carry out what the author indicates for you.

I. Action

The stage takes away the living truth. We put it back from the nature of our actions. The facts are boring. What can I contribute to them? Know the difference between showing and doing. Know the difference between the convention of doing and the life of doing. To act is easy; not to act is hard. *Don't give nature to life; take nature from life.*

An action can be won or lost, simple or complicated.

Complicate action. Reflect on complication. Like and immediately respond to things. Get off your pedestrian ass onto your theatrical feet. You're ready to act when you're full of material.

Listen actively. Give up resistance—stop holding back. Don't talk away the subject. When and where does the action start? If it starts in you, the words will then tumble out. It will finish when it stops in you.

An action is doable. It takes place somewhere. It has its nature. Nothing physical can be "acted"—no speech defect or regional dialect or anything else. It must be done by a technique which has become second nature. Everything physical done on the stage must be second nature to the actor.

Whatever is needed for an action, nature can supply. One will always be truthful to any action if one lets nature be his guide. Give your action only what it needs.

Everything you do has a nature. Never do things because they are comfortable. Always do things because of their nature. Understand the nature of the most simple action and give the truth to it. Don't just bring your own mannerisms to it. The person who bores me most is the person who is dying to show me what a temperament he has.

Know how to do the action and then smarten it up—know the difference between the stage reality and the life reality. Create a real attention as you do it. The attention must be multiple. The audience is interested in the complexity of the actor much more than in the facts.

EXERCISE:

Choose an action—e.g, sit down in chair, powder your nose, put on a sweater, comb your hair, read a paper—and do it simply. Do it again and complicate it. Then complicate it again. Change the action but not the nature of the action.

The nature of Total Listening is IN. The nature of Total Looking is OUT. The nature of Total Speaking is OUT. The nature of Total Relating with others is both out and in.

Reach! Don't pull back from people. Ask, "Where do I pull back when I shouldn't?" If you have nothing else to do, LOOK. Don't pull voice, body, feeling, or anything else back. GO OUT. Truly give the action its own life and follow through to its end. DO it— don't say it. Use the set and prop objects truthfully, letting their nature feed you. PERSONALIZE the doing by putting yourself and your life into your actions.

Concentrating on the doing of the action will lessen distraction and give you coordination free from tension and actor's anxiety. Distraction is countered by what you're doing, if you're really doing it. But have spontaneity. If you like something, respond quickly to the thing about it that excites you. ACTING IS DOING. Fill yourself with material by seeing and then go to the image. See the image— but particularize and economize it. Don't let unspecific chatter drain your image. DON'T BE GENERAL!

Always be able to finish anything you are asked to do. Knowing the END of a direction will give you the security of doing the action. Always carry out your action fully each time. Each time, *do* it—don't *repeat* it! The nature of the theater is having to do things over and over again. They must be really DONE each time.

Life, too, has a way of making us lose things from repetition. But in art, every time you create it must feed you and you must feed it. Real life exhausts itself. Facts are not for actors. In acting, the thought provokes everything. You don't repeat. You find it again. Don't ever listen to another actor on stage without thought. Be active and personal in your listening. TRAIN YOUR EAR TO THINK.

Actions must be DOABLE. Break down the overall action into its doable elements. Action means doing, not feeling. Find the things you like and can do to advance the plot. Don't make artificial choices. Start with what most involves you and see where it takes you. Use the circumstances to feed your action and give it life. Put yourself into the facts you use.

EXERCISE:

Take ten "activity" actions from Ibsen and Strindberg and Chekhov scenes and put yourself into what is needed. Take action that needs a great deal of doing, like trimming the Christmas tree in *Doll's House,* for example. Think of everything that must be done with trimming that tree. Let the lines come out of the action—don't pick the thing you cannot do. Ask what can you *do* rather than what can you *feel.* Turn the fiction into reality—use the thing that makes it personal for you. In preparing the food for the big holiday meal, personalize and talk about it before you go to the line "Such a big turkey!"

Inner justification is the thing that belongs to the actor. It does not come from the object. Provoke action through justification. Justify it without the words, because the words stink. Live in the circumstances for an hour without saying a word.

In realism, you enlarge the big life-and-death arguments by enlarging the justification. That element of need must be added, and it will help. Always justify every action. You build your attitude toward your partner through justification, too.

Who am I? Where am I? What am I doing? Why am I doing it?

Inner justification has to do with what is behind the text. It has less to do with the object than with *why* the object is used in a certain way. The WHY belongs to the actor. Choose something you need for justification. When you reach for the justification, stay within the realm of your own believability. What happens before must influence the justification as the plot builds. If you take the thing that really works for you and your action, then the words will come out of an inner experience.

Motivate everything you do. If you do an action, the reason must help you. *Spontaneous* justification gets you to go.

EXERCISE:

Pick a scene from Chekhov and do all your movements in it unmotivated. Then go through the movements and motivate them all. See and feel the difference.

EXERCISE:

Take and do the same action spontaneously ten times for different reasons: e.g., the act of shaking hands, saying goodbye, trying on gloves. Get your different circumstances each time, know what you need, and justify what you do. Break the action down into all of its component parts and spontaneously justify each one. Make the justifications fit the circumstances.

EXERCISE:

Choose a partner and improvise several variations of a scene with a different spontaneous justification for each one: e.g., a man comes into a room and a girl must stop him from doing whatever he is doing or wants to do. The first time, she rejects him. The second time, she helps him. The third, she stalls. Different justifications excite truly different temperament switches. Why does she help him take the car or keep him from taking it? Speak to each other from different places in the room.

*　　*　　*

Provoke the circumstances to complicate your actions. The physical things you do are part of an action in circumstances. In realism, life is fed to the actor through circumstances. Live off the circumstances. If the circumstances are truly created, an actor can justify his use of them in a personal way, making logical and correct choices.

Pay attention to *sequence:* An action must grow up or down, or you better just give it up. Find the growth in the action through the plot. Emotion comes out of action. Never look for the emotion—you'll drive it away. Let it come out of what you're doing. You draw from the circumstances of the play. Improvise first, to totally involve yourself in the moment—then later go back to the play. There's not always time to find the moment in our lives—go to the circumstances.

If you are having a picnic and it starts to rain, know and justify the things you do when you are enjoying or tiring of something. What can you do to drag out or speed up the action of leaving the picnic? Let the life of the doing come through in your use of the objects. If you pack the blanket, let the truth that's in the blanket come through. Go from one thing to another continuing the action and living truthfully in the circumstances.

Remember that you are looking for the *doable* actions, so go quickly but specifically to the details you can use. Take the act of waiting, for example. When waiting, don't just sit back and be bored. That leads to lethargy. The action of waiting can be boring, but there is a world around you. An action always takes place in a world. Waiting in a subway is different from waiting in a theatrical office for an audition or waiting for your costume to be mended right before your entrance. Know the difference. Take the things you would humanly use in that circumstance and filter it through your imagination until it belongs to you.

Don't stay with a detail unless you see that it grows. Then go on with the detail and add lines. It all starts to develop from the action. Do lines out of the action.

Sometimes things that happen have nothing to do with the action. Let life come into the action. The phone rings. It's irrelevant—one doesn't give up the action for the irrelevant, but life often intrudes on your action, and you can use it in the circumstances. Let the outside life in.

Improvisation: You are playing a small role or chorus part in a show. You are in the dressing room getting into costume, but you're having a hell of a time getting your girdle on. Put on the girdle, take off the girdle, look for another one. . . . Suddenly the stage manager comes in and says one of the leads is sick, and you're the understudy. You're caught in the middle of this girdle thing. You call in another actress for help. Maybe she's your sister. She thinks it's funny. You don't. Or maybe you do, in part. The lines come from your circumstances with those girdles. Filter them through your imagination, experiencing that which makes it difficult or easy. Then let the lines spill out.

The truth comes out of the humanity of the doing. Be in the truth of *living* in that circumstance. You know consciously about one millionth of what you know. Be more conscious in your knowing. If you really *see* the details of that dressing room and select the right ones, they will grow and lead you to the doing.

How do you do that? By cultivating new and better ways of *seeing*. Start with stream-of-consciousness association. Take an object and see where it leads you. Shop for the image that feeds. Be *very personal* in your selection: it can be used again—enlarged and changed, according to your needs on stage. When it is alive in you, you can give it out and it will awaken your audience. Get to your image fast and have it fully in you, but don't do more than it gives you. Take the life from the image to the degree that it truly exists. Don't force more from the image. Pick up each other's images and see it for yourself, and see *more* in it *from* yourself. There is no inner insecurity when one really sees the image. Put your image in a place. When the next person takes it, he should put it in another place. Make the growth a little bigger each time.

EXERCISE:

Work on memory enhancement. Get as close as you can to a photo-
graphic memory. Pass a shop and see, to the count of ten, everything
in the window. Wherever you are, count people, chairs, dogs,
trees. . . . Look at a thing and see it completely, no matter how
quickly you look. Count the lights and notice every object in the
room you enter. Really see imaginatively: be able to describe the
fabulous coat you saw in Saks' window, down to the tiniest detail.
Practice seeing throughout the day until you can do it without its
being evident to anyone else.

EXERCISE:

Find ten different colors of white in ten things. Give the life of each
white. The life of what you see is drawn from within the memory
sources of your own life. Don't see things in a lifeless way. Find a
dozen red things: see their particular redness. A dozen black things:
their particular blackness.

EXERCISE:

Do something while some prose or poetry is being read in a group
visualization-association rhythm. Prepare a story that describes
something lyrical-beautiful in nature. Hear yourself talk. Make
sense. When many people talk at once, you must adjust to them and
use each other. Really listen—become engaged and respond spontaneously. *To act is to* REACT! But you tend to listen without thought
onstage. If you listen and pick up the group rhythm, it will carry
you forward and your concentration will not only be intact but
stronger than before.

*   *   *

The actor must find a way to be private onstage with his partner, to speak humanly and to be at home in the circumstances. Become deeply attached to your partner. What does he or she need from you? Really *watch*—find something in your partner that affects you deeply. Stanislavsky told a young actor, "In acting you must give back—if not, your partner is stranded."

Partners must find the part of their relationship wherein they don't talk, they *do.* Find the *now,* the urgency. Don't "clarify" the play for your partner. Don't "tell" or flirt. Real sex never shows itself. But action is reaction, and you can only build your own attitude through your partner's. You must give each other something.

EXERCISE:

See if you and your partners can distinguish each other by touching hands with your eyes closed. See if you can distinguish them by touching their hair.

The growth of the relationship and the idea is not only for you and your partner. It is to be given to the audience. That is why the play was written. So is the growth of an action: to win an action, to lose an action, to change an action, requires the actor and his partner to *be* the growing size of the idea. Which means, never "know" how you're going to do an action in advance. Just arrange it and then do it.

Anything physical that you do on stage must be second nature. It is simply a matter of physical control. The aim of mastering all physical controls is to theatricalize the actor. You can act a lisp, a limp—anything. You just have to work scientifically on where the control lies, which is what we will do next.

II. Physical Objects and Controls

Natasha in *Three Sisters* can move a lot. In the lower middle class she belongs to, they do that. They move that way. But in the sisters' class, Chekhov says, beauty is in two movements—not four or five. Their sense of aesthetics is in two movements. You make too many movements on the stage. Because you are comfortable, you make any movements you want. But I am telling you, this class does not. Know that. Don't do too much. Just do what is needed to give the physical control its truth.

Anything physical must be practiced until it is so second nature that you can forget about it. All movements, gestures, expressions, dialects—every physical control—must be down completely before you can act.

Start with your own face.

Study it. Know its structure and what can be done with it. Memorize its every detail. Your greatest value is in self-realization, not imitation. What are your assets? Your faults? Don't underestimate the assets.

Then go to movement—falls, wrestling, physical pushings and stumblings. But start with the thing you need and use most on stage: walking. Notice and place the many different walks in life— just their physical controls, without character.

EXERCISE:

Throw away your own walk and learn three new ones. Find what you need. Choose the most difficult ones. Live with them and make them your own. Walk with them—three different ways—in a room, on the street, and then on a frozen pond. Locate where the ice is solid, where it is thin.

EXERCISE:

Practice various national salutes and social protocols: Nazi arm raising and heel clicking, Communist proletarian greetings, handshakes with dignitaries, men's bows and women's curtsies to royalty, Oriental obeisances.

Go next from the body to the physical controls of speech. Buy a book or a set of tapes on dialects. Come up with a whole range of accents. Locate the most difficult examples you can find of the French *r* versus the German *r*. For dialects and physical disabilities—WATCH, LISTEN, AND OBSERVE. Go to life for the various speech patterns. Only take things that can be controlled. Be able to improvise on a subject or read an essay with a lisp. When you steal accents, steal what you need!

EXERCISE:

Practice saying the alphabet with a lisp. Choose the most difficult words to practice with a lisp: "necessarily," "starlight," "Mississippi," "sister," "strange," "Stella," "stupendous," "stupid" . . . When you add a lisp to a speech or an essay, add it to the *idea*—don't feature it. Try out your lisp or dialect when ordering your groceries or going to a bookstore.

EXERCISE:

Go to the zoo and listen to the animal sounds. Choose certain ones. Find the whole thing about them, but mostly the sound. It's not enough to be free when you do it—you must be unashamed. Wear tights and bring in the sounds you've really heard. Do the animal sound you hear from the animal; don't imitate yourself.

*   *   *

Realism's prose style deals with middle-class problems—the toughness of life in unembroidered, realistic circumstances. Artificiality had to be cut out. To put over an idea in realism, speech and place must go together. The place—the room—must be known and used by the actor.

You never act in space. You act in a place. Where are you in your scene? Always know and think of this before stepping on stage. Understand and remember the difference between being in a library, a bedroom, a restaurant, and a garden. What do people do in these different places? You must not be dependent on the director to tell you. You must be intimately in contact. You must live in the room of the play, not play on a set. The use of every section of the stage and set must be clear to you. What you do, you do differently depending on where you are.

E X E R C I S E :

Perform the act of washing out a pair of socks in a hotel bathroom and at a pond. Add your imagination and personal life. The life of the object on the stage is put there by you.

Perform the act of washing your hands in ten different places. Let the action filter through your imagination and location. It is more interesting if you make some selections based on that instead of just focusing on the cold fact or act itself.

The fact itself is dead material; finished. The actor must contribute life to it—different kinds of life, depending on the place, the characters, and the objects: a wife waits to have her cigarette lit; a career girl whips out her own matches.

Props

If the room has a table, be completely familiar with that table and every object around that cognac bottle. The actor must live utterly in the room for the style of realism. If there is a window, how does it open and what does it open onto? If there is a cupboard or a bureau, what's in it?

You must know everything pertaining to a room, even if you do not use it all, during the first stage of rehearsal. Understand and be familiar with every object in the room. The life of the objects around you is half the battle in realism. If you use a prop, you are responsible for having the knowledge of the place in which you use it. The stage will take the life out of the props if they—and the world you are in—are not filtered through your imagination.

"Know your world like you know your underwear," Stanislavsky said. Live with your props as your wordless partners in the circumstances. If you can't see the organic circumstances, don't act. If you can, use them through your imagination to put life into the objects you use.

EXERCISE:

Bring four or five unusual objects—maybe a sword, a snuff box, a pipe, a cane, a watch, a piece of linoleum, an antique chair—and work on very precise actions with them: fixing the watch, cutting the linoleum, painting the chair. . . . Each time you do the action, REALLY DO IT. Personalize it. Become intimate with everything needed to bring life to the fact of painting the chair or handling the sword. Think about its complete history. Where does one put a cane when one enters a room? How does one approach a watch that needs to be repaired?

Know the object instead of just *handling* it. There must be for you the humanity of what you handle. The reality of the props will feed you. Don't use a folding fan just for "something to do" with your hands. Use it for all its purposes—to shoo mosquitoes away, to put off odors, to cool off. Don't go to bed in a prop bed. Go to bed in the bed your character actually sleeps in. In realism, you don't have big orations or poetry. All you have is humanity.

Costumes

You don't have to be a genius to see that the same thing applies to costumes. How are you dressed and groomed in your scene? Know this and *be* this and think of this when you come on.

If an element of your costume is a high hat, know the life and the place of that hat. Know the background of the hat or cane—how that fashion came into being. Play and live with it until the life of the hat or cane sinks into you.

A costume will not help you unless your body fits into it. Know what your body requires for it. EXPERIENCE IT! Select what awakens you! Choose the costume element that gives you what you need. If you cannot handle a certain element, don't take it. Know when the costume was worn and what it needs from you, the actor, in your body line. Let the costume affect you. Question what it does for you as an actor. Find out how to live with trains, long skirts, lace cuffs, in drinking and dancing for each period. If you're in Venice, use the Venetian lanterns and streets to help you make use of the costume. Find out how one stands on the Rialto. When the choice of costume and period is made, use the life around the period—the furniture, the jewels. Treat them with the attitude that they need and deserve.

EXERCISE:

Learn how to handle different kinds and conditions of SHOES. See and describe those *bashmaki*—Russian peasant boots the servants wear—and Japanese wedding slippers, men's and women's both.

Don't be totally historical. Once you know them, re-create them imaginatively.

Practice "sense memory" with different shoe problems—e.g., shoes with gum or dog excrement on the bottom. Let those sensations stimulate you.

EXERCISE:

Take out your old family photo albums and closely examine the differences in how people dressed and were photographed in the 1920s versus the 1940s. Let the pictures help you detect the change in morals and manners. Be specific about those changes. Don't be general. See from the clothes that as the taboos broke down, the attitude between the sexes changed and new conflicts came about: women moved into areas of life that had been closed to them and became a threat to men socially and professionally. Women's dress went from a more modest to a more naked mode; the old symbols of femininity changed. See that the need was not just to be more comfortable but to observe or to break certain traditions. See that many of those traditions and social habits still remain unsettled, unresolved today. Bring in a couple of such costume elements that make the actor feel tough. Also a couple of elements which make one feel meek. How would *you* use and interpret them? How would *you* behave in them?

A crown makes an actor keep his head erect. Keep the experience of that feeling even after the crown is put aside. Sense what the costume does for you and keep the experience. The long skirt helps to discipline the body. One walks, sits, and moves with more grace. The costume must go *into* the actor.

From the Greeks to Shakespeare to Chekhov's time, and until very recently, props and costumes were not commercially produced but made by hand with special skill. If your character wears a monocle or pince-nez, it is not "for effect." Glasses were not supposed to give the external convention. *Avoid the result.* Use the prop with its nature—find that nature, then motivate. Get the nature of handling one prop or costume element completely, and then you can do it with another. Practice some action in a costume element or with a prop without *demonstrating*. Get used to USING the prop or costume, not demonstrating it.

This is essential in every play, especially in a realistic play. But nowhere is it more essential than in Chekhov.

III. Mood and Soul

When you say "Chekhov," you know you are in a certain mood of extreme tension and extreme nontension. The abolition of serfdom, the liberation of politics—these are the immediate aims of the time. The more distant aims are happiness, God, life beyond the grave. Realists paint life as it is. That is done particularly well by the Russians, from Tolstoy to Gorky. But when Chekhov comes along, in addition to seeing life as it is, you are captivated with life as it should be.

Chekhov said to his editor, "Tell me in all conscience, which of my contemporaries have given the world a single drop of this flame, this alcohol, which makes you aim high?" He says the playwrights of his day are lemonade, including himself. He says science and technology are developing at a fast pace but the arts are flabby, sour, and dull. The cause of the flabbiness is not to be found in our stupidity or lack of talent or in our silence. He says we are not stupid. He says it's a disease which, for the artist, is worse than syphilis. We lack something which is true. We have nothing in mind; we are not going anywhere. When we lift the skirt of our muse, we discover there is nothing underneath. We lack inspiration.

This is the main source of the problem with Chekhov's characters and their interrelationships.

How do you know that a couple in a restaurant are husband and wife? They eat, but they don't talk to each other. You have to understand that relationships have nothing to do with what people say or don't say—and, thus, that you must establish the relationship before you attack the words. You must ask: "Who am I in relation to the Doctor? In relation to my younger sister?" Understand that their relationship is complex. Don't make the relationships simple or empty. Every relationship has everybody else in it.

In *Seagull,* Stanislavsky gives Arkadina tea and cake. Know what to do with them to help reveal the relationships. Arkadina would certainly give Dr. Dorn the bad part of the cake. If she gave him the best piece by mistake, she would take it back from him and eat it herself. It would tell you something.

Use it for that. Use everything. I would play with the food and be very coquettish. How do Russians drink tea? It is an absolute symphony of noise. You have to make noise because you drink it when it's boiling hot. The Russians slurp—you are supposed to, and it's fun. Great during somebody else's speech. It's not impolite. Play with it while the other people are talking.

Arkadina gets up, brushes off the crumbs, waltzes in a big circle to show off her figure in front of Masha. Dorn watches her and knows she shouldn't do this in front of somebody who is devastated. Dorn sees this as she dances—this fight for life, this splendid vulgarity, and can't help loving her for it. Arkadina takes an apple, throws it to Dorn—it is not what you think. What is it?

All this is better and more useful than just waiting for your turn to talk. You have to make it interesting.

Russians have the ability to gather into a community of family which is compatible with one another. In the large sense of this, Chekhov, Tolstoy, and Gorky were friends. They traveled together. They had a need to relate and identify with people like themselves. Tolstoy went to Gorky and Gorky went to Chekhov and Chekhov went to Tolstoy. They were a family of trying to understand each other. Small units of people find and gravitate to each other. I say to a poet, "Would you like to come over and bring somebody?" He brings four poets. In *The Seagull,* everybody exists in community terms of the theater. The three sisters exist in terms of mutual spiritual necessity. They are together looking for a way to live their lives in their isolation.

You find in each Chekhov play a community that is isolated from the larger community, which intensifies a need in the Russian soul to express itself within the family life. They all complement each other in some way.

I read that there are one hundred Russian immigrants arriving in the United States daily now, and that they can't understand the unfriendliness of the Americans. They are so used to being part of a group. They know how to live together. They say, "I want to love you." It is all love. The men in Russia hold each other and kiss each other. That "Shake hands like a man!" business doesn't exist for them. You express yourself soulfully by giving yourself away. It's so alien to us, unfortunately, except in the theater. Theater people are the most demonstrative here—all my students kiss me and hold each other. Once in a while we get somebody from Bryn Mawr, and it takes her about six months longer than anybody else. She gets there very slowly, but she gets there. But outside of artists, that thing doesn't really exist in the American soul.

The Russian soul is different. The Russians don't attach great importance to success or professions or institutions. They get bored very quickly with all that. They understand that those things don't give your soul or inner needs any answers. Science and philosophy don't give you the answers because they all have a method that goes from A to B to C and they think that makes it right. If you go to law school, they tell you one answer; if you study architecture, they tell you another. Chekhov realized that each human soul, each person inside, wanted an answer of his own that he couldn't be "told."

Where are you going to find it?

Nobody in Chekhov speaks of religion; that solace is not there. Nobody in the plays says, "I'm a nihilist," or "Nietzsche has the answer." If you do that, people leave the room. What they don't leave is the lonely desperation of someone saying, "What happened to me? I wanted to go to Moscow." You remain with your own loneliness, trying to express what is godly in you and in what we call civilization.

The elegance of the Russian spirit is without a sense of money and possessions. Money is rarely talked about. There is no conversation in America which doesn't end with "How much is it?" Chekhov's characters are not blessed with the ability of tying up the economic or practical loose ends. What they want is not tangible, and neither is God. They go to their particular spiritual source. In every play, their individual soul leads them somewhere.

Masha's last speech in *Three Sisters,* when she knows there is no answer, is that she sees the cranes flying to freedom. This need to free the soul is in the Russian spirit. They all have it—Tolstoy has it, Turgenev has it. Nobody else has it like the Russians. Nobody else writes about the desperation of living but with the hope of the soul giving birth or rebirth to itself in some higher form. Chekhov says these are limited people who find one another and express man's universal need when God deserts him and he is left to solve his own problems.

In every character, the personal truth that comes through is different. Each person is not a stage character who promotes action. He simply needs to live truthfully.

Chekhov deals with the souls of the people in the play. He dealt with his own soul as a doctor, too. He served medicine without love, and he understood what that did to him: it killed his feeling for everything. To do without love is to kill yourself. But, knowing that, he still says it is better to knock your head against the wall than to say, "Science has the answer," or "Just take six lessons with Madame Lasagna and she'll give you exactly what you need." When the answers aren't there that way, the other way of doing it is to submit. That is what his doctors do in each play. They submit, even when they are screaming at you. It's tribal, isn't it? Chekhov says it is so big, so atavistic for man to scream out, and he has always done so. Man still has in him this sense of "Leave me out of it—I must go someplace which will be there throughout the ages."

Andrei protests and then he says, "You know, I'm dead. This is the truth of my life." It is good for you to learn to give away the inside. It's hard to give that away, but don't, for God's sake, hold on to it or think it's not "masculine" or any other stupid thing. Don't do that. Big actors understand that maybe you have to practice it in life a little bit before you can do it. At the moment, I'm working with an actor—an angel of a man, but when he goes on stage, he doesn't know how to confess. He doesn't know how to say, "Look at me, I'm naked." Do it. It is possible for you to achieve this openness.

It is only Chekhov who allows the situation not to progress. Everybody talks and nothing happens. Another playwright says, this happens, and then after that somebody comes in and something else happens, and then. . . . But Chekhov wants nothing to happen. If you understand that lack of logic, it will save you on the stage. It will give you an inner life that is not dependent on the text. Most playwrights after Chekhov don't want you to depend on the text. If you just *talk* Chekhov—if you take the line without adding what's underneath—it is terrible.

Harold Clurman said that when people drink, they have no nationality—they're all the same. You can see by the way Masha pours drinks in *The Seagull* that she is an expert at it. She drinks like a real man. It's like Sorin's assumed gaiety in the same scene—people in deep tragedy. I say, you have to be born with a broken heart for the theater—you can't get it, it has to be there. If suicide is there, they can take a drink and laugh.

The scene is complicated. The lack of logic. In life, you can be sitting with somebody in the drugstore having a Coke and you say, "Listen, I tried to kill myself this morning," and the other guy is having a double pistachio ice cream and says, "Yeah, can I give you a cigarette?" You don't have to connect, you can swim over it. The need to talk comes from a depth which says, "I have to express this." It doesn't have to make sense. Play the scene without the lines.

Chekhov created a form of play which is minimal in statement and which, for the first time in history, really belongs to the actor. If you are playing Masha—in *Seagull* or *Three Sisters*—you are not just "doing a role," you are drawing a portrait.

The drawing of portraits is a Russian characteristic. When you go to Russian literature—to *Anna Karenina* and *Dead Souls*—people like Tolstoy and Gogol and Chekhov don't write "stories," they paint portraits. Every portrait became a name. A century later we say, "She's a Masha," or "He's an Oblomov." Read the plays and look for the portraits—don't look for the dialogue.

Think of Maria Callas, for example, in our own time. When you saw or heard her in the beginning she was fat and married and wanted to be a singer. Then she didn't want that man and became a great singer. Then you see her further and she is great, but she is losing her voice and losing the man she loves. Then you see her teaching, very quiet, and then you see her in her hotel room, sick and dying.* Chekhov lets you see characters like this in all stages. There is no finality. You go from one stage to the other. In understanding the three sisters, you must realize that four years go by. They change and go on. At the end, there are definite changes but no conclusion.

---

*Adler's passage on Callas here anticipates and predates Terrence McNally's *Master Class* by twenty years.

It is the technique of this particular author not to settle his characters with the kind of conviction that other authors have. Ibsen has a type of conviction. Strindberg has a conviction about man, woman, and fate. But not Chekhov.

Chekhov says each man evolves in his own way. His characters are part of a big thing—the evolution is seen through his tiny microscopic characters. They are little people, but that is what gives their story its greatness.

Masha says, "I can't remember what my mother looked like. Isn't that funny, I really can't. I suppose when I die, people won't remember me, either. . . . " That is the beginning of evolution. I went to school and, my God, I got a bad mark and it was just terrible, but when you think about it you realize it was terrible *then* but now it isn't important at all. Think about your own past in that sense of traveling time. It's good to understand not only the play but ourselves. We see that what was serious one year is not serious the next. That is our evolution.

The difference between Ibsen and Chekhov is that Ibsen's doctor in *Enemy of the People* says, "I practice medicine and I know what I'm doing," whereas Chekhov's doctor in *Three Sisters* does not. Chekhov's doctors understand what is wrong but never do anything. Chekhov's sense of social responsibility is not doable, it is only talkable. Dr. Dorn in *The Seagull* is always singing. What is it that makes him sing? It is his secret. You don't have a career unless you have a secret on the stage. There must be a lot of secrets. I don't want to tell you why Dr. Dorn sings, because I have to keep it for me. Get it for yourself.

Vershinin says, "Don't look for happiness for yourself. You won't find it." Tuzenbakh says, "I'm happy." Vershinin says, "No, you're not." He says this in front of Masha, whom he loves deeply. Masha laughs. Why? You will never know. That is her secret. You will never know what she hears in this that makes her laugh. That gets the audience interested. He asks, "Why are you laughing?" She says, "I don't know, I've been laughing all day." It's Masha's secret and the secret of the actress who plays her. For me to tell it to you would be almost sacrilege.

There are certain things you never tell. Stella's Rules: Never tell anyone how you feel. Never tell anyone about your health. Never tell anybody how you got here. Never tell anybody how enthusiastic you are about something you saw that they didn't see. It is the height of vulgarity and stupidity.

In Chekhov, you cannot act as you have ever acted before. You are in a very special moment in theater where a man named Chekhov and a man named Stanislavsky got together to create an absolutely new way of acting the truth in the individual.

Stanislavsky was the genius who made it possible to perform the plays of another genius who didn't write anything except what the actor had to bring out. If you don't have an actor in Chekhov, you have nothing. Everybody can do Shaw. Shaw's ideas are answerable. Chekhov's are not. That is why they required a new kind of acting.

The Chekhov idea comes from a character who says, "I am lost. How did it happen? What is the answer?" In the Russian culture, this dilemma produced a number of writers and a style deeply involved in the need to express the human problem. Somebody says, "Study Indian philosophy, that will give you an answer," or "The Bible has the answer." Everybody is ready to fill the gap. But Chekhov makes it quite clear that the people who have answers are not right—they are just spouting general concepts and formulas. Everybody in *The Seagull* needs to answer something in their lives, but there is no formula. The one person who has a formula—Trigorin—is the most miserable person there.

Chekhov knows science and concepts and formulas, but he says, "They don't help me, I'm lost. Who am I going to ask for an answer to my soul?" There is no one. That is why, in Chekhov, the experiential need comes first. That is why you have, for the first time in theater history, the inner technique—which corresponds to the need to understand.

The Russian writers were intellectuals and they understood the scientific age. But they gave it up. The Russians were the only ones who weren't so intrigued by it. Americans are so intrigued with it—with the formulas, the patterns. The Russians said, "I know what it is—you can have it." Chekhov understood; he was a doctor. He was interested in science but he said it had worn him out and created a morgue in him. It did not in any way save him. He is the only playwright who has no voice in his own plays. He is just a listener.

You rarely hear in a Chekhov play any reference to the outside world. They don't need the outside. Like I don't need *The New York Times,* thank God. It was a prayer answered from heaven when I gave up *The New York Times.* It was just reading in a void, not getting to know anything. God looked down and said, "Stella—" sometimes he calls me Stella—"get rid of it!" It is not writing that can really be read. It is good for people who have no inner need for Dostoyevsky or Mozart or for coming to this class. But who wants to read *The New York Times* if you can read Chekhov or come here?

Chekhov is able in one sentence to convey the most shattering experience—the suffering of having lost yourself without it being your fault. He can do it sometimes in four words—"Help me, save me!" Tennessee learned that from him. What does Blanche DuBois say in the last act? She says, "Fire, fire!" She is reaching out in a very Chekhovian way—"Save me!" Do you see that if you understand Chekhov, you'll understand Blanche and Tennessee Williams, too?

In movies and television when you are jumping on a horse or into a spaceship to kill fourteen people, it's exciting, but it means you don't have to solve the problem of how to live. All you have to solve is how to kill the enemy.

The tendency in most people is to locate the enemy. Take Mrs. Jean Harris, again. Dr. Tarnower abandoned her and left her alone with no way of recovering her charm, her youth. Her sense of loving, her sense of being—it was all over. He didn't love her. Happens all the time. Nobody loves anybody in Chekhov. So Mrs. Harris reached out for some equivalent of the scream. She said, "He's the guilty one!" and got a gun. If life doesn't give you what you want, you can shoot the guy, but it's useless. It doesn't resolve her problem. Actually, I think she *should* have shot him. It's all right. But she still has to face what she is.

In Chekhov, they either shoot themselves or—like Uncle Vanya—when they locate the enemy, they shoot twice but miss him. All of us would like to shoot the person who is guilty. It is Chekhov's way of saying, "*He's* not guilty—*life* is guilty."

Chekhov says, finally you must accept your loneliness.

Stanislavsky says, "It is not what is transmitted by the words but what is underneath them." It can't be done in TV because there's nothing underneath and nothing to transmit. The nature of TV is action, period.

The nature of theater is a mixture of action and nonaction. In *The Glass Menagerie,* there is a girl who has no action in the whole play. Laura sits; she is lame. She is like a character from Chekhov. What dominates is her passivity. You get in her passive state of living that it is not life, it is just passing through. In Strindberg the father says "I want the child!" and there is a big fight and the mother wins and the father dies. You don't get that kind of playwriting from Chekhov.

All three of the sisters lose. They lose the hope of achieving their deepest desires. But in exchange they have gained real insight into the human condition. Insight is not granted to happy people. Through suffering, the sisters learn that work—not happiness—is the human destiny. They are stranded. The people are stranded in *Uncle Vanya* and *The Cherry Orchard* and *The Seagull,* too. Chekhov characters are not happy at the beginning or at the end.

Chekhov shows you that it is not important to be happy but to understand. Through the futile quest for happiness you gain insight into how to live. It is not gained by being happy. You don't need so much happiness. What you need is the penetration that gives you a sense of truth to endure the blows. Was it worth it? Yes. I understand life better, and I am stronger now.

Three Sisters is Chekhov's masterpiece because it best reveals the shifting nature of life. Our lives are transitory. That transitory quality, when you catch it, is tremendously moving—people caught in the sadness and beauty of the passing moment. What Chekhov caught was the poetry of life, constantly changing like a summer cloud—now this shape, now another one. It is *poetic realism.* After Chekhov, you could have Yeats and de Maupassant and eventually Pinter—a whole new literature. We like Pinter because he's so abstract. When he says nothing, I know exactly what it means because he doesn't *tell* me what it means. He is a child of Chekhov.

Stanislavsky thought he understood literature, but he didn't understand Chekhov at first. Chekhov presented him with a problem of *creation in the void*. It was a terrible problem for modern theater. Stanislavsky had to create a way of acting for a man to say, "I've been here for thirty-five years and I don't understand what happened to me. What happened? Why did it all happen?"

Creation in the void is all man has left, nothing else. Time goes on, and the only thing left of Athens is the idea of beauty and ruins of the Parthenon. Finally, that's about all that remains of every culture—all that man can rescue from the void. Understand that it is there to keep you from dying out. Most people do die out. One senses in Chekhov one's personal death—the dying out in oneself of that thing in a human being which needs to be in itself a god. This sense of death is in his characters. The three sisters' struggle against it is a cry in the night. Chekhov is not the poet of hope, really. He is really the poet of death.

Only your own deep need to salvage something from the void—to act or to write or to create, not to have a "profession"—can keep you from the commonplace and from dying out. But you must have a deep recognition of your solitude to live the way you should live, not the way it is agreed upon, and not to fall for this big thing around you.

Being in the theater means learning about yourself. You have to dump the insignificant and enrich yourself with its truths. When Vershinin goes off with the army, he'll be lonely but he'll have his work. He has a real dedication to those boys. But Masha goes off with Kuligin into nothingness, into an endless compromise without poetry. You must understand the difference between the suffering of this man and this woman. Her talent is killed because she has no courage and sees no way out.

Be careful what happens to your talent. Sometimes a student of mine goes away and gets married, lives in Scarsdale, has the kids—one day comes back and says, "Hello, Stella," with that sad, dead look in her eyes. I wait . . . try to think of something to say. . . .

Listen to that voice inside that helps you. Be very careful. Don't let the source get dried up. It happens all the time in Hollywood, because the source of talent is not nourished by the way the product is made—it dries up the ability to run the character through in your mind. I did a film once with Sam Wanamaker, and he was absolutely lost about where to go or how to come into the scene. It is hard to start a scene when you are dead and you don't know how you died.

It wears out that creative talent. Do it, but be careful that you don't take their way but you put in *your* way of working. That means a great deal of discipline. Like Marlon—"You want me? I'll do what I want." That is agreed from the beginning.

I have a recording of Orson Welles doing a commercial. This brilliant man—doing a commercial—says, "in the planes . . ." Two producers say, "No, it's 'IN the planes.'" Orson says, "There isn't a sentence in the English language that can start with the stress on 'IN the planes.'" He tries to explain this to them. They say, "But, Mr. Welles, you've done such great things, couldn't you just do it our way?" Finally he says, "Tell me, in the depths of your ignorance, what do you want?" He was worn out. If you have talent, this wearing-down by life gets to you and hurts you.

Guard against it. Fight it your whole life.

I'll tell you something else: you can't give anybody anything that is not already in them. All you can do is awaken it.

A NOTE ON THE TYPE

The text of this book was set in Garamond No. 3.
It is not a true copy of any of the designs of Claude Garamond
(ca. 1480–1561), but an adaptation of his types, which set the
European standard for two centuries. It probably owes as much
to the designs of Jean Jannon, a Protestant printer working in
Sedan in the early seventeenth century, who had worked with
Garamond's romans earlier, in Paris, but who was denied their
use because of Catholic censorship. Jannon's matrices came into
the possession of the Imprimerie Nationale, where they were
thought to be by Garamond himself, and were so described when
the Imprimerie revived the type in 1900. This particular version
is based on an adaptation by Morris Fuller Benton.

Composed by NK Graphics, Keene, New Hampshire

Printed and Bound by Quebecor Printing, Fairfield, Pennsylvania

Designed by Iris Weinstein